# Unmasking
# Administrative
# Evil

# Unmasking Administrative Evil

## FOURTH EDITION

**Guy B. Adams** and **Danny L. Balfour**

*M.E.Sharpe*
Armonk, New York
London, England

The EuroSlavic fonts used to create this work are © 1986–2014 Payne Loving Trust.
EuroSlavic is available from Linguist's Software, Inc.,
www.linguistsoftware.com, P.O. Box 580, Edmonds, WA 98020-0580 USA
tel (425) 775-1130.

**Library of Congress Cataloging-in-Publication Data**

Adams, Guy B.
Unmasking administrative evil / by Guy B. Adams and Danny L. Balfour.—Fourth edition.
    pages cm
Includes bibliographical references and index.
ISBN 978-0-7656-4290-5 (hardcover : alk. paper)—ISBN 978-0-7656-4291-2 (pbk. : alk. paper)
1. Public administration—Moral and ethical aspects. I. Balfour, Danny L. II. Title.

JF1525.E8A33 2015
172′.2—dc23                                                                                    2014009999

Printed in the United States of America

The paper used in this publication meets the minimum requirements of
American National Standard for Information Sciences
Permanence of Paper for Printed Library Materials,
ANSI Z 39.48-1984.

∞

GP (c)    10    9    8    7    6    5    4    3    2    1
GP (p)    10    9    8    7    6    5    4    3    2    1

# Contents

# Acknowledgments

The authors of this book first met in 1993, and only discovered nearly two years later that we had a common interest in the Holocaust and its implications for public affairs. As academics, we have both read many books. Some have had a lasting and profound impact. But few have affected us more or changed as significantly our outlook on the world and on our chosen field of study than *The Cunning of History: The Holocaust and the American Future*, by Richard L. Rubenstein (1975). Although not written expressly for public policy and administration, the book showed us that the Holocaust was an important, perhaps the most important, historical event in the history of our field, although it had been in no way recognized as such by most other scholars and practitioners. Both of us continue to teach this book to our students.

Rubenstein's book opened up a new and disturbing perspective on public policy and administration (and all professions in public life), a perspective that does not allow us to be satisfied with conventional understandings of the field in general, and of public service ethics in particular. To a considerable extent, our book represents an attempt to deal with the profound issues raised by Rubenstein (and now a number of other scholars), and to suggest new directions for public life that take into account a fuller history of the field and the reality of administrative evil. We both value and respect public service and are ardent defenders of the good that our field and other professions can and do accomplish. At the same time, we believe that our future is imperiled by the field's lack of historical consciousness and attendant blindness to the potential for administrative evil to erupt in our midst.

Researching, writing, and updating *Unmasking Administrative Evil* for nearly two decades has been a valuable learning experience for both authors.

This is due in large measure to the many friends and colleagues who have helped us throughout the process. Professor Henry Kass of Portland State University; Catherine Rossbach, our original editor; Professor Bayard Catron of George Washington University; and Dr. Stuart Gilman of the United Nations Office on Drugs and Crime were all invaluable commentators and critics as we wrote the first edition. Harry Briggs, our editor at M.E. Sharpe, has been a complete pleasure to work with. Professor Curtis Ventriss of the University of Vermont both provided useful feedback and wrote the Foreword for the first edition. We greatly appreciate the willingness of Professor Charles Perrow of Yale University to contribute a Foreword to the revised edition. The Foreword to the third edition was written by Professor Philip Zimbardo of Stanford University, whose book, *The Lucifer Effect,* parallels our arguments in almost every respect: we are very grateful for his support of our work. All three of these forewords may now be found in the appendixes to this fourth edition of *Unmasking Administrative Evil.*

We appreciate the expert assistance of several individuals. Dr. Michael Neufeld, curator at the National Air and Space Museum in Washington, D.C., was very generous with his time and offered useful advice in dealing with the history of the von Braun team of rocket scientists and engineers. From a different perspective, Dr. Steven Luckert of the United States Holocaust Memorial Museum, and Mr. Eli Rosenbaum, Director of the Office of Special Investigations in the U.S. Department of Justice, were also helpful in this same area. Mr. Roger Boisjoly read the entire manuscript and provided useful technical assistance on space shuttle issues. Dr. George E. Reed, formerly on faculty at the U.S. Army War College and now at the University of San Diego, was a full partner in our initial research on the events in Abu Ghraib prison and co-author of our 2006 article in *Public Administration Review* (Adams, Balfour, and Reed, 2006), which won the Marshall Dimock award for best lead article; we appreciate his willingness to let us use parts of this research in Chapter 7.

*Unmasking Administrative Evil* received three national book awards: the 1998 Louis Brownlow Book Award, the National Academy of Public Administration's highest award for excellence in public administration scholarship, and two from the Academy of Management; the 1998 Best Book Award from the Public and Nonprofit Division; and the 2002 Best Book Award from the Social Issues in Management Division. This last award, from the Social Issues in Management Division, is only open to books that have been in print for at least three years, which makes it a bit different, but most welcome. The first edition was reviewed in thirteen scholarly journals, mostly favorably, and was widely adopted in public policy and administration courses, as well as courses in other fields and disciplines, around the nation. The revised and third editions have remained widely used for many years. We have learned much from the comments and reactions of our colleagues and students. We hope this fourth (and final) edition speaks well to the extensive commentary and critique we have received. Further, we welcome your thoughts on this edition (e-mail us at adams@missouri.edu and balfourd@gvsu.edu).

Guy Adams would like to thank his colleagues in the Harry S. Truman School of Public Affairs at the University of Missouri. His family—Martha, Kate, and Dave—gave not only their special kind of support and encouragement, but also provided the best possible antidote to dwelling so much on the topic of evil.

Danny Balfour would like to thank his colleagues and students at Grand Valley State University for their advice and support. Special appreciation goes to the late Professor Raul Hilberg, Professor Peter Hayes, and the United States Holocaust Memorial Museum for invaluable weeks of study and research on the Holocaust. Finally, to his wife, Mayumi, and son, Trevor: It is you who make it all worthwhile and provide hope for the future.

Guy B. Adams                                           Danny L. Balfour
Columbia, Missouri                          Grand Rapids, Michigan

# Introduction and Overview

A Century of Progress
—*title of the 1933 Chicago World's Fair*

Science Explores, Technology Executes, Mankind Conforms
—*motto of the 1933 Chicago World's Fair*

In the acclaimed novel *The Remains of the Day,* by Kazuo Ishiguro (1988), the central character, Mr. Stevens, reflects on his life of faithful service as butler to Lord Darlington (a British aristocrat and diplomat). Mr. Stevens takes great pride in his high standards of professionalism and the supporting role he played in Lord Darlington's attempts to keep the peace in Europe and support accommodative policies toward a defeated Germany during the years between the world wars. Lord Darlington arranged numerous informal meetings of key politicians and diplomats at his palatial home in the English countryside where great affairs of state were negotiated over fine food, wine, and cigars. But Mr. Stevens must also struggle with the fact that his employer lost faith in democracy, succumbing to the temptations of fascism in difficult times, and failed to appreciate the true nature of Hitler and his regime, even to the point of supporting anti-Semitism and lauding the "achievements" of Nazism in the mid-1930s. Lord Darlington's efforts were ultimately discredited, and he died in disgrace soon after World War II.

Mr. Stevens, a consummate professional, sees no connection between his service to the household and the moral and strategic failures of his employer. In a remarkable example of perverse moral reasoning, Stevens comes to the conclusion that his professional behavior shields him from any moral responsibility for his employer's actions (Ishiguro, 1988, 201):

How can one possibly be held to blame in any sense because, say, the passage of time has shown that Lord Darlington's efforts were misguided, even foolish? Throughout the years I served him, it was he and he alone who weighed up evidence and judged it best to proceed in the way he did, while I simply confined myself, quite properly, to affairs within my own professional realm. And as far as I am concerned, I carried out my duties to the best of my abilities, indeed to a standard which many may consider "first rate." It is hardly my fault if his lordship's life and work have turned out today to look, at best, a sad waste—and it is quite illogical that I should feel any regret or shame on my own account.

Mr. Stevens's justification of his role and abdication of responsibility in Lord Darlington's affairs provides a clear example of what we have termed *administrative evil*. The common characteristic of administrative evil is that ordinary people within their normal professional and administrative roles can engage in acts of evil without being aware that they are doing anything wrong. While a "professional" butler may perhaps seem an odd exemplar of administrative evil, Stevens pursues every new technique and practice in his chosen profession with the greatest diligence. Yet, his myopic focus on his administrative role and professional "standards" serves to mask his own contributions to the evil that stemmed from Darlington's moral failures. "Just following orders," his dismissal of two housekeepers, whose only offense was that they were Jewish, does not stir his conscience. Mr. Stevens carries on, stubbornly denying that he did anything wrong and asserting instead that he actually did everything right.

In this book, we explore the phenomenon so poignantly expressed in this literary example. Administrative evil has been and remains a central feature of both public and private organizations in the modern era. We wish it were otherwise, that we could report progress in the unmasking of administrative evil in the sixteen years since this book was first published. Instead we include new and revised sections in this edition on administrative evil in the twenty-first century. The same reasoning and behaviors employed by Mr. Stevens continue to mask the supporting role, played by far too many professionals and administrators in acts that dehumanize, injure, and even kill, their fellow human beings. We still hope for improvement, but offer a fourth edition of this book with the tragic understanding that administrative evil has reappeared with a vengeance in a country that depends on the organizations and professions that systematically reproduce it.

Since the first edition of this book in 1998, we have seen a continued escalation of violence and uncertainty worldwide, punctuated for Americans by the events of September 11, 2001 (on the sources of this violence, see

Juergensmeyer, 2000; Lifton, 1999; Volkan, 1997), by the "Global War on Terror," and the misplaced invasion of Iraq. All these events have led to the escalation of references to "evil" in public discourse. Bernstein notes how 9/11 changed our discourse (2002, x):

> Few would hesitate to name what happened on that day as evil—indeed, the very epitome of evil in our time. Yet, despite the complex emotions and responses that the events have evoked, there is a great deal of uncertainty about what is meant by calling them evil. There is an all too familiar popular rhetoric of "evil" that becomes fashionable at such critical moments, which actually obscures and blocks serious thinking about the meaning of evil. "Evil" is used to silence thinking and to demonize what we refuse to understand.

Although it might initially seem odd for us not to welcome greater use of a term that we have argued is in fact underused in the social science literature, we agree completely with Bernstein that the proliferation of "evil talk" in public discourse undermines our understanding of dynamics about which we very much need all the insight we can gain. At the same time, there has been an increased attention to the topic of evil in the scholarly literature, epitomized by Bernstein (2002, 2005), Neiman (2002), and Zimbardo (2007); this development we welcome wholeheartedly, because much of this new scholarship supports our argument in key areas.

Some readers misconstrued our argument in earlier editions, thinking that administrative evil occurs only or primarily in public organizations. We have attempted vigorously in our revisions to communicate that administrative evil is a social phenomenon, and as such is ubiquitous in complex organizations of all kinds. There are certainly any number of private sector cases that could be included in a book on administrative evil: The Dalkon Shield, a contraceptive device made by the Robins Company, caused severe health problems for many women (Mintz, 1985); the American tobacco industry's decades-long distortion of the health effects of cigarettes (Hurt and Robertson, 1998); the Goodrich Corporation's subcontract with the LTV Corporation that resulted in a cover-up of dysfunctional brakes in A7D military aircraft (fortunately without loss of life; Darley, 1996); and Morton Thiokol's involvement as a private company contracted to build the solid rocket booster for the space shuttle program (see Chapter 5).

The appearance of administrative evil in private organizations is drawing some notice (Vardi and Weitz, 2004). Commenting on what they call "craft ethics" (closely similar in some respects to professional ethics as discussed in Chapter 2), Browne, Kubasek, and Giampetro-Meyer state (1995, 26):

[A] kind of corporate cultural relativism exists in firms today. It is a relativism whereby what is right and wrong is determined by what those at the upper reaches of the corporate hierarchy say is right or wrong. And in most corporations, it could be summed up by the phrase, "whatever it takes to get the job done." As an ethical moral agent, the manager's overriding responsibility is to interpret and follow the corporate culture.

Finally, in a *Journal of Management Inquiry* article entitled "'Evil' Manifested in Destructive Individual Behavior: A Senior Leadership Challenge," Andre Delbecq offers the following conclusion (2001, 225): "I believe by seldom addressing the possibility of deeply hurtful behavior in our management literature, we have given evil undue power." In sum, administrative evil is just as much at home, if not more so, in private organizations as in public ones, a phenomenon that we address in detail in a revised Chapter 8. Having offered some context for the latest edition of this book, we want to turn now more specifically to how we have revised our discussion of administrative evil.

This fourth edition of *Unmasking Administrative Evil* contains new material on administrative evil in the twenty-first century, but the overall argument remains essentially the same. In Chapter 1, we provide our characterizations and definition of evil and administrative evil, and incorporate some excellent new literature on the subject. Chapters 2 through 7 have been updated and lightly revised. We have extensive new material in Chapter 8, focusing on what we have termed "Praetorian" times and the relationship between administrative evil and public ethics in the twenty-first century. We also seek some viable ground for public ethics moving forward. In a new afterword we discuss how cultures, organizations and individuals can respond in the aftermath of evil and administrative evil, and present the Forewords to previous editions in a new appendix.

In sum, we believe our argument in *Unmasking Administrative Evil* has been clarified, extended, and strengthened with these revisions, and is more clearly encompassing of all professions involved in public life and organizations both public and private, and has now demonstrated, much to our disappointment, that both evil and administrative evil represent a clear and present danger in twenty-first-century America, as well as the rest of the world.

## Overview of the Book

In Chapter 1, "The Dynamics of Evil and Administrative Evil," we explore the nature of evil in general and of administrative evil in particular. The connection between evil and public affairs (and other related fields and professions) is discussed, as is the failure to recognize instances of administrative evil. In an attempt to better understand evil itself, we provide a framework based on the insights of object-relations psychology and also examine the role of distance, perspective, and moral disengagement, as well as language and dehumanization, in the dynamics of evil. Next, a social constructionist perspective is used in an attempt to understand the apparent ease with which people participate in acts of administrative evil. Finally, we show how individual, organizational, and social behaviors interact in ways that can lead to administrative evil. This chapter strives to lay the foundation for understanding the examples of administrative evil discussed in subsequent chapters.

A central theme of the modern age is the emphasis on the value of technical rationality and the attendant narrowing of the concepts of reason, professionalism, ethics, and politics. When linked to bureaucracy and organization, the result can be an unintentional tendency toward compliance to authority, and the elevation of technical progress and processes over human values and dignity. Advances in information and communication systems are as likely to exacerbate these tendencies as to empower or liberate. Chapter 2, "Compliance, Technical Rationality, and Administrative Evil," focuses on the social and organizational dynamics that lead individuals to comply with authority, even when the consequences of their actions are detrimental to other human beings. The Stanford Prison and Milgram experiments provide powerful evidence of our willingness to harm others, and to wear the mask of administrative evil, when the responsibility for our actions can be placed on others who represent legitimate authority and the values of technical rationality. This edition includes updates from important new scholarship on both experiments.

Chapter 3, "Administrative Evil Unmasked: The Holocaust and Public Service," reviews interpretations of the Holocaust with a primary focus on its management and administration. Here we show how the combination of state power and authority and advances in modern, technical-rational administrative practice were central to the implementation of this paradigmatic case of administrative evil. In fact, the existence of an advanced, administrative infrastructure allowed the Nazis to surpass all others in the magnitude and efficiency of their killing. Public administration, in the form of ordinary civil servants (and business organizations) carrying out legally sanctioned and routine bureaucratic processes, played a key role in all stages of the Holocaust, including the composition and management of the civil service; the compiling of lists and management of files; defining the legal status of victims and their property; the organization of ghetto communities; transportation management; the administration of death/ slave labor camps; and the coordination of these and other activities. In short, the Holocaust was a massive administrative undertaking that required the complicity of thousands of professionals and administrators, most of whom were not "committed" Nazis. This leads us to consider how so many came to participate in mass murder and whether modern public service may be at its most effective and efficient operating levels when engaging in programs of dehumanization and destruction—even if the very thought is repugnant.

Chapter 4, "Administrative Evil Masked: From Mittelbau-Dora and Peenemünde to the Marshall Space Flight Center," reviews a case in which we begin to see the increasing difficulty of identifying clear instances of administrative evil within our own culture and time. Here we show how the instrumental aim of attaining technical superiority over all others resulted in American military intelligence officers and other public servants crossing legal and moral boundaries to bring the von Braun team of German rocket scientists and engineers to our country after World War II. We discuss the roles played by Wernher von Braun and several other team members in proposing and then making extensive use of slave labor to construct V-2 rockets as part of the Third Reich's war effort. First at Peenemünde, the Nazi rocket development and production facility, then at Mittelbau-Dora, the last of the SS concentration camps and the only one devoted solely to weapons production, some of the von Braun team members, including Wernher von Braun himself, engaged in activities for which others were convicted of war crimes in post-war Germany. Brought to the United States under Operations Overcast and Paperclip, their past was ignored, misrepresented, and then kept hidden, as the von Braun team went on to play a key role in American space exploration at the Marshall Space Flight Center, including building the Saturn rockets that launched *Apollo* to the moon. This small group of Germans, whose past was sullied by their actions in the Nazi Third Reich, had highly successful careers as executives in both the public and private sectors, suggesting that the specialized skills of managing in a technical-rational context transferred readily from the Third Reich to the post-war United States. While it is true that such questions are more easily raised in hindsight, we ask whether the price for these achievements was too high—20,000 dead in less than two years at Mittelbau-Dora, with American public servants overlooking the direct participation of von Braun and a few others in the decisions and actions leading to those deaths because their technical expertise was so desirable.

Chapter 5, "Organizational Dynamics and Administrative Evil: The Marshall Space Flight Center, NASA, and the Space Shuttles *Challenger* and *Columbia*," shows how less visible dynamics of organizational culture can lead to administrative evil. We view Marshall, NASA, and the space shuttles *Challenger* and *Columbia* as an opaque and complex case in which the identification of administrative evil is problematic. We focus on the role of the Marshall Space Flight Center not only in the *Challenger* disaster, but more significantly within the overall space program. A defensive organizational culture, created by the von Braun team as a natural response to their feelings of isolation, and of being slighted and even attacked by outsiders within NASA and in society at large, turned destructive under the leadership of Dr. William Lucas in the 1970s and 1980s. Even if the *Challenger* launch could somehow have been stopped, Marshall's destructive organizational culture, which ensured that critical information was either blocked or not acted upon, practically guaranteed a space shuttle disaster. Those same dynamics were at work in the more recent *Columbia* disaster. In the return-to-flight process following the *Columbia* tragedy, NASA's organizational culture continues to exhibit the same dynamics, now placing the next-generation space vehicle at apparent risk.

Chapter 6, "Public Policy and Administrative Evil," explores the implications of "problem solving" as a metaphor for how public policy is formulated and implemented, with a focus on the messy and intractable policy problems that may involve "surplus populations" (Rubenstein, 1975, 1983) and the potential for public policies of destruction based on moral inversions. What is especially problematic is the extent to which technical-rational problem solving has attained an unquestioned (and unspoken) dominance in the policy arena with little or no reflection on the possible destructive consequences of addressing social problems in this way. In the United States, many social problems persist, in part, because we choose to maintain what Berlin (1991) terms an "uneasy equilibrium" between competing values rather than to pursue final, and potentially inhuman, solutions to social problems. In other words, the drive or desire to solve social problems such as poverty, crime, drug abuse, and illegal immigration has been balanced with concern for protecting political and human rights.

But this equilibrium is threatened when the problem to be solved involves surplus populations. When public policy programs deal with populations that are considered expendable—portrayed as unwanted vermin or diseases, or as some other blight on society (Bauman, 1989)—such moral inversions can lead toward policies of destruction and elimination. There are too many examples in American history of these destructive tendencies and policies. The decimation of Native American populations from the earliest days of national expansion, the expropriation of property and forced internment of Japanese Americans in Relocation Centers during World War II, the Tuskegee and other exploitative experiments, and Operations Overcast and Paperclip are all disturbing reminders that our own American public service also possesses a well-developed capacity for administrative evil.

Chapter 7, "Administrative Evil in the Twenty-First Century: Abu Ghraib, Moral Inversion, and Torture Policy," presents a contemporary U.S. case—the torture and abuse of detainees at Abu Ghraib prison and at other sites in Iraq, Afghanistan, and Cuba. This case raises disturbing questions that have few, if any, easy answers. Were these intentionally evil acts committed by a few bad apples who took advantage of the power they wielded over the detainees? Or were they examples of administrative evil in which the obvious evil of torture and abuse was hidden from the perpetrators, including those who performed subsidiary and supportive functions? The more fundamental question is, are torture and abuse always wrong? How did the United States arrive at a moral inversion in this case? We show in this chapter how a climate was created that essentially gave permission for the torture and abuse that occurred. Now, in the sad aftermath of Abu Ghraib, questions remain about the interrogation practices of the CIA, special operations units, and civilian contract personnel, and about the possibility of U.S. officials being indicted on war crimes charges either at home or in international courts.

Chapter 8, "Administrative Evil and Public Ethics in Praetorian Times," begins by exploring the relationship between public ethics and administrative evil. The cultural context of administrative ethics has become even more challenging in what we term "Praetorian times," when unethical behavior has become the norm in many organizations, both public and private. We go on to examine the nature of and prospects for ethics in public life, living as we do in the shadow of evil and administrative evil. Within our liberal democratic polity, at least two versions of public ethics seem plausible. The first is based on a liberalism of fear and expects relatively little of us based on our rather dismal historical track record. In this version, "putting cruelty first," we posit only a minimalist public ethics—one that offers only small protection against administrative evil. The second version is based on deliberative democracy and suggests that we humans can do better and that perhaps we can strengthen our public ethics through the rigor and tribulations of the deliberative process. This version offers a more robust defense against administrative evil.

Finally, in a new afterword, we explore how cultures, organizations, and individuals can find a way forward in the wake of evil and administrative evil. While some aspects of evil's aftermath are clear enough through the trail of mass graves, broken bodies and lives, and transgenerational reverberations, the possibilities of expiating evil, including administrative evil, through processes of forgiveness, reconciliation, and reparation, especially on the part of organizations and states, remain underexplored.

In the end, *Unmasking Administrative Evil* does not provide a definitive direction or set of recommendations on how to avoid administrative evil in the future. The profound challenges that evil presents are such that it would be presumptuous to propose that we have any authoritative answers to them. At the same time, we do not want to suggest that public life is necessarily and permanently caught in a sort of Sartrean "no exit." We do believe that the unmasking of administrative evil means a sharp departure from the unquestioned dominance of the modern, technical-rational conception of organizations and public policies. We offer some hopeful prospects for a public service that might eschew, to some extent, the mask of administrative evil.

# 1

# The Dynamics of Evil and Administrative Evil

> We see through a glass darkly when we seek to understand the cause and nature of evil. . . . But we see more profoundly when we know it is through a dark glass that we see, than if we pretend to have clear light on this profound problem.
>
> —*Reinhold Niebuhr,* 1986 (246)

We begin with the premise that evil is an essential concept for understanding the human condition. As one examines the sweep of human history, clearly there have been many great and good deeds and achievements, and real progress in the quality of at least many humans' lives. We also see century after century of mind-numbing, human-initiated violence, betrayal, and tragedy. We name as evil the actions of human beings that unjustly or needlessly inflict pain and suffering and death on other human beings. However, evil is one of those phenomena in human life that defies easy definition and understanding (Adams and Merrihew, 1990; Formosa, 2006, 2008; Garrard, 2002; Hammer, 2000; Kahn, 2007; Katz, 1988; Mathewes, 2000; McGinn, 1997; Parkin, 1985; Russell, 1988; Sanford, 1981; Steiner, 2002; Zimbardo, 2007; Zycinski, 2000).

Those readers who can look at human history and see no evil may find little interest in this book. Others who acknowledge negative interaction and tragedy in human affairs, but prefer more modern terminology, say, "dysfunctional behavior," may find our use of a very old word—evil—uncomfortable or even misguided. Still others may readily acknowledge evil in human affairs and find our argument—that evil appears in a new and dangerous form in the modern age—fairly easy to follow, but will also be cautioned by the counsel of Aldous Huxley (1952, 192):

> The effects which follow too constant and intense a concentration upon evil are always disastrous. Those who crusade not for God in themselves, but against the devil in others, never succeed in making the world better, but leave it either as it was, or sometimes even perceptibly worse than it was, before the crusade began. By thinking primarily of evil we tend, however excellent our intentions, to create occasions for evil to manifest itself.

## Modernity, Technical Rationality, and Administrative Evil

The modern age, especially in the last century and a half, has had as its hallmark what we call *technical rationality*. Technical rationality underlies a way of thinking and living (a culture) that emphasizes the scientific-analytic mindset and the belief in technological progress (Adams, 1992). We explain this notion and its historical evolution at greater length in Chapter 2. For our purposes here, the culture of technical rationality enables a new and bewildering form of evil that we call *administrative evil*. As our title implies, administrative evil is different because its appearance is *masked*. Administrative evil may be masked in many different ways, but the common characteristic is that people can engage in acts of evil unaware that they are in fact doing anything at all wrong. Indeed, ordinary people may simply act appropriately in their organizational role—in essence, just doing what those around them would agree they should be doing—and at the same time, participate in what a critical and reasonable observer, usually well after the fact, would call evil. Even worse, under conditions of what we call *moral inversion*, in which something evil has been redefined convincingly as good, ordinary people can all too easily engage in acts of administrative evil while believing that what they are doing is not only correct, but in fact, good.

The basic difference between evil as it has appeared throughout human history, and administrative evil, a fundamentally modern phenomenon, is that the latter is less easily recognized as evil. People have always been able to delude themselves into thinking that their evil acts are not really so bad, and we have certainly had moral inversions in times past. But there are three very important differences in administrative evil. One is our modern inclination to *un-name* evil, an old concept that does not lend itself well to the scientific-analytic mindset (Bernstein, 2002; Neiman, 2002). The second difference is found in the structure of the modern, complex organization, which diffuses individual responsibility and requires the compartmentalized accomplishment of role expectations in order to perform work on a daily basis (Staub, 1992,

84). The third difference is the way in which the culture of technical rationality has analytically narrowed the processes by which public policy is formulated and implemented, so that moral inversions are now more likely. Our goal in this book is to illuminate at least some of the dynamics in organizations and in public policy that can lead to administrative evil.

Our understanding of administrative evil has its roots in the genocide perpetrated by Nazi Germany during World War II. While the evil—the pain and suffering and death—that was inflicted on millions of "others" in the Holocaust (Glass, 1997) was so horrific as to almost defy our comprehension, it was also clearly an instance of administrative evil. Here we refer to administrative evil as unmasked (although much of it was masked at the time), and we suggest that identifying administrative evil is easier today because the Holocaust was perpetrated by the Nazis (and others complicit with them) and because it occurred well over half a century ago.

The Holocaust occurred in modern times in a culture suffused with technical rationality, and most of its activity was accomplished within organizational roles and within legitimated public policy. While the results of the Holocaust were horrific and arguably without precedent in human history, ordinary Germans fulfilling ordinary roles carried out extraordinary destruction in ways that had been successfully packaged as socially normal and appropriate (Arendt, 1963). Nothing else in human history really compares with this event, and certainly all else in modern times pales before its example. Although the Holocaust provides the lens through which we can unmask contemporary examples of administrative evil, we are concerned to point out most emphatically that we do not equate our American examples of administrative evil with the Holocaust.

## Evil in the Modern Age

Evil remains only a barely accepted entry in the lexicon of the social sciences. Social scientists much prefer to *describe* behavior, avoiding ethically loaded or judgmental rubrics—to say nothing of what is often considered religious phraseology (Miller, Gordon, and Buddie, 1999). Yet, evil reverberates down through the centuries of human history, showing little sign of weakening in the first decades of the twenty-first century and the apex of modernity (Lang, 1991). As Claudia Card (2002, 28) notes:

> The denial of evil has become an important strand of twentieth century secular Western culture. Some critics find evil a chimera, like Santa Claus or the tooth fairy, but a dangerous one that calls forth disturbing emotions, such as hatred, and leads to such disturbing projects as revenge. . . . Many reject the idea of

evil because, like Nietzsche, they find it a *bad* idea. . . . Nietzsche's critique
has helped engineer a shift from questions of what to do to prevent, reduce or
redress evils to skeptical psychological questions about what inclines people
to make judgments of evil in the first place, what functions such judgments
have served.

In the modern age, we are greatly enamored with the notion of progress,
of the belief that civilization develops in a positive direction, with the present age at the pinnacle of human achievement. These beliefs, along with the
denial of evil, constrain us from acknowledging the implications of the fact
that the twentieth century was one of the bloodiest, both in absolute and relative terms, in human history, and that we continue to develop the capacity for
even greater mass destruction (Rummel, 1994).

Nearly 200 million human beings were slaughtered or otherwise killed as
a direct or indirect consequence of the epidemic of wars and state-sponsored
violence in the twentieth century (Bauman, 1989; Eliot, 1972; Glover, 1999;
Rummel, 1994). Administrative mass murder and genocide have become
a demonstrated capacity within the human social repertoire (Rubenstein,
1975, 1983), and simply because such events have occurred, new instances
of genocide and dehumanization become more likely (Arendt, 1963). As
Bernstein (2002, iv) states:

> Looking back over the horrendous twentieth century, few of us would hesitate
> to speak of evil. Many people believe that the evils witnessed in the twentieth
> century exceed anything that has ever been recorded in past history. Most of
> us do not hesitate to speak about these extreme events—genocides, massacres,
> torture, terrorist attacks, the infliction of gratuitous suffering—as evil.

If we are to have any realistic hope for ameliorating this trajectory in the
twenty-first century, administrative evil needs to be unmasked and better understood, especially by those likely to participate in any future acts of mass
destruction—professionals and citizens who are active in public affairs.

Despite its enormous scale and tragic result, it took more than twenty-five
years for the Holocaust to emerge as the major topic of study and public
discussion that we know it as today. But knowing more about the Holocaust
does not necessarily mean that we really understand it, or that future genocides will be prevented (Power, 2002). As we move into Chapters 4 through
7 progressively to examples that occur within our own culture, closer to our
own time, and eventually into the present, the dynamics of administrative
evil become more subtle and opaque. Here we refer to administrative evil as
masked. This is one of the central points of our argument; that administra-

tive evil is not easily recognized as such because its appearance is masked; moreover, in our ordinary roles with our taken-for-granted assumptions about the modern world, *we wear the mask.*

### Is Administrative Evil Public or Private?

While our own academic home is in public policy and administration, and the arguments and examples in the book are largely from the public sector, we believe the arguments hold for all professions and disciplines involved in public life most generally. In other words, as a phenomenon of the modern world, administrative evil is confined to neither the public nor the private sector. Rather, it is a social phenomenon, and its appearance in private or public organizations is likely to vary according to the political and economic arrangements of particular countries. Further, we believe a similar argument about administrative evil could be made from the perspective of the private sector (Hills, 1987; Mintz, 1985). An obvious starting point could be the American tobacco industry (Hurt and Robertson, 1998). We are convinced that administrative evil is a phenomenon of the culture of technical rationality, and as such is socially ubiquitous and certainly not confined to the public sector.

Nevertheless, we argue and present evidence that the tendency toward administrative evil, as manifested primarily in acts of dehumanization and genocide, is deeply woven into the identity of public affairs (and also in other fields and professions in public life). The reality of evil has been suppressed and masked despite, or perhaps because of, its profound and far-reaching implications for the future of both public and private organizations.

Despite what may initially seem to be a negative treatment of the public service, it is not our intention to somehow diminish public service, engage in "bureaucrat-bashing," or give credence to misguided arguments that governments and their agents are necessarily or inherently evil. In fact, our aim is quite the opposite: to get beyond the superficial critiques and lay the groundwork for a more ethical and democratic public life, one that recognizes its potential for evil and thereby creates greater possibilities for avoiding the many pathways toward state-sponsored dehumanization and destruction. Nonetheless, this approach (as with any attempt to rethink aspects of the field) is bound to bring us into conflict with conventional wisdom. A passage from Hirsch (1995, 75–76) conveys one aspect of this issue:

> Genocide is a controversial topic that may very well pit the researcher against the state. If the nation-state has been the major perpetrator of genocide or some other form of atrocity, then any researcher investigating this topic must begin to

ask critical questions about the nature of the state in general and his or her state in particular. Social scientists are sometimes reluctant to raise critical questions because serious contemplation of them may force the scientists to evaluate or re-evaluate their principles or their connection to their government.

Substituting "torture" for "genocide" in the quotation above demonstrates its contemporary relevance, as we shall see in Chapter 7. Our critical stance toward public affairs aims not so much at any particular formulation of public life, but more at what has not been addressed—the failure to recognize administrative evil as part and parcel of its identity. Administrative evil should be as much a part of public policy and administration as other well-worn concepts such as efficiency, effectiveness, accountability, and productivity.

### Administrative Evil and Public Affairs

Likewise, public affairs cannot, in light of this realization, be described only in terms of progress in the "art, science, and profession" of public policy and administration (see, for example, Lynn, 1996) without recognizing that acts of administrative evil consist of something other than uncontrolled, sporadic deviations from the norms of technical-rational public policy and administrative practice, which are often simply assumed to be ethical (Denhardt, 1981). Practitioners and scholars of public affairs, as well as other related fields and professions, should recognize that the pathways to administrative evil, while sometimes built from the outside by seductive leaders, most often emanate from within, ready to coax and nudge any professional down a surprisingly familiar route: first toward moral inversion, then to complicity in crimes against humanity.

Efficient and legitimate institutions can be used for constructive or destructive purposes. The fundamental problem for public affairs, given the ubiquity of administrative evil, is to develop and nurture a critical, reflexive attitude toward public institutions, the exercise of authority, and the culture at large. And as difficult as this may be to imagine, much less to accomplish, even this offers no final guarantee against administrative evil. Responsibility for the prevention of future acts of administrative evil rests, in part, with both theorists and practitioners who understand their role and identity in such a way that they can resist seductive and cunning temptations within moral inversions, to apply expedient or ideological solutions to the many difficult issues that confront contemporary public life.

In this view, public administration certainly encompasses, but is not centered on, the use of sophisticated organizational and management techniques in the implementation of public policy. Public administration must also, and primarily, cultivate a historical consciousness aware of the fearsome potential for evil on the part of the state and its agents, and a societal role and identity infused not just with personal and professional ethics, but also with a social and political consciousness—a public ethics—that can recognize the masks of administrative evil and refuse to act as its accomplice.

Based on the premise that the concept of evil remains relevant and essential for understanding the human condition in the twenty-first century, we make several key arguments in this book:

1. The modern age, with its scientific-analytic mindset and technical-rational approach to social and political problems, enables a new and bewildering form of evil—administrative evil. It is bewildering because it wears many masks, making it easy for ordinary people to do evil, even when they do not intend to do so.

2. Because administrative evil wears a mask, no one has to accept an overt invitation to commit an evil act; because such overt invitations are very rarely issued. Rather, the invitation may come in the form of an expert or technical role, couched in the appropriate language, or it may even come packaged as a good and worthy project, representing what we call a *moral inversion*, in which something evil or destructive has been redefined as good and worthy.

3. We examine closely two of administrative evil's most favored masks. First, within modern organizations (both public and private), because so much of what occurs is *underneath* our awareness of it, we find people engaged in patterns and activities that can—and sometimes do—culminate in evil, without recognizing them as evil until after the fact (and often, not even then). Second, we look at social and public policies that can culminate in evil; these most often involve either an instrumental or technical goal (which drives out ethics) or a moral inversion unseen by those pursuing such a policy.

4. Because public service ethics, and professional ethics more generally, are both anchored in the scientific-analytic mindset, in a technical-rational approach to administrative or social problems, and in the professions themselves, they are most often ineffective when faced with administrative evil. Since administrative evil wears many masks, it is entirely possible to adhere to the tenets of public service and professional ethics and participate in even a great evil, and remain unaware of it, until it is too late (or perhaps not at all). Thus, finding a moral basis for public service or professional ethics in the face of administrative evil is problematic at best.

### Dirty Hands

Those in public life have always had to deal with questions of conscience that arise when one chooses what one hopes is a "small evil" in order to achieve a greater good on behalf of others. Machiavelli (1961, orig. c. 1520), in *The Prince,* still offers perhaps the clearest expression of the *dirty hands* conundrum in political action and public life (Wijze, 2002). *Raisons d'état,* or reasons of state, are advanced as good and valid reasons for engaging in minor, and sometimes not so minor, acts of evil. The problem of dirty hands has always had within it a subtle temptation, which has at times led to great evil in human history. Jean-Paul Sartre, the French existential philosopher, wrote a play, *Les mains sales* (Dirty Hands; 1948), precisely on this subject, which one author (Sutherland, 1995, 490) has described as "a fatalistic mockery of the bold adventurer in politics who feels fit to decide for others as though the future were a game of chess in an empty room; the play insists that one cannot predict what will happen as a result of one's act, from the basis of what one might want to think one had intended to happen." But the arrogant, utilitarian flaw of dirty hands is different altogether from administrative evil.

The dirty hands choice means that one inflicts knowingly and deliberately (hopefully limited) pain and suffering on others, *for a presumed good reason—for the greater good of the polity.* Whether and when such a choice is justified has been widely debated, but it does not bear significantly on the topic of this book. Administrative evil is different in part because the culture of technical rationality tends to drive the consideration of ethics out of the picture altogether, not to mention the rational calculation of how much good can legitimately be traded off against evil. Because administrative evil is masked, ethics are not considered in the situation at all, meaning that we do not even see a choice about which we might calculate degrees of good.

### Hubris

Another venerable word, hubris, means an inflated pride or sense of self—a phenomenon often connected with "dirty hands" as just discussed. Hubris, although a frequent companion of evil throughout human history, while not a necessary component of administrative evil, can combine with it to produce particularly deadly results. Hubris can be an individual trait and a social and political characteristic, as in Nazi Germany. Although not discussed in great depth here, the career of Albert Speer, Hitler's Minister of Armaments, shows with remarkable clarity how hubris and administrative evil can combine with terrible results (Sereny, 1995; Speer, 1970). Wernher von Braun, whose career is treated in some detail in Chapters 4 and 5, was also marked by hubris. We suspect those more recently involved in policies and practices that enabled the United States to torture detainees in the "Global War on Terror" and recklessly lead the world into economic decline may have embodied hubris as well. Hubris might be compared to an accelerant, which when added to an existing fire (administrative evil) can easily escalate something seemingly small into a conflagration.

## Understanding Evil

The *Oxford English Dictionary* defines evil as the antithesis of good in all its principal senses. Claudia Card (2002, 3) defines it as "foreseeable intolerable harm produced by culpable wrongdoing." Elias Staub (1992, 25) offers another characterization: "Evil is not a scientific concept with an agreed meaning, but the idea of evil is part of a broadly shared human cultural heritage. The essence of evil is the destruction of human beings. . . . By evil I mean *actions* that have such consequences." Philip Zimbardo suggests the following definition (2007, 5): "Evil consists in intentionally behaving in ways that harm, abuse, demean, dehumanize or destroy innocent others—or using one's authority and systemic power to encourage or permit others to do so on your behalf." Finally, Geddes (2003, 105) emphasizes that

> evil is relational. . . . For evil occurs between people: one or more persons do evil (and are thereby understood to be evil or connected to evil) and someone else, or some other group, suffers evil. As Paul Ricouer (1995, 250) notes, "To do evil is always, either directly or indirectly, to make someone else suffer. In its dialogic structure evil committed by someone finds its other half in the evil suffered by someone else."

These definitions, while helpful, can be further refined. We propose a continuum of evil and wrongdoing, with horrible, mass eruptions of evil, such as the Holocaust and other, lesser instances of mass murder, at one extreme, and the "small" white lie, which is somewhat hurtful, at the other (Staub, 1992, xi). Somewhere along this continuum, wrongdoing turns into evil. At the white-lie end of the continuum, use of the term wrongdoing seems more apt. However, Sissela Bok (1978) has argued persuasively that even so-called white lies can have serious personal and social consequences, especially as they accrue over time. For the most part, we discuss the end of the continuum where the recognition of evil may be easier and more obvious (at least when it is unmasked). Nonetheless, the small-scale end of the continuum remains important, because the road to great evil often begins with seemingly small, first steps of wrongdoing (Zimbardo, 2007). Staub (1992, xi) notes that "Extreme destructiveness . . . is usually the last of many steps along a continuum of destruction." Evil, in many cases, hides within cunning and seductive processes that can lead ordinary people in ordinary times down the proverbial slippery slope.

Thousands of years of human religious history have provided ample commentary on evil, and philosophers have certainly discussed it at length (Bernstein, 2002; Card, 1998; Cole, 2006; Dews, 2008; Garrard, 1998; Hallie, 1997; Haybron, 2002; Kateb, 1983; Kekes, 1990, 2005; Morton, 2004; Norden, 2000; Perrett, 2002; Petrik, 2000; Rorty, 2001; Schrift, 2005; Stivers, 1982; Twitchell, 1985). While locating evil in the symbolic persona of the devil once provided adequate explanation of its origins, the modern scientific era both demands a more comprehensive explanation of the origins of evil and makes it nearly impossible to provide one. One author has argued that the modern age has been engaged in a process of un-naming evil, such that we now have a "crisis of incompetence" toward evil: "A gulf has opened up in our [modern] culture between the visibility of evil and the intellectual resources available for coping with it" (Delbanco, 1995, 3). And Bernstein (2002, 2) further notes:

> Philosophers and political theorists are much more comfortable speaking about injustice, the violation of human rights, what is immoral and unethical, than about evil. When theologians and philosophers of religion speak about "the problem of evil," they typically mean something quite specific—the problem of how to reconcile the appearance of evil with a belief in God. . . . It is almost as if the language of evil has been dropped from contemporary moral and ethical discourse.

Evil may not have become undiscussable or unnamable, but in its administrative manifestations it usually goes unrecognized. Identifying evil depends on our approach and stance toward it, but in the modern age, we risk not seeing it at all, for administrative evil wears many masks.

The masking of administrative evil suggests that evil also occurs along another continuum: from acts committed in relative ignorance to those committed knowingly and deliberately, or what we would characterize as masked and unmasked evil. Plato maintained that no one would knowingly commit an evil act. The fact that someone did something evil indicates his ignorance. In fact, individuals and groups can and often do engage in evil acts without recognizing the consequences of their behavior, or when convinced their actions are justified or serving the greater good, as Staub (1992, 25) notes:

> We cannot judge evil by conscious intentions, because psychological distortions tend to hide even from the perpetrators themselves their true intentions. They are unaware, for example, of their own unconscious hostility or that they are scapegoating others. Frequently, their intention is to create a "better world," but in the course of doing so they . . . destroy the lives of human

beings. Perpetrators of evil often intend to make people suffer but see their actions as necessary or serving a higher good. In addition, people tend to hide their negative intentions from others and justify negative actions by higher ideals or the victims' evil nature.

Administrative evil falls within the part of the continuum in which people engage in or contribute to acts of evil without recognizing that they are doing anything wrong.

Lang (1991) argues that, in the case of genocide, it is difficult to maintain that evil occurs without the knowledge of the actor. Genocide is a deliberate act; mass murderers know that they are doing evil. Katz (1993) recounts several instances in which deliberate acts of evil have occurred in bureaucratic settings (such as those based on the testimonies of the commandants of the death camps of Auschwitz and Sobibor). However, the direct act of mass murder or torture, even when facilitated by public institutions, is not what we call administrative evil, or at least represents its most extreme, and unmasked, manifestation. Before and surrounding such overt acts of evil, there are many more and much less obviously evil administrative activities that lead to and support the worst forms of human behavior. Moreover, without these instances of masked evil, the more overt and unmasked acts are less likely to occur (Staub, 1992, 20–21).

If administrative evil means that people inflict pain and suffering and death on others, but do so *not* knowingly or deliberately, can they be held responsible for their actions? We believe the answer is yes, but when ordinary people inflict pain and suffering and even death on others in the course of performing their "normal" organizational or policy role, they usually justify their actions by saying that they were just following orders and doing their job. This reflects the difficulty of identifying administrative evil, and the possibility of missing it altogether, or perhaps worse, calling mistakes or misjudgments evil.

We maintain that identifying administrative evil is most difficult within one's own culture and historical time period. In Chapter 7, we examine how the torture and abuse of detainees received, at a minimum, tacit approval from the U.S. government. The opaque nature of administrative evil should not lead us to conclude that it cannot be recognized or that evil cannot be prevented from developing into its worst manifestations. The Holocaust provides an example of the latter, when evil, both masked and unmasked, ran unchecked. We remember it now as an instance of administrative evil, but only after several decades of denial and suppressed memories. Other examples, which we recount in later chapters, show how what we remember is often not as important as what remains unseen or forgotten beneath the mask of administrative evil.

## The Roots of Administrative Evil: A Psychological Perspective

We know that human beings are killers. We are (at least most of us) meat-eaters who must kill for the sustenance of life. We are in the food chain and are at minimum killers of plant life. We have also learned, during the course of human history, to kill for high social purposes; that is, for political, religious, and/or economic beliefs and systems. As uncomfortable as it may be to acknowledge, evil lurks as close to all of us as ourselves. Most versions of psychology, from Freud to Jung and beyond, explore the potentially destructive tendencies of human behavior, including aggression, anger, and rage. Richard Bernstein (2002, 231) summarizes Freud's stance quite well:

> The most important lesson to be learned from Freud concerns the depth and inescapability of psychological ambivalence—an ambivalence ultimately rooted in the unconscious. Freud's reflections on civilization and its discontents serve as a warning against the idea that as civilization develops, so this powerful psychic ambivalence decreases. On the contrary, civilization leads to greater repression and an increased sense of guilt. And Freud well understood how, as a consequence of this psychic ambivalence, we are always threatened by the possibility of destructive and self-destructive outbursts of repressed aggressiveness. This is the sense in which we must understand Freud's claim that, "*In reality, there is no such thing as 'eradicating' evil.*"

Melanie Klein (1964), perhaps the preeminent object-relations psychologist, understands aggression, and other emotions as well, as relationships with "objects" (which are in most cases other human beings). As Greenberg and Mitchell (1983, 139–146) point out: "Drives, for Klein, are relationships." One such manifestation is hating those we love the most (as infants and children). Such a psychic contradiction is emotional dynamite and is defused through "splitting." Unlike repression, which drives unwanted or intolerable emotions underground into the unconscious, splitting allows these contradictory feelings to co-exist, albeit separately, in the human consciousness. Normally, the good aspect is held internally, and the bad aspect is split off and projected outward to some external person (the "object"). This is known as "projective identification." Developmentally, these phenomena interact in the following way (Alford, 1990, 11):

> Primal splitting-and-idealization thus involves a delicate balancing act. Too little, and the child cannot protect itself from its own aggression, living in constant fear that its bad objects will overcome its good ones, and itself. Too much separation, on the other hand, will prevent the good and bad object from

ever being recognized as one, an insight that is the foundation of the depressive position, in which the child despairs of ever being able to restore to wholeness the good object, which he now recognizes is inseparable from the bad object that he has destroyed in fantasy a thousand times. For Klein, the depressive position is not an illness, but a crucial step in emotional development, by which love and hate are integrated.

These insights help us understand the construction of social and organizational evil in adults. The tendency to "split off" unwelcome and negative feelings and emotions, and to project them onto others, manifests in both individual and group behavior. Zimbardo (2007, 230) states:

> The fundamental human need to belong comes from the desire to associate with others, to cooperate, to accept group norms. However . . . the need to belong can also be perverted into excessive conformity, compliance, and in-group versus out-group hostility. The need for autonomy and control, the central forces toward self-direction and planning, can be perverted into an excessive exercise of power to dominate others or into learned helplessness.

And as Staub (1992, 17) notes, "Blaming others, scapegoating, diminishes our own responsibility. By pointing to a cause of the problems, it offers understanding, which, although false, has great psychological usefulness. It promises a solution to problems by action against the scapegoat." Our focus here is on group behavior, and Staub clarifies these dynamics at the group level (1992, 17): "people . . . feel connected as they join to scapegoat others. The groups that are attractive in hard times often provide an ideological blueprint for a better world and an enemy that must be destroyed to fulfill the ideology. . . . These psychological tendencies have violent potentials."

### Distance, Perspective, and Moral Disengagement

*Distance* is important, in terms of both space and time, in understanding evil. It is clearly more difficult to name evil, and do so accurately, in one's own historical time period. The introduction and proliferation of the language of evil in political discourse, as in President George W. Bush's "Axis of Evil" speech in 2003, only muddies the waters further. Consider the genocide in Rwanda and ethnic cleansing in the former Yugoslavia. Even from the distant perspective of a concerned nation—the United States—evidence during the time of those events was spotty. While we would argue that sufficient evidence existed for the United States to take earlier and stronger action, the point is that a social or political consensus to resist evil is not so easily achieved as events unfold and the situation remains murky (Power, 2002). In hindsight, and when no longer called upon to do anything, it is much easier to name such events as evil with widespread agreement (but only if a Serb and Bosnian or Kosovar, or Hutu and Tutsi, are not part of the discourse). Geographic and cultural (or racial) distance matter as well. The horrors of the Rwandan genocide occurred, after all, in Africa (Prunier, 1995). The genocide in Darfur generated impassioned discussion for several years, but effective preventive action emerged slowly and after many deaths. Naming the Holocaust as evil became easier because of the obvious horrors of the camps discovered at the end of the war, but even so, it took the passage of nearly twenty-five years before there was much discussion of this signal event in the United States (Hilberg, 2003).

*Perspective* is equally important in recognizing evil actions. In recognizing when evil has been done, the perspective of the victim has authority. The body or psyche of the victim (and sometimes both) bears the marks of evil. The witness and testimony of the victim(s) carry moral authority as well, and provide the foundation for making judgments of good and evil. Still, there is a distortion from the victim's perspective, from which an act of cruelty or violence (or the perpetrator of that act—or both) is typically described as evil—most typically, as wholly evil. Baumeister (1997, 17) refers to this as the *myth of pure evil.*

The myth of pure evil is compounded by at least two related tendencies. First of all, the psychological concept of splitting, as discussed earlier, projects those aspects of the psyche seen as "all bad" outward onto some object (typically a person or persons). Second, American culture has a propensity, considerably exacerbated by popular media and particularly by television, to cast moral questions in stark contrasts, all good or all bad terms. Villains appear as wholly evil, and heroes as all good. In the political arena, national leaders must have a flawless and spotless past. The myth of pure evil thus represents a dangerous propensity to cast moral questions in absolute terms, which in turn makes them easier to reverse, facilitating moral inversion (see Staub [1992, 83], for a closely similar argument).

The perpetrator's description of the same act differs from that of the victim, often dramatically. Baumeister (1997, 18) refers to this as the *magnitude gap:*

> The importance of what takes place is almost always much greater for the victim than for the perpetrator. When trying to understand evil, one is always asking, "How could they do such a horrible thing?" But the horror is usually being measured in the victim's terms. To the perpetrator, it is often a very small thing. As we saw earlier, perpetrators generally have less emotion about

their acts than do victims. It is almost impossible to submit to rape, pillage, impoverishment or possible murder without strong emotional reactions, but it is quite possible to perform those crimes without emotion. In fact, it makes it easier in many ways.

The magnitude gap is centrally important for understanding evil. From the victims' perspective and most often in hindsight, evil is more readily identified. But perpetrators rarely recognize their acts as evil. From the perpetrator's perspective, the act of cruelty or violence seems "not so good" (not to say, evil), but considering other factors, say, necessity, prior injustices or some provocation, perpetrators rather easily produce rationales and justifications for even the most heinous acts (Baumeister, 1997, 307): "The combination of desire and minimally plausible evidence is a powerful recipe for distorted conclusions." The importance of perspective in recognizing evil may be captured by the old adage "Whether one sees evil depends upon where one stands." One can stand elsewhere only by a mental act of critical reflexivity, in which one reflects critically on one's own position, which actively engages both context and empathy—seeing from the perspective of others.

*Moral disengagement* is central to the magnitude gap. Although it is not easy to accept, moral standards and self-control are selective; they can be "switched" on and off, as the extensive research of Albert Bandura and others (Bandura, Underwood, and Fromsen, 1975) has demonstrated. There are at least four ways to switch off our moral compass. First, harmful behavior may be repackaged as positive (as in what we call moral inversions). Second, we can create distance between our actions and the destructive activity; this is easy within administrative evil because, after all, one is just doing one's job. Third, we can minimize or use euphemisms to diminish the destructive activity, thus convincing ourselves that nothing really bad happened. And finally, we can use dehumanization (further discussed later) to portray the victims as deserving of their treatment.

Distance, perspective, and moral disengagement are powerful constituents of the mask of administrative evil. Naming any evil that those in public service have committed, even many years ago, remains difficult because we have no distance from our own culture and profession. Recognizing administrative evil in our own time is most problematic of all because we have neither distance nor perspective—and perhaps not even moral engagement—without an explicit and somewhat difficult effort to create them (critical reflexivity). In subsequent chapters, we name evil done by those in public service, but realize that there will be no easy agreement on the part of at least some readers with our diagnosis. Unmasking administrative evil in our time and in our culture is fraught with difficulty because, essentially, we wear the mask.

### *Language and Dehumanization*

Given that much of what we do on a daily basis is taken for granted or tacit (Polanyi, 1966), two additional elements make us especially susceptible to participation in evil, without "knowing" what we are doing. The first of these is *language.* The use of euphemism or of technical language often helps provide emotional distance from our actions (Orwell, 1984, orig. 1950). "Collateral damage" from bombing raids is a euphemism for killing civilian noncombatants and reducing nonmilitary property to rubble. In the Holocaust, code words were used for killing: "evacuation," "special treatment," and the now well-known "final solution." In cases of moral inversion, euphemism or technical language can enable us to disconnect our actions from our normal, moral categories of right and wrong, good and evil (Arendt, 1963). Deportation—that is, the uprooting of entire communities, the expropriation of their property, and their evacuation to forced labor or death camps—was called "resettlement" or "labor in the East." Such language provided the minimal evidence needed to convince people that this activity was *not* evil, and that, to the contrary, it was socially appropriate or even necessary. Language often masks administrative evil.

*Dehumanization* is another powerful ally in the conduct of evil (Staub, 1992, 3). As Zimbardo (2007, 222) notes: "One of the worst things we can do to our fellow human beings is deprive them of their humanity, render them worthless by exercising the psychological process of dehumanization." If one does something cruel or violent to a fellow human being, it may well be morally disturbing. But if that person belongs to a group of people deemed (that is, redefined as) not "normal," not like the majority, or even dangerous, such action becomes easier. Furthermore, if a people can be defined as less than human, "all bad," rather like bugs or roaches (a classic moral inversion), extermination can all too easily be seen as the appropriate action. "They" brought it on themselves, after all. As Albert Speer, Hitler's Minister of Armaments, said about Jews (Speer, 1970, 315): "If I had continued to see them as human beings, I would not have remained a Nazi. I did not hate them. I was indifferent to them." Dehumanization also often masks administrative evil.

### *The Taken-for-Granted*

Tacit knowing—the taken-for-granted nature of our daily habits of action—is essential to our ability to function in a social world (Polanyi, 1966) in which even the simplest activity is enormously and dauntingly complex if each component and step has to be articulated and thought about explicitly. But the taken-for-granted also bears on our human capacity to participate in evil, as Baumeister (1997, 268) notes:

Another factor that reduces self-control and fosters the crossing of moral boundaries is a certain kind of mental state. This state is marked by a very concrete narrow, rigid way of thinking, with the focus on the here and now, on the details of what one is doing. It is the state that characterizes someone who is fully absorbed in working with tools or playing a video game. One does not pause to reflect on broader implications or grand principles or events far removed in time (past or future).

Most of our daily life in social institutions and organizations occurs within the realm of the taken for granted. Not only do we not stop and think about everything that we do (which would socially paralyze us), we hardly stop and think about anything. We do not have to make a decision about which side of the road to drive on when we start our automobile; indeed, "side of the road" does not come up on our conscious "radar screen." In most of what we do on a daily or routine basis, we simply engage in well-worn habits of action. Nothing prompts us to stop and question. So it is with administrative evil. In a culture that emphasizes technical rationality, being "at work" means maintaining a narrow focus on the task at hand. This typical focus of aware-ness drives out, or at least minimizes, our subsidiary awareness of ethics and morality (and other contextual matters as well). Acts of administrative evil can all too easily be taken for granted as well.

**The Social Construction of Evil**

Individualism, one of the core values of American culture, forms a barrier to our understanding of group and organizational dynamics—and adminis-trative evil (Zimbardo, 2007, 212). In our culture, we often assume that an individual's actions are freely and independently chosen. When we examine an individual's behavior in isolation or even in aggregate, as we often do, that notion can be reinforced. However, such assumptions about individuals blind us to group and organizational dynamics, which typically play a far more powerful role in shaping human behavior than we assume (Mynatt and Sherman, 1975; Wallach, Kogan, and Bem, 1962). As Zimbardo (2007) suggests, it is useful to distinguish between dispositional, situational, and systemic understandings.

It is an easy but important error to personalize evil in the form of the excep-tional psychopath, such as Charles Manson or Jeffrey Dahmer (often without considering how they might be a product of our culture). This dispositional understanding—the default option in a society such as ours that so highly values individualism—draws a cloak over social and organizational evil. Yet the term "mob psychology" still has resonance. The United States had a long history of public lynching, clearly a recurring example of social evil. Even more to the point, thousands of people have been subjected to administrative evil in dehumanizing experiments, internment camps, and other destructive acts by public agencies, often in the name of science and/or the national interest (Nevitt and Comstock, 1971; Stannard, 1992). Situational factors are far more significant than we typically imagine.

As we argue in Chapter 2, the modern age has been dominated by the scientific-analytic mindset. We have approached social and political problems with the tools of science, thinking of social and human phenomena as if they had the same tangibility and properties as physical reality. But societies and cultures are human artifacts, created and enacted by human activities through time (Zimbardo, 2007, 221): "It is the meaning that people assign to various components of the situation that creates its social reality." Social and political institutions, indeed all organizations, are thus socially constructed (Berger and Luckmann, 1967). This means, of course, that they are not immutable: what human beings create and enact can be reenacted in some different way. However, this does not mean that organizations and institutions are easily malleable.

To say that human social and cultural institutions and organizations are socially constructed may seem to imply that at some point groups of people rationally choose to meet together, and consciously and intentionally set about to devise an institution. Such an activity, of course, is the very rare exception. Rather, organizations and institutions more typically emerge and develop incrementally over a long period of time. As children, we are socialized into a culture that already has a vast array of institutions, practices, and rules of the road. For the most part, these all come to feel natural to us, or, more aptly, like second nature. During a person's lifetime, most organizations or institutions will change some, but usually not dramatically. Still, they *could* change dramatically. Revolutions, economic depressions, and even natural cataclysms can prompt rapid and dramatic change in a society. And of course, there are new institutions. Television and the Internet as social institutions developed within the lifetime of recent generations. Given this context of social construction, how does evil find its way in?

**Individual, Organization, and Society**

So far, we have seen how cultural predispositions can blind us to aspects of human behavior crucial for understanding administrative evil. But how do we develop these behavioral tendencies and bring them to organizations, and how do these dynamics link with our larger social and cultural context? Shapiro and Carr explore these connections in their book, *Lost in Familiar Places:*

*Creating New Connections Between the Individual and Society* (1991). Both families and organizations, along with other social institutions, are *familiar* places for us; after all, we spend our lives in them. Yet, as the authors note, we increasingly experience a sense of strangeness in these places—hence the phrase "lost in familiar places." Old ways of understanding a family, for example, seem overwhelmed by changes that impact the ways in which, over time, we negotiate a sense of meaning in our lives (social construction). The old anchors do not reach bottom, and we are cast adrift. A more or less stable, shared understanding of the family or of the church or of the work organization in the past served in part as a buffer for the ideology of individualism so pervasive in American society. For most of us, our socialization into various institutions is no longer "automatic," and the socialization that we do receive is increasingly fragmented and complex.

Shapiro and Carr discuss meaning, and in particular, the process by which we develop meaning, as negotiated collaborative interpretation—a fundamentally relational process. And they focus on the primary human group—the family, as the context in which we first learn this process, and as providing the initial model with which we subsequently attempt to make meaningful sense out of organizational life. As they develop a phenomenology of family life, the authors suggest that curiosity is a central constant in healthy families, that is to say, the parents' (or caregivers') stance toward the child is captured by the question, "What is your experience?" rather than by versions of the command, "Your experience is . . ." The question builds, over time, a capacity for negotiated, collaborative interpretation (the child pieces together boundaries that define "who I am"), while the command cuts off negotiation and imposes a definition of self on the child, leading potentially to a fragmented, defensive, and often neurotic personality. In this case, the child is apt to carry unintegrated rage and aggression into adult life, along with its characteristic splitting and projective identification.

Alternatively, the split good and bad objects can be successfully reintegrated into the self, which may lead to reparation. Reparation, which we address in more depth in the Afterword, is the motivation in mature human beings to complete worthy tasks and to render things whole again, and to do so in the recognition that there is capacity for both great good and great evil in each of us. This then is a recognition that moves one past splitting and projective identification, processes we learn as children to cope with the unbearable knowledge that we experience hate and rage toward those we love, and the concomitant anxiety that those feelings induce. Alternatively, destructive patterns of interaction quite common in organizational life enable us to maintain the projections we grew used to as children, or even to be ready accomplices to administrative evil.

Shapiro and Carr go on to make interesting linkages to broader social institutions, such as religion. Here the key concept is the notion of a holding environment (or container), which has to do with how families (or other organizations) manage the emotional issues of their members. In the successful holding environment, empathic interpretation, valuing the experiences of others, and containment of aggression and sexuality are managed in ways that sustain the integrity of members. Organizations, social institutions, and countries also function as holding environments, or containers (see, for example, Volkan, 1997). Religious institutions may be thought of as ritualized symbolic structures that contain chaotic experiences; that is, act as holding environments for these difficult feelings and emotions: "Our proposition is that a key holding environment is continually being negotiated and created through the unconscious interaction between members of a society and its religious institutions" (Shapiro and Carr, 1991, 159). However, the concept of administrative evil shows how organizations, institutions, and countries can also serve as masked holding environments for evil. People who need direction—a target, really—for their unintegrated rage and aggression, who split off the "bad" and project it out, hear all too well the siren call of groups and organizations that will contain this psychic energy for them. The price tag is almost always obedience and loyalty, sometimes moral inversion and administrative evil, and occasionally the price is very dear indeed—those truly evil eruptions that become the great moral debacles of human history.

# 2

# Compliance, Technical Rationality, and Administrative Evil

No one knows who will live in this cage in the future, or whether at the end of this tremendous development entirely new prophets will arise, or there will be a great rebirth of old ideas and ideals, or, if neither, mechanized petrification, embellished with a sort of convulsive self-importance. For of the last stage of this cultural development, it might well be truly said: "Specialists without spirit, sensualists without heart; this nullity imagines that it has attained a level of civilization never before achieved."

—*Max Weber,* 1905 (182)

Compliance stems in part from the human need for order. Our political and legal systems provide the foundation for order in social terms through law, norms, and the like. When the public order is threatened, as it was in post-9/11 United States, the response of the citizenry is a visceral one. The powerful social motivation for the preservation of social order is fueled by a fear of chaotic conditions. This fundamental need for social order helps in understanding just how strong the inclination to obey authority is for most people most of the time. Compliance accounts of human behavior also help in understanding how ordinary people become engaged in administrative evil. When compliance is wedded to organizations and institutions within a culture of technical rationality, we begin to see the social and political dynamics that can result in eruptions of evil.

## Evil and Organizations

Organizations, social institutions, and even countries can be holding environments (or "containers") for both good and evil purposes. After all, it was a
church organization that conceived and carried out the Inquisition and Cru-
sades in centuries past. When an organization, institution, or polity "contains"
the unintegrated aggression and rage (the projective identification of the
split-off "bad" parts) of its members, one has the phenomenon identified in
the title of a book by Vamik Volkan (1988), *The Need to Have Enemies and
Allies*. The belief system, or ideology, that is manifested by the organization
or polity gives the anxiety (which results from the unintegrated aggression)
a name and mitigates it by making it less confusing whom to love and whom
to hate (Staub, 1992, 4). In essence, the organization or polity communicates
some version (which varies according to the nature of the felt anxiety) of the
following to its individual members (Alford, 1990, 13):

> You really are being persecuted. Let me help you by naming your persecutors,
> and telling you who your true friends are, friends who are also being attacked
> by these persecutors. Together you and your true friends can fight the persecu-
> tors, and praise each other's righteousness, which will help you realize that the
> source of aggression and evil is out there, in the real world. And you thought
> it was all in your head.

The organization or polity has reduced the members' anxiety, but reinforced
the splitting off of the bad object(s) and the projective identification. Thus,
the unintegrated hatred and aggression that is the source of evil is called out,
and given organization and direction (Alford, 2001). This dynamic may be as
benign as an amateur softball team that makes its rival teams into "enemies."
However, when combined with a moral inversion, in which the bad becomes
good, this dynamic can lead to eruptions of evil (Alford, 1990, 15): "To seek
to destroy the bad object with all the hatred and aggression at one's command
becomes good, because doing so protects the self from badness." From a psychological perspective, unintegrated rage and aggression—part of the normal
repertoire of human emotional responses—represent the source of evil. How
these dynamics can escalate into genocide is described by Staub (1992, 5):

> Genocide does not result directly. There is usually a progression of actions. Earlier,
> less harmful acts cause changes in individual perpetrators, bystanders and the
> whole group that make more harmful acts possible. The victims are further deval-
> ued. The self concept of the perpetrators changes and allows them to inflict greater
> harm—for "justifiable" reasons. Ultimately, there is a commitment to genocide

or mass killing or to ideological goals that require mass killing or genocide. The motivation and the psychological possibility evolve gradually.

Other individual and group dynamics also play a part in the eruptions of evil. With regard to human interaction in organizations, then, our deep cultural value of individualism blinds us to the power of groups and of social conditioning over the actions of individuals. Experiments in the social construction of compliance help reveal what we may typically overlook and how ordinary people get caught up in evil activity.

## The Social Construction of Compliance:
## The Stanford Prison Experiment

An experiment in compliance conducted in the basement of the psychology department at Stanford University shows how people can comfortably adopt behaviors that are destructive to others (Haney, Banks, and Zimbardo, 1974; Zimbardo, 2007). Zimbardo and his colleagues selected twenty-two of the most normal male undergraduates they could find at Stanford. They specifically tested for individual "dispositional characteristics" that might have inclined subjects toward higher degrees of either passive or aggressive behavior. The plan was to create a simulated prison in the basement of their building in which eleven subjects were randomly assigned to be prisoners, and eleven others to be guards (with two in each group to be backups in case of illness). Nine prisoners were to occupy three cells in groups of three, and the nine guards were divided equally into three shifts of eight hours each. Zimbardo (2007, 31–32) was "interested in discovering what it means psychologically to be a prisoner or a prison guard. What changes does a person undergo in the process of adapting to that new role? Is it possible in the short time of only a few weeks to take on a new identity that is different from one's usual self?"

The "contract" offered to the subjects at the beginning of the experiment gave assurances of adequate diet, clothing, housing, and medical care—and more generally, "humane conditions." Prisoners were told they could expect to be under surveillance and have some basic civil rights suspended, but that there would be no physical abuse. Direction for the guards was simple: "maintain the reasonable degree of order within the prison necessary for its effective functioning." Prisoners were provided a loose, muslin smock with a number on the front and back, no underclothes, a light chain and lock around one ankle, rubber sandals, and a nylon stocking skullcap. Guards were given a uniform of plain khaki shirts and pants, a whistle, a police nightstick, and reflecting sunglasses (making eye contact impossible). The Palo Alto police department helped out by "arresting" each prisoner and running them through standard booking procedures. The situation was loaded with social cues to mimic the experience of prison, but unlike the Milgram experiments, to be discussed later in this chapter, here there was no "scientist" or other authority figure standing ready to assume the responsibility for the choices made by the participants.

Prisoners followed rules that were developed by the guards: three supervised toilet visits, two hours for reading or letter writing, work assignments (to "earn" the $15 per day that all participants were paid), two visiting periods per week, movie rights, and exercise periods. Three times a day, at the beginning of each shift, there was a lineup for a "count" (with nine prisoners, this was hardly difficult). The first of these lasted ten minutes, but these were spontaneously increased in length by the guards until some lasted several hours. Interactions between guards and prisoners quickly assumed a negative tone, with prisoners assuming a passive, sullen role of "learned helplessness" (Zimbardo, 2007, 196), and guards an aggressive, initiating role, characterized by verbal affronts.

Without orders or prompting, the guards became increasingly aggressive and abusive, even after prisoners had ceased any resistance and were visibly deteriorating. Prisoner rights were redefined as privileges, to be earned by obedient behavior. The experiment was planned for two weeks, but was terminated after six days. Five prisoners were released because of extreme emotional depression, crying, rage, and/or acute anxiety. Guards forced the prisoners to chant filthy songs, to defecate in buckets that were not emptied, and to clean toilets with their bare hands. They acted as if the prisoners were less than human, and so did the prisoners (Haney, Banks, and Zimbardo, 1974, 94):

> At the end of only six days we had to close down our mock prison because what we saw was frightening. It was no longer apparent to us or most of the subjects where they ended and their roles began. The majority had indeed become "prisoners" or "guards," no longer able to clearly differentiate between role-playing and self. There were dramatic changes in virtually every aspect of their behavior, thinking and feeling. In less than a week, the experience of imprisonment undid (temporarily) a lifetime of learning; human values were suspended, self-concepts were challenged, and the ugliest, most base, pathological side of human nature surfaced. We were horrified because we saw some boys ("guards") treat other boys as if they were despicable animals, taking pleasure in cruelty, while other boys ("prisoners") became servile, dehumanized robots who thought only of escape, of their own individual survival, and of their mounting hatred of the guards.

The subjects of the experiment adapted to and developed their new roles more rapidly and fervently than was ever anticipated, thus demonstrating how social roles and structures play a far more powerful part in everyday human behavior than our American belief in individualism can admit. And we can see clearly how individual morality and ethics can be swallowed and effectively erased by the dynamics of social situations (Zimbardo, 2007, 197):

> At the start of the experiment, there were no differences between the two groups; less than a week later, there were no similarities between them. It is reasonable . . . to conclude that the pathologies were elicited by the set of situational forces . . . in this prisonlike setting. . . . Neither the guards nor the prisoners could be considered "bad apples" prior to the time when they were so powerfully impacted by being embedded in a "bad barrel."

How does this happen? One is rarely confronted with a clear, up-or-down decision on an ethical issue; rather, a series of small, usually ambiguous choices are made, and the weight of commitments, social pressures, and of habit drives out morality until the next "logical" action is something that would have been unthinkable earlier. The skids are further greased if the situation is defined or presented as technical, or calling for expert judgment, or is legitimated by organizational or professional authority, as we shall see next. It becomes an even easier choice if the immoral behavior has itself been masked, redefined, and sanitized through a moral inversion as the "good" or "right" thing to do.

## Modernity and the Dominance of Technical Rationality

While the subjects of the Stanford experiment were caged in a mock prison, people in the modern world are caged by the less visible, but no less powerful, constraints of technical rationality. Here, we provide a brief historical context for technical rationality, which helps further our understanding of its role in administrative evil. The most important aspect of this historical context is how technical rationality has come to pervade the culture at large, which today may be characterized as one of *modernity* (Turner, 1990; see also Bauman, 1989; Bernstein, 1985; and Rabinbach, 1990). Modernity is the culmination of a centuries-long process of modernization. Intellectual strands of modernity reach back to the sixteenth and seventeenth centuries, but as the defining characteristic of our own culture, modernity coalesced in the last century and a half. Modernity describes a social, political, and economic world increasingly characterized by "secularization, the universalistic claims of instrumental rationality, the differentiation of the various spheres of the life-world, the bureaucratization of economic, political and military practices, and the growing monetarization of values" (Turner, 1990, 6).

Our culture of modernity has as one of its chief constituents technical rationality (Barrett, 1979; Ellul, 1954; Vanderburg, 2000; Yankelovich, 1991). Technical rationality is a way of thinking and living that elevates the scientific-analytical mindset and the belief in technological progress over all other forms of rationality. Indeed, it becomes synonymous with rationality itself (Vanderburg, 2005). In the United States, technical rationality developed in full form in the late nineteenth and early twentieth centuries. Two streams converged during this period, and released a potent set of ideas and practices into the social and political world—ideas and practices that are still in ascendancy (Wiebe, 1967, 145–163). The first stream arose from the development of epistemology in Western culture and comprised the scientific-analytical mindset that was the legacy of seventeenth-century Enlightenment thinking and the shift from a belief in divine authority to a belief in the power of individual reason. The second stream was the product of the Great Transformation of the nineteenth century and comprised the unparalleled technological progress characteristic of this period of rapid industrialization.

Beginning in the late nineteenth and early twentieth centuries, technical rationality was applied to the social and political world. "Functional rationality," as characterized by Karl Mannheim (1940), is quite similar to technical rationality. Mannheim saw functional rationality as the logical organization of tasks into smaller units, originally in the interest of efficiency. He contrasted this with "substantive rationality"—the ability to understand the purposeful nature of the whole system of which a particular task is a part. Max Horkheimer's (1947) notion of "instrumental reason" is also closely akin to technical rationality. Instrumental reason is the narrow application of human reason solely in the service of instrumental aims. Until the modern era, reason was conceived as a process incorporating ethical and normative concerns as well as the consideration of instrumental aims.

To understand how technical rationality became so pervasive in the social and political world, a brief look at the recent history of epistemology (the branch of philosophy that examines the nature, limits, and validity of knowledge) may help. By the time of the seventeenth-century Enlightenment, science, as physical science, had emerged on the scene and had begun to exert a powerful influence. Epistemology became preoccupied with a quest for the irreducible facts of existence. By the eighteenth century, the split between European and Anglo-American epistemology and philosophy had begun to be visible (this split has blurred considerably more recently). European philosophy may be represented as a series of attempts to resuscitate epistemology and metaphysics from the problems posed by science and its method of empiricism (Hegel, 1965, orig. 1807; Heidegger, 1977, orig. 1926; Nietzsche, 1956, orig. 1872). Anglo-American philosophy, on the other hand, may be represented as a series of attempts to reconstruct the concerns of philosophy according to the insights of science and its method (Whitehead and Russell, 1910; Wittgenstein, 1922). In our culture, the scientific-analytical mindset captured the way we think, and the study of epistemology was largely reduced to commentaries on the history of science. The scientific-analytical mindset, then, represents one part of the confluence that occurred in the early years of the twentieth century; technological developments comprised the other.

The astonishing succession of technological developments during the Great Transformation of the nineteenth century provided the physical, tangible embodiment of the sheer power of scientific thinking. What could have been more convincing? It must have seemed an obvious step to apply technical rationality to the social world in order to achieve science-like precision and objectivity. Frederick Taylor found a ready audience for the notion of scientific management during this period (Haber, 1964; Merkle, 1980). Technical rationality became a new ideal in the social and political world, prompting new groups of professionals, managers, behaviorists, social scientists, and industrial psychologists toward a worldview in which human conflicts were recast as problems fit for engineering solutions (Bendix, 1956; see also Ellul, 1954). As William Barrett (1979, 229) has sagely noted, "it would be silly for anyone to announce that he is 'against' technology, whatever that might mean. We should have to be against ourselves in our present historical existence. We have now become dependent upon the increasingly complex and interlocking network of production for our barest necessities." Donald Schon (1983, 21) and others have argued that technical rationality has been the most powerful influence on thinking about the professions and the institutional relations of research, government, and business. William Vanderburg (1985, 2000, 2005) argues that technical rationality represents the first universal culture of humankind.

## Technical Rationality and the Evolution of Modern Professionalism

The combination of the scientific-analytical mindset and technological progress also formed the foundation of modern professionalism, the social mechanism for translating scientific discovery and expert knowledge into practical application. Technical rationality led to specialized, expert knowledge, the life-blood of the professional, and to the proliferation of professional associations in the latter half of the nineteenth and early part of the twentieth centuries (Bendix, 1956; Graebner, 1987; Larson, 1977). The legitimacy derived from specialized knowledge enabled the professional to aspire to—and sometimes to gain—the social status and the autonomy and control over the practice of the profession that are the ultimate goals, even if sometimes unstated, of every profession. But the compartmentalization of knowledge demanded by technical rationality also inevitably led to a contextless, or timeless, practice. Thus, we find a lack of historical consciousness across the professions and academic disciplines, and more broadly, pervasive in the culture at large (Smith, 1990). The practice of a profession with little or no sense of context precludes meaningful engagement with the larger ethical and political concerns of a society (Guerreiro-Ramos, 1981). Put another way, professionalism, fed and nurtured by technical rationality, has contributed significantly to a naked public square (Arendt, 1954).

This emerging, modern model of professionalism was conceived and tried out in the late nineteenth and early twentieth centuries. The development of professional associations of all kinds began in the mid-nineteenth century, at first more rapidly in England and then burgeoning in the United States (Larson, 1977, 246). The characteristics of professions, which are fully visible around the turn of the twentieth century, include a professional association, a cognitive scientific base, institutionalized training (usually within higher education), licensing, work autonomy, colleague control, and a code of ethics (Larson, 1977, 208). Larson emphasizes the connection between the development of professionalism and the broader process of modernization (1977, xiii), "the advance of science and cognitive rationality and the progressive differentiation and rationalization of the division of labor in industrial societies."

Some professional associations were academic, and some emerged in the various professions themselves. Turning first to the academic associations, Haskell traced the history of the old American Social Science Association (ASSA), founded in 1865, as it confronted what he called a "crisis of professional authority" (1977, vi). Reform and advocacy coexisted, albeit somewhat uneasily, with science and objectivity during most of the latter half of the nineteenth century within the ASSA. Members of the ASSA came not only from the academy, but also included practitioners interested in charity work and in prison reform, among other causes. Many were involved in the Social Gospel, Chautauqua, and urban reform movements as well (Ross, 1979, 118). David Rothman's *The Discovery of the Asylum* (1971) is a good example of the reform roots of those who later turned to a rising professionalism during the latter half of the nineteenth century. Increasingly, however, the professional associations moved to become more and more separate, academic, and scientific (Ross, 1991, 125), leaving the practitioners behind and advocating a different brand of reform. Thus, in the professional organizations, the tensions grew and eventually choices had to be made. Haskell (1977, vii) places the crucial turning point during the "watershed decade" of the 1890s.

In his founding address to the American Economic Association (AEA) in 1886, Richard Ely attempted to preserve both directions, yet he called prominently for the scientific study of economics. The founding AEA platform captured the ambiguity as well (Levy, 1982, 282):

> We regard the state as an educational and ethical agency whose positive aid is an indispensable condition of human progress . . . we hold that the doctrine of laissez-faire is unsafe in politics and unsound in morals. . . .
>
> We hold that the conflict of labor and capital has brought to the front a vast number of social problems whose solution is impossible without the united efforts of Church, state and science.

The formation of the AEA in the 1880s, along with the American History Association and the American Statistics Association, was indicative both of the growing specialization of the social sciences and of the fatal contradiction in the ASSA. By the time the American Political Science Association and the American Sociological Association were founded in 1903, the demise of the ASSA was becoming inevitable. Franklin H. Giddings of Columbia University made it clear to the ASSA as early as their 1894 meeting that social science, as they had conceived it, was dying, and its heir was to be *scientific* sociology (Haskell, 1977, 204). The comments of Albion W. Small, the founding editor of the *American Journal of Sociology* and chair of the Sociology Department at the University of Chicago, about the ASSA are representative (1916, 729): "it represented humanitarian sentiment more distinctly than a desire for critical methodology."

Outside the academy, a similar process was occurring in a variety of professional associations formed in the nineteenth century, including dentists (1840), medical doctors (1847), pharmacists (1852), architects (1857), civil engineers (1867), lawyers (1878), and accountants (1887). The American Medical Association (AMA), reorganized in 1903 under the banner of scientific medicine, is representative. The AMA's Council on Medical Education, relying on visits to medical schools by Abraham Flexner, set about to ensure the conformity of medical education to the principles of "scientific medicine." Larson (1977, 163) notes that this process was characterized by "the same general principles that guided the general movement of reform in the nineties and in the first decades of the twentieth century: centralization, consolidation into larger units, efficient management by experts, and the inevitable accent on technology." Reform became equated with science and technical expertise. Flexner's conclusions—"fewer and better doctors"—were firmly and colorfully stated: "the privileges of the medical school can no longer be open to casual strollers from the highway" (Larson, 1977, 163). Flexner operationalized this dictum by recommending that the 131 medical schools in the United States be cut down to the 31 that could teach on the "modern, scientific bases" (Larson, 1977, 163).

The evolution of professional associations in the latter half of the nineteenth century reveals much about the moral and ethical impotence of professionalism—and professional ethics—in the face of administrative evil. Advocacy and reform, although in differing versions, were an integral part of the ethos of most professions until the turn of the nineteenth century and represent a trajectory incorporating moral norms and ethical values that has been largely lost in our culture. Put simply, technical expertise and social prestige won out over reform and advocacy (Furner, 1975). But this victory spawned unintended consequences in the areas of morals and ethics, as the science-based technical rationality undermined normative judgments and relegated ethical considerations to afterthoughts. In the next section, we examine the consequences of this abdication.

### The Moral Vacuity of Technical-Rational Professionalism

Within the first two decades of the twentieth century, professionalization had come to mean the reliance on science and the scientific-analytic mindset, and the growing specialization and expertise of the professions. It also meant the sloughing off of reform and advocacy as a trademark of professionalism. We want to suggest here that the tenets of advocacy and reform, when they were part and parcel of the ethos of professionalism (as they were in the latter half of the nineteenth century), represented a large part of the substance of both the *public service ideal* and the *ethical standards* of the professions. Their loss left a technically expert, but morally impoverished professionalism susceptible to moral inversion and administrative evil (Browne, Kubasek, and Giampetro-Meyer, 1995).

Professions drawing on science and social scientific approaches generally postulate an ethic based on some form of neutral objectivity. Such an approach presupposes that ethical standards can be rigorously and objectively applied, rendering judgments by "applying abstract principles to moral problems in an almost computational way, giving a procedure for deducing the morally correct answer in any given circumstances" (Clarke and Simpson, 1989, 2). Typically, the abstract principles include respect for persons, beneficence, and justice. Actors are presumed to be rational and autonomous, proceeding rigorously from some point assumed to be true.

In such an environment, prescribed ethical behavior becomes mere window dressing, which accounts for the confusion that arose within the professions over behavior that benefits a profession and ethical behavior. John Kultgen, in his book *Ethics and Professionalism* (1988, 212) states:

Codes contribute to the professional project in two ways. The professional ideology maintains that every genuine profession has an ethic. An occupation's code conveys the impression that this is true for it and hence that it is a profession. Second, the code formulates what leaders of the profession would have the public think its operative ethic is. This is intended to instill trust in its actual practices.

The emphasis on scientific method and procedure clearly narrowed the conception of ethics within professionalism. Writing in 1922, the architect Robert Kohn expressed the moral vacuity of modern professionalism quite clearly (4):

> Nothing is more evident than that today the inexpert is listened to more frequently, perhaps more trustfully than the expert, on questions of public policy. Even when the expert speaks officially as representative of his particular professional body, he is weak because of the suspicion as to his motives. The right technique, that is to say the technique best qualified, can be brought to bear upon our government affairs only when the professions as professions join together.

As both MacIntyre (1984) and Poole (1991) have argued, modernity has produced a way of thinking—an epistemology—that renders moral reasoning necessary but superfluous. Note how ethics is simply subsumed in professionalism in this statement by Kearney and Sinha (1988, 575):

> In a sense, the profession provides the professional administrator with a Rosetta Stone for deciphering and responding to various elements of the public interest. Professional accountability as embodied in norms and standards also serves as an inner check on an administrator's behavior. . . . When joined with a code of ethics or conduct and the oath of office, professionalism establishes a value system that serves as a frame of reference for decision making . . . and creates a special form of social control conducive to bureaucratic responsiveness.

Professionals do not see the technical-rational model of professionalism as eschewing ethics; quite the contrary: they see the role model of "professional" as satisfying the need for a system of ethical standards. To be professional is to be ethical.

## Compliance in a Culture of Technical Rationality

The culture of technical rationality fosters a model of professionalism that exacerbates tendencies toward compliance—and administrative evil—in groups and organizations in our culture. Consider the Milgram experiments, which cloaked legitimate authority in the mantle of science and professionalism. In the mid-1960s, Professor Stanley Milgram of Yale University set up an experiment designed to show that Americans were less prone to obey the dictates of authority than their German counterparts who had given themselves over to a totalitarian regime and obeyed it to the extremes of mass murder and genocide. He initially intended to conduct the experiment with psychology students in the United States and Germany as the test subjects, but he quickly abandoned the comparison after finding that American students were remarkably willing to obey legitimate authority, even when the consequences entailed harming another human being.

Milgram then set out to test a wider population of Americans and placed an advertisement in a New Haven, Connecticut, newspaper seeking volunteers for a "study of memory" (Milgram, 1974). Volunteers were promised payment of $4.50 for their time and trouble. Participants were placed in a room with a "scientist in a white coat" who ran the experiment, and another subject, who was actually an actor. The "scientist" explained that the experiment was a study of memory with a "teacher" and a "learner." The other "subject," the actor, was chosen through a rigged lottery to be the "learner," always leaving the only real subject in the role of "teacher."

The role of the teacher was to read a series of word pairs to the learner, who then attempted to recite them from memory. A correct answer was simply acknowledged, but upon hearing an incorrect answer, the teacher's task was to press the button on the rather elaborate console in front of him, which delivered an electric shock to the learner. The teacher was given a 45-volt shock before beginning the questions, in order to have some direct sense of the learner's experience. A 45-volt shock is quite sufficient to get one's attention. That, of course, was the only real electric shock anyone actually received in the experiment, but the teacher did not know this, and acted under the assumption that he was actually administering a series of shocks to the learner. The learner was literally strapped into a chair, with electrodes attached to one bare arm.

The console of the shock generator had 30 ascending levels of shocks, starting at 15 volts and continuing in 15-volt increments all the way to 450 volts. The console was further labeled by groups of four, with the first group called "slight shock," the next "moderate shock," then "strong shock," which ended at 180 volts. The scale continued with "very strong shock," "intense shock," "extreme intensity shock," "danger: severe shock," and finally, the simple "XXX." It was anticipated that many subjects would express hesitations or objections as the experiment progressed and they were called upon to deliver ever-increasing shocks. A series of "prods" was established, such that the first time the teacher expressed hesitation, the scientist in the white coat said, "Please continue." After the next three such expressions by the teacher, the remaining three prods in order were: "The experiment requires that you continue"; "It is absolutely essential that you continue"; and "You have no other choice, you must go on." A fifth balk by the teacher terminated the experiment.

Professor Milgram asked various samples of people what they thought the subjects' response would be. He canvassed psychiatrists, graduate students, sophomores, and a middle-class group from New Haven. All of them indicated that they personally would break off at some point early in the experiment and predicted that only a pathological few (less than 1 percent) subjects would deliver shocks all the way to 450 volts.

While the experiment came to have many variants, the initial one was the so-called voice-proximity version. In this version, the learner was positioned in a room adjacent to the teacher, but with the door open, so his voice could be heard. The learner of course rapidly began giving far more incorrect responses on the word pair questions, and at the fifth level—75 volts—he grunted audibly. At 120 volts, the learner complained verbally that the shocks were painful. Two levels later, at 150 volts, the learner demanded release. At 270 volts, the learner began delivering an agonized scream after each shock, and from 300 to 330 volts, no answer was offered, only the scream. The scientist in the white coat explained that no answer was to be considered as an incorrect answer. After 330 volts, there was no further response from the learner at all.

In the voice-proximity version, 62.5 percent of the subjects went through all 30 levels on the console, delivering the final two shocks of 435 and 450 volts in the XXX category. If you used the willingness to deliver a "strong shock" of 135 volts as the measure of compliance, then fully 99 percent of the subjects complied. And remember, at 120 volts the learner complained about the pain of the shocks. In other versions of the experiment, by moving the learner into the same room as the teacher, the percentage of fully obedient subjects was reduced, but was still at 40 percent. On the other hand, when placed in a group setting, subjects were almost 100 percent compliant and willing to cause harm to the learner, especially when another teacher administered the shocks. No version of this experiment of which we are aware—Milgram's or others'—has produced what we would call comforting results.

This kind of experiment would never pass muster before a human subjects review panel today (Nicholson, 2011). The scientist and the learner misrepresented what was going on. They lied to the subjects, many of whom experienced considerable stress and discomfort until they were informed that the learner was unharmed. Still, the teacher found himself in a rather typical social situation. A legitimate authority figure, a scientist, backed by the stature of a major university, presented an experiment that ostensibly would help to discover more about learning. The learner was a volunteer, just like the teacher. When the situation induced discomfort, which it did for large numbers of participants, the scientist authoritatively took full responsibility for the experiment and its consequences. Once the procedure began—15 volts is insignificant—role acceptance was in place and the situation was loaded so that a clear and strong individual response was needed to break free of the setting.

In this culture, which so highly values individualism, our expectation is that the individual response will trump the social situation and nearly everyone will break off, and most assuredly not fully comply. However, we find instead that these Americans, much like the "guards" in the Stanford prison experiments, found it acceptable to harm others and to play the role of "shock technician" or perhaps even "executioner," as long as they embraced the roles of "teacher" or "guard" and a professional in a technical-rational mantle of authority took full responsibility. Recent studies that revisit the Milgram and Stanford experiments (Reicher et.al, 2012; Russell and Gregory, 2011) find them more in consonance with each other than previously thought, due to attributing subject compliance less with obedience and more with identification with and acceptance of the values of the experiment. That is, subjects complied with the experiment to the extent that they found it morally acceptable and broke off only when confronted with a competing value (e.g., the well-being of the "learner"). "Teachers" who continued to administer shocks to helpless "learners" or "guards" who punished an "inmate" engaged in a moral inversion, putting their role in the experiment ahead of the pain and suffering of another human being. In at least this context, and perhaps in others, American culture seems well adapted for administrative evil, and demonstrated this capacity at Abu Ghraib prison.

**Failing to See Administrative Evil**

In considering eruptions of evil throughout our history, it is commonplace to assume, as Stanley Milgram initially did, that such acts emanate from a unique context; for example, a uniquely compliant German culture. We want to believe that they occur at a particular historical moment and within a specific culture. While this is clearly true, at least in part, it also holds a cunning deception: the effect of understanding great eruptions of evil as historical aberrations is that we safely wall them off from our own time and space, and from ordinary people in ordinary times. A lack of attention to what we believe to be a vitally important concept can be explained by this understandable, yet unfortunate, tendency to lament acts of administrative evil, while dismissing them as temporary and isolated aberrations or deviations from proper administrative behavior and rational public policy.

It is not unusual for the Holocaust (and other state-sponsored atrocities) to be viewed in such terms: that, in the midst of extraordinary circumstances, Hitler led Germany out of the fold of Western culture and into a deviant, criminal culture. But as Rubenstein (1975) and Bauman (1989) have argued, the Holocaust, rather than being a deviation from Western civilization, was one of its inherent (although not inevitable) possibilities, carried out in large part by the most advanced, technical-rational mechanisms and procedures of modern society. Further, it was the public service and advanced administrative procedures that made the mass slaughter possible (Bauman, 1989, 17):

> The Final Solution did not clash at any stage with the rational pursuit of efficient, optimal goal implementation. On the contrary, *it arose out of a genuinely rational concern, and it was generated by bureaucracy true to its form and purpose* [italics in original]. The Holocaust . . . was a legitimate resident in the house of modernity; indeed, one who would not be at home in any other house.

The same can be said of administrative evil in the history of American government and public service, such as importing hundreds of Germans—some of them "committed" Nazis and some who engaged in activities for which other Germans were convicted of war crimes—to our country after World War II in order to spearhead our rocket research and development (see Chapter 4). While sometimes recognized well after the fact as immoral acts and even crimes, few have been able to perceive that such administrative evil is consistent with, and even an outcome of, the rational pursuit of instrumental goals in the tradition of modern civilization and organizations (both public and private).

In the twentieth century, modern civilization unfolded as a paradox of unparalleled progress, order, and civility on the one hand, and mass murder and barbarity on the other. Rubenstein (1975, 91) argues, therefore, that the Holocaust, "bears witness to the advance of civilization," where progress is Janus-like, with two faces, one benevolent, the other destructive. For any profession in public life to identify itself exclusively with the face that represents order, efficiency, productivity, creativity, and the great achievements of modern civilization is, in effect, to mask the existence of a fundamental and recurring aspect of its own history and identity—the destructive and even evil face (Rubenstein, 1975, 195):

> The world of the death camps and the society it engenders reveals the progressively intensifying night side of Judeo-Christian civilization. Civilization means slavery, wars, exploitation, and death camps. It also means medical hygiene, elevated religious ideas, beautiful art, and exquisite music. It is an error to imagine that civilization and savage cruelty are antithesis. . . . In our times, the

cruelties, like most other aspects of our world, have become far more effectively administered than ever before. They have not and will not cease to exist. Both creation and destruction are inseparable aspects of what we call civilization.

Robert Bellah (1971) reached similar conclusions about American culture in reflections prompted by the massacre of hundreds of civilians, mostly women and children, by American soldiers in the 1960s in the Vietnamese hamlet of My Lai. He stated, "both the assertion of the fundamental unity of man and the assertion that whole groups of people are defective and justly subject to extreme aggression are genuinely part of our tradition" (178). From this perspective, there are not two American traditions, one good and another evil, but one tradition consisting of a paradox wherein progress in technology and human rights is accompanied by brutality, exploitation, and even the potential for mass murder. Just as Thomas Mann observed that the demonic and supremely creative were entwined in the German soul (Bellah, 1971), so freedom and exploitation are entwined in the heart of America. In the first decade of the twenty-first century, these twin impulses played out in the invasion and occupation of Iraq, with unfortunate consequences that we explore at some length in Chapter 7.

As compliance accounts of human behavior suggest, social structures and roles are far more powerful in shaping our behavior than we typically think. Within a culture of technical rationality, a model of professionalism that drives out ethics and moral reasoning offers all too fertile soil for administrative evil to emerge. Bauman (1989) and Rubenstein (1975) advance the notion that the conditions and values of modernity have unleashed the most destructive and dehumanizing forces known in human history. Bauman (1989, 73–77) argues that the core values of the culture of technical rationality—the engineering approach to society, the institution of expertise, and the practice of scientific management—are essential components of the Holocaust and other instances of contemporary racism and mass exterminations: "For these reasons, the exterminatory version of anti-Semitism ought to be seen as a thoroughly modern phenomenon; that is, something which could occur only in an advanced state of modernity. To achieve its destructive goals, modern exterminatory anti-Semitism had to be married to modern bureaucracy." Professionals and citizens alike would do well to consider not only that genocide and other acts of administrative evil required modern organizations, but also the extent to which modern management in part is founded upon and sustained by systematic dehumanization, exploitation, and even extermination. To the extent that this is true, and we will argue that it is, we must reconstruct our ethical foundation into one that unmasks and confronts the reality of administrative evil.

# Administrative Evil Unmasked

## *The Holocaust and Public Service*

> Mass murder demands organization. Repeated killing is not a deed, a single act, but an activity with all the distinguishing features of work: a task done methodically, according to plan, over time, oriented to a goal, marked by bureaucratic efficiency and routine.
>
> —*Wolfgang Sofsky,* 1997 (111)

The Holocaust is the signal event in human history that unmasks the reality of administrative evil. Despite the fact that a number of prominent authors (e.g., Allen, 2002; Arendt, 1963; Bauman, 1989; Browning, 1983; Hilberg, 1989, 2003; Rubenstein, 1975) have documented and discussed the role of the public service and private corporations in the destruction of Europe's Jews, little consideration has been given to the notion that the Holocaust is directly relevant to the theory and practice of public policy and administration. This inattention to the meaning of the Holocaust for public affairs reflects the field's deficit of historical consciousness and represents a dangerous gap in self-understanding, one that contributes to a blindness to the potential for administrative evil and to the fragility of the field's ethical foundations.

This chapter connects public policy and administration to the Holocaust by demonstrating the centrality of routine administrative processes and ordinary bureaucrats to the implementation of the Holocaust. We show that the nature and dynamics of these deadly bureaucratic processes are not unique to Nazi Germany or the Holocaust, but are entirely consistent with modern organizations and the technical-rational approach to administration. The significance of the connection between the Holocaust and the civil service in Germany is such that responsibility for the event extends not only to the central perpetrators who planned and committed overt acts of killing innocent human beings, but also to thousands of ordinary public administrators who carried out seemingly routine and morally neutral tasks. Indeed, without the full complicity of professional civil servants (and myriad other professionals and businesses), it is virtually inconceivable that the mass murder of Europe's Jews could have been accomplished. The role of public servants as perpetrators of the Holocaust requires that we seriously call into question the adequacy of the ethical foundations of modern public administration.

## The Holocaust and Administrative Evil

Prior to World War II, there were more than nine million Jews living throughout Europe. By the end of the war, approximately two-thirds, or nearly six million of them, were dead (Berenbaum, 1993; Hilberg, 2003). In Poland and other Eastern European countries, over 90 percent of the Jews were annihilated. The vast majority of these people died, not as casualties of war, but as innocent victims of a massive, deliberate effort by Nazi Germany to rid all of Europe of its Jewish population. In addition to Jews, the Nazis murdered hundreds of thousands of other victims, including Gypsies (Roma), the mentally and physically disabled, "asocials," homosexuals, and political prisoners from Poland, Russia, and other Eastern European countries.

The genocide of the Jews and these other "undesirables" was carried out by several means, culminating in the infamous death camps of Auschwitz-Birkenau, Belzec, Chelmno, Sobibor, and Treblinka, among others. In these camps, nearly four million Jews and thousands of other victims were systematically murdered. Most were gassed with carbon monoxide or the insecticide (Zyklon-B) in the massive gas chambers, but many others died in transit to the camps, or from starvation, disease, and overwork as slaves working in the most inhumane and unsanitary conditions imaginable in these and hundreds of other SS concentration camps.

Another one and a half to two million Jews were executed by mobile killing squads (known as *Einsatzgruppen*), and by other military and police death squads. The job of these squads in the early stages of the German invasion of the Soviet Union was to round up all the Jews in a town, transport them to a remote location, force them to dig their own mass grave, and then shoot everyone except those deemed (temporarily) useful as slave laborers (Browning, 1992; Rhodes, 2002). Many of the victims of these execution squads (and the majority gassed in the death camps) were women, children, and the elderly. The gas chambers and crematoria were subsequently developed as a means of killing without the horrors of mass shootings and to solve the difficulties of disposing of so many dead bodies.

## Historical Interpretations of the Holocaust and the Role of Public Service

Historical interpretations of the Holocaust center around two conceptual frameworks: one *intentional,* the other *functional* (Balfour, 1996; Browning, 1989; Mason, 1981). Both frameworks have important implications for the role of the public service in the Holocaust and what it means for the field today. The intentional interpretation (much like Allison's Model I or rational actor, 1971) centers on understanding the unfolding of events that led to the Holocaust as stemming from Hitler's explicit intention to annihilate the Jews and other "undesirable" peoples. This sinister objective was derived from his racist ideology and implemented by his henchmen through the deliberate plans and centralized commands of an all-powerful totalitarian dictatorship.

Intentional interpretations of the Holocaust emphasize its uniqueness in history as an unprecedented event, both in terms of its enormous scale and the inhumanity of the killing processes. The physical destruction of Europe's Jews is seen as a fixed goal in Hitler's mind from the beginning, certainly by the early 1920s. Events that transpired subsequent to that decision were orchestrated steps on the road to realizing this twisted vision. When the circumstances of the war provided the opportunity, Hitler decided to finally accomplish his goal of annihilating the Jews. The most important of the two decision points is the earlier one, when Hitler decided what must be done. The decision as to how and where was relatively incidental and entirely consistent with his original vision, which was conceptualized twenty-some years before its implementation (Dawidowicz, 1975). In this framework, evil stems from Hitler's hatred of the Jews, and the role of public administration in the Holocaust is a secondary one, as civil servants act as extensions of and in response to the Nazi dictatorship.

Functional interpretations of the Holocaust (which resemble aspects of Allison's Model II, organizational processes, and Model III, governmental politics, 1971), downplay the importance of Hitler's intentions and the role of central planning, emphasizing instead how the final solution emerged from the chaotic interplay of state-sponsored anti-Semitism, changing circumstances, separate and often competing organizational structures, established bureaucratic procedures, failed population policies, improvised decision processes, and local initiatives in a war zone. This perspective focuses on the somewhat anarchical nature of the Nazi state, its internal competition, and contingent decision making, which encouraged continuous improvisation at the local or micro level (Broszat, 1981; Browning, 1989). In contrast to the intentional approach, the role of Hitler and the central Nazi leadership is seen more as a catalyst for these disparate forces than that of central planner or controlling decision maker. The Holocaust was implemented by a multipronged operation of a decentralized apparatus or web of organizations that depended as much on administrative input and discretion as on a top-down, centralized command hierarchy (Hilberg, 1989).

The functional perspective sees no meaningful distinction between the conceptualization and implementation of the final solution (Browning, 1989, 98–99): The final solution did not result so much from explicit orders systematically disseminated from the top leadership as through self-recruitment by the zealous and ambitious servants of the Third Reich in response to the impulses and hints they perceived emanating from the centers of power. While Hitler's ideological fixation assured that a final solution to the "Jewish problem" would be sought, it did not specify the form it would take. As circumstances changed, especially after the invasion of the Soviet Union, so did the definition of the problem and its possible solution. Only after considering and experimenting with a number of definitions of and solutions to the Jewish problem did the final solution emerge. Even the infamous death camp at Auschwitz was not created at once for its ultimate role, but evolved through a succession of purposes in a step-wise process, culminating in extermination (Adam, 1989; Dwork and Van Pelt, 1996).

Functionalists (for example, Broszat, 1981; Browning, 1989; Hilberg, 1989) argue that the intent to pursue mass murder as the final solution was more latent than manifest until it crystallized in the minds of decision makers as population engineering policies focused on deportation and resettlement proved increasingly unworkable (Aly, 1999). That is, mass murder as an intentional strategy was reconstructed as decision makers became aware of the path they were following and the consequences of their actions. The goal of killing all the Jews emerged from organizational practice and the escalation of killing operations (*Einsatzgruppen*) during the invasion of the Soviet Union (Rhodes, 2002).

The functionalist emphasis on process tends to highlight not the uniqueness and enormity of the Holocaust, but rather micro-level processes and the extent to which they reflect much "that is familiar and even commonplace in the context of contemporary institutions and practices" (Hilberg, 1989, 119). The Nazi dictatorship, German anti-Semitism, and Hitler's racist ideology represent necessary but not sufficient conditions for the Holocaust to occur (Bauman, 1989; Browning, 1989). Just as important were latent tendencies toward dehumanization within routine bureaucratic processes, "performed by thousands of functionaries in public offices and private enterprises

. . . embedded in habit, routine, and tradition" (Hilberg, 1989, 119). Those involved in these processes did not merely respond to the Nazi dictatorship, but also provided impetus and direction to the genocide.

Ultimately, however, neither the intentionalist nor the functionalist interpretation of the Holocaust provides an entirely satisfactory explanation for what happened. While we cannot penetrate Hitler's mind or even his conversations with his inner circle of advisors, the actions of the Third Reich during the 1930s do not reflect a consistent intention to murder Europe's, or even Germany's, entire Jewish population (Kaplan, 1998). Several strategies aimed at removing Jews, first from German society and then from the rest of Europe, were tried before changing circumstances and failed population policies led Hitler and the Third Reich to their final solution to the Jewish problem (Aly, 1999; Bloxham, 2009). On the other hand, a purely functionalist explanation for the Holocaust tends to marginalize the intentions and influence of Hitler and the SS and obscures Hitler's role in leading Germany toward the final solution (also see Friedlander, 1997; 2007, 1–6).

Appreciating the contributions of both perspectives contributes to a better understanding of how the Holocaust occurred: not as the result of exclusively intentional or functional processes, but as the confluence of historical and political forces including racist ideology and anti-Semitism, organizational competition, the lack of moral constraints in the "bloodlands" of Central and Eastern Europe (Snyder, 2010), and the bureaucratic processes of a highly developed modern society. The combination of planning and opportunism, of tight control and improvisation, of rational preparation and intuitive action, was characteristic of how the Nazis gained, exercised, and eventually fell from power (Browning, 1989; Burleigh, 2000; Yahil, 1990, 54).

To the extent that both perspectives, intentional and functional, contribute to understanding the Holocaust, organizational structure and modern bureaucratic processes should comprise at least as much of the overall picture as the intentions and directives of the Nazi dictatorship. Functional processes formed the foundation for the vast and systematic mass killing operations, and the Holocaust cannot be understood apart from the contribution of relatively mundane bureaucratic processes. Bureaucratic procedures carried out by regular civil servants were essential to both the formulation and the implementation of the Holocaust. The perpetrators did not operate only in a specialized agency or department, but within all the public bureaucracies, national and local, and within businesses and corporations (Matthaus, 2004). No separate agency or commission was created to deal with the Jewish problem. Existing organizations (centering on and eventually directed by the SS) adapted and contributed to the evolving task of separating Jews from the society of the Third Reich to the point where their destruction became the logical and efficient solution to an administrative problem.

### Legalizing Evil: The German Civil Service and the Third Reich

Yahil (1990) identifies three basic tools that Hitler used to establish and maintain his fascist state: terror (including the SS and Gestapo), legislation, and propaganda. To these we must add the public service (see also Neumann, 1944). Hitler used all of these simultaneously (and sometimes at odds with each other) to achieve his ends and create an aura of legitimacy for his dictatorship. This approach allowed Hitler to justify his actions both to the international community and to Germany's civil service, who were essential to administering first the Nazi state and later the Holocaust. Germany's professional civil servants and the courts probably would have resisted a regime that lacked legal and constitutional legitimacy, as they had opposed the 1923 putsch (Brecht, 1944), and the 1933 boycott of Jewish businesses.

Following his appointment to the chancellory and in the wake of the Reichstag fire, Hitler pushed through two key pieces of legislation in the spring of 1933. First, the "Emergency Regulation in Defense of the People and the State" abolished the basic individual rights and legal protections of a democratic society. Second, the "Enabling Act," or "Law for Removing the Distress of People and the Reich," provided the legal instrument to sanction and strengthen his dictatorship. These were justified in the name of suppressing an imminent communist revolution (Burleigh, 2000). The Enabling Act invested Hitler with direct legislative authority, and he used it to pass numerous laws aimed at putting the government fully under the control of the National Socialists (Yahil, 1990, 54–55). It also placed the civil service at the disposal of Hitler's cabinet for whatever it deemed fit to decree. Once Hitler was elected and the Enabling Act passed according to constitutional requirements, civil servants had little choice but to fall in line with the new regime or be at odds with an overwhelming power.

According to Brecht (1944), their professional duty, as they understood it, demanded that civil servants apply decrees issued within the limits of the Enabling Act, whether they personally approved of them or not. The individual public employee was faced with a limited range of choices. He could (1) withdraw and lose employment, with potentially dire consequences, (2) stay in office and warn or advise during the preparation stages of new measures, or (3) try to undermine the regime. As Brecht noted (1944, 105):

> Only someone who is well acquainted with the German civil servant is able to estimate the torment through which many of them have gone since Hitler's

access to power. But the legalistic measures of the Nazi regime left little opportunity for concerted resistance. Once a decree based on the Enabling Act
was issued, civil servants felt obligated to execute measures that fell under
their jurisdiction.

But there is evidence that many bureaucrats may have been more than
grudging participants in the consolidation of Nazi power. Several enabling
acts had been passed as emergency measures during the Weimar Republic and
were welcomed by the civil service, which had long been frustrated with, and
disdainful of, the disorganized and contentious politics of the Reichstag. The
Enabling Act of 1933 was seen as another example of the legislature's failure
to govern effectively, and as necessary to combat revolutionary (Marxist)
forces. Thus, governing by decree was nothing new in Germany, and civil
servants were well prepared to govern without democratic processes. But
this Enabling Act eventually went further than previous ones. Any decrees
published in the German equivalent of the Federal Register gained the force
of law, effectively creating government by the executive and the civil service
(Noakes and Pridham, 1984). In a classic case of moral inversion, many
public servants believed that they were doing what was best for Germany in
troubled times.

The importance of a cooperative and dutiful public bureaucracy to the
Third Reich is reflected in the fact that the first basic statute passed under
the Enabling Act was the "Law for the Restoration of the Professional Civil
Service," promulgated on April 7, 1933, together with a statute that restricted
the independence of the secondary states in favor of the central government.
The intent of this legislation was to remove Jews and other "unreliables"
from important government posts (Browning, 1983; Yahil, 1990, 64), and it
represented a key first step in separating Jews from German society. Yet not
all Jews were removed at first. At President Hindenburg's insistence, World
War I veterans were retained and those who were dismissed received their
regular pensions. Even "unreliables" received 75 percent pensions. These
were not revoked until the end of 1938 (Brecht, 1944, 110).

According to Brecht (1944, 110–111), the majority of dismissals came
from the ranks of the higher civil service. Out of 1,663 Prussian members
of the higher civil service in field positions, 469, or 28 percent, were either
dismissed as "unreliable" or Jewish (12.5 percent), or were demoted to lower
positions for "administrative reasons" (15.5 percent). In the middle brackets of
the civil service, including the clerical class, only 3.46 percent were affected
(1.13 percent "unreliable"; 2.33 percent for "other reasons").

These developments should not lead to the conclusion that most remaining
civil servants belonged to the Nazi Party. The great majority did not, espe-

cially during the 1930s. Most civil servants were neither minions of the Nazi state nor hardcore anti-Semites. They were career professionals who valued competence, efficiency, and their ability to overcome obstacles and adverse conditions, and they often took pride in knowing what to do without asking for direction (Hilberg, 1989, 132–133). They wanted to keep their jobs and were allowed to do so because they were needed to administer the state and their functions were considered politically neutral, constituting no political danger to the rule of National Socialism. Indeed, widespread dismissals to install Nazi Party members would have posed a much greater threat to the regime's stability. The legislative and legalistic measures taken by the new government reassured most civil servants that their actions were legally justifiable and maintained their continued reliability as administrators in nonpolitical posts.

One of the immediate effects of the Law for the Restoration of the Professional Civil Service was that civil servants throughout Germany became deeply involved in the highly bureaucratic process of determining who was or was not a Jew. The law contained the first official definition of a Jew, and genealogical and medical records had to be tracked down and verified for thousands of individuals, that is, for anyone suspected of being Jewish. These investigations led to the dismissals of thousands of Jews from civil service positions, to prohibitions from the practice of law and medicine, and to many other prohibitions and restrictions in all areas of political, social, and cultural affairs (Friedlander, 1997). There is little evidence that government employees objected to these background investigations or questioned the policy of separating Jews from German society.

Thus there appears to have been very little direct prodding, and certainly no wholesale purging, of the German public service (Hilberg, 1989, 129). Most civil servants were relatively comfortable in positions that entailed "morally neutral" functions, such as economic affairs, tax collection, social security, statistics, railroad service, foreign currency, municipal government, and so forth, meaning that their work could not be directly implicated in acts they would judge to be immoral, illegal, or unethical. Direct acts of murder and cruelty generally were the provenance of the SS, and were not assigned to permanent officials. If indirectly involved in such actions, civil servants would try to be fair to the victims, and attend to the details of administration within the boundaries of the law. Being of such service may have brought some moral conflict to civil servants in the Third Reich, but most reasoned that matters would only be worse if they failed to cooperate and do their duty (Brecht, 1944, 106). However, a closer examination of these so-called "morally neutral" functions will show that such activities were not as neutral or peripheral to the killing process as civil servants might have liked to believe.

As Hilberg (1989, 129) points out, they contributed their share to the destruction of the Jews as a matter of course.

## Implementing Evil: The German Civil Service and the Holocaust

Most generally, the Holocaust evolved from the efforts of the Nazi state to solve the Jewish problem, or to accomplish the elimination of the Jews from German society, and eventually, from all of Europe. This task became, essentially, a vast and complex administrative problem. As the policy evolved, it was up to the various components of both public and private organizations to figure out how to accomplish it. The difficulty of the problem stemmed from the fact that, despite centuries of anti-Semitism, Jews were fully entwined with every aspect of German (and European) society: economic, political, social, and cultural. No matter how virulent Hitler's hatred of the Jews and the zeal of his followers, Jews could not suddenly be exiled or killed without severely disrupting the social fabric and political economy of German society (Browning, 1989). Hitler had to first consolidate his political power before beginning his campaign against the Jews. The first victims of the Nazi regime were its communist, liberal, and other internal opponents. Of course, some Jews were caught up in this dragnet, but they were not its focus (Gellately, 2001; Johnson, 1999).

Anti-Jewish legislation of the 1930s reflects the gradual escalation of a policy to remove Jews from German society: legally, economically, and socially (Bauman, 1989; Kaplan, 1998; Rubenstein, 1975; Yahil, 1990). A variety of measures were needed to sever these connections without violating the rights or interests of the non-Jewish population. The necessary actions to implement anti-Jewish legislation thus had to be taken by technical, professional specialists: accountants, lawyers and judges, engineers, physicians, and so forth, many of whom worked in the public service. Numerous technical and legal problems had to be solved, such as: Who was (or was not) a Jew? What about a mixed marriage? How was a "Jewish enterprise" to be defined? How were its assets to be disbursed? Where would Jews be allowed to live? These legal procedures and accounting routines were essential to the process of removing Jews from German society, through an administrative apparatus that was attempting to preserve non-Jewish rights and to balance the books at all times. Administrative problems relating to the Jews were dealt with, like any other, in bureaucratic memoranda, correspondence, meetings, and discussions (Hilberg, 1989, 120, 121). By following proper procedures, the German public servant could feel satisfied that his actions were appropriate and legal. He could separate his actions from their inhuman consequences by equating correctness with rightness and accuracy with accountability. In this way, the German bureaucracy and businesses adapted to the evolution of Nazi anti-Jewish policy from legislative discrimination and expropriation to emigration and then deportation and extermination (Browning, 1983, 147; Hayes, 2004).

The de-nationalization decrees of the 1930s empowered the Minister of the Interior to cancel naturalization granted since the end of World War I, and provided that all German citizens residing outside of the Reich could be deprived of their citizenship. The ultimate impact of this decree was felt in 1941 when the Reich Citizenship Law (one of the 1935 Nuremburg Laws) was amended to provide that Jews "who take up residence abroad" were no longer Reich nationals and their property was to be confiscated by the state. As soon as the Gestapo transported Jews beyond the German border, regardless of their unwillingness to go, they lost all rights as citizens. No government was concerned for their fate, and thus, the Nazis eliminated all legal impediments to carrying out the final solution (Rubenstein, 1975, 32–33). The legal conversion of Jews from citizens into aliens preceded their destruction. Before they were executed, the Jews ceased to exist as members of a political community. Perhaps the most frightening aspect of the Holocaust is that these measures were implemented in large part by the public service and private organizations carrying out routine functions as if virtually nothing was out of the ordinary (Hilberg, 1989, 128): "In the final phases, not even orders were needed. Everyone knew what had to be done, and no one was in doubt about directions and goals. The fact is that the initiators, formulators, and expediters, who at critical junctures moved the bureaucratic apparatus from one point to the next, came from within the apparatus."

While, understandably, history has focused on Hitler and his inner circle, the brutality of the SS, the Gestapo, and infamous concentration camp doctors and guards, much less attention has been given to the thousands of public administrators such as those in the Finance Ministry who engaged in confiscations, the armament inspectors who organized forced labor, municipal authorities who helped create and maintain ghettos and death camps throughout Poland and Eastern Europe, corporations that profited from slave labor, and women who served in roles from secretaries to concentration camp staff members (Allen, 2002; Hayes, 2004; Kaplan, 1998; Lower, 2013). The destruction of the Jews became procedurally indistinguishable from any other modern organizational process. Great attention was given to precise definition, to detailed regulation, to compliance with the law, and to record keeping. In other words, the modern, technical-rational approach to public service was adhered to in every aspect.

For example, one difficult administrative problem involved the financing of rail transport, which was essential to the destruction process. Jews were transported out of Germany and other European countries to the death camps, a process that stripped them of all legal protections and allowed the Nazis to execute them at a distance from major population centers. But bureaucratic procedure had to be followed, and this dictated that no agency, including the Gestapo or the SS, could just use the trains as they saw fit. The German Rail Authority derived its revenue from individual clients or organizations requiring space on its trains. The client for the trains to the death camps was the Gestapo. The travelers were Jews. The fare, payable by Gestapo offices, was calculated at the passenger rate, third class, for the number of track kilometers, one way only, with discounts for children. Group rates were applied to transports exceeding 400 individuals. For the guards, the round-trip fare had to be paid (Hilberg, 1989, 129–131). With this routine, matter-of-fact calculation, whole communities were transported to their deaths.

However, the Gestapo had no budget for transport, and there was no precedent for simply charging such expenses to the Finance Ministry. The Gestapo solved the problem by developing a "self-financing" scheme that shifted the burden of funding to authorities in the foreign areas where Jewish properties had been expropriated or even to the Jewish communities themselves. Levies were collected and deposited in special accounts "W," which the Gestapo controlled and then paid to the rail authority. The Finance Ministry condoned this practice even though it constituted an evasion of the basic principle that only the ministry could collect funds for the Reich and disburse them to agencies. By allowing the Gestapo to find and implement a creative solution, albeit one of questionable legality, to the financing problem, the basic framework of routine bureaucratic procedures could be preserved, allowing civil servants to focus on their administrative responsibilities with a minimum of disruption or moral discomfort.

The financing of rail transport illustrates the combination of technical-rational administrative procedures with the improvisation and opportunism that characterized the many activities contributing to the Holocaust. Every effort was made to preserve the facade of legality and proper procedures at all times, and to find the most efficient solution to the problem. The approach was consistently impersonal and dehumanizing. Hilberg points out how this approach is reflected in the reporting system. Offices and field units would make reference to the final solution in long summaries of diverse activities, following a rigid format and matter-of-fact style that masked the nature of the activities (Hilberg, 1989, 131): "The Jews are absorbed in the daily passage of events, and there is seldom any disconcerting emphasis on their ultimate fate." Jews basically became a subheading under normal bureaucratic lists of wages, rations, taxes, transport, and so forth.

It is important to recognize, however, that the routine duties and procedures carried out by civil servants contributed to the Holocaust—to mass murder—

in more direct ways. Concentration and death camps generated externalities that affected the surrounding communities and environment. The SS and Gestapo found that they could not carry out their grim mission without the aid of competent and diligent public servants. While the SS had complete control over what happened in their camps once they were built, they had to conform to normal planning and inspection procedures while the camps were under construction. Public officials dealt with the establishment and maintenance of death camps in much the same way as they would any other public facility or private industry, as illustrated by the following comments by a provincial planner in the Auschwitz region (Van Pelt, 1994, 134):

> When I gave my permission some time ago to create a concentration camp, I made it clear that a camp of this enormous size, located in such an extraordinarily well-located place for industry . . . would be expected to accept many conditions in the interest of other parties or for the common good.

But problems commonly dealt with by public bureaucracies took on horrific and dehumanizing properties in the context of genocide and the Holocaust.

A particularly vexing problem at the larger concentration and death camps involved the processing and disposal of human waste (a separate issue from the disposal of ashes from the crematoriums). The attempt to dispose of waste in the most efficient manner (most output for the least cost) resulted in systems that stripped inmates of the last vestiges of their humanity and wreaked havoc on the surrounding environment and communities (Van Pelt, 1994). The initial reluctance of the SS to invest resources and manpower in the construction of adequate latrines and wastewater facilities at Auschwitz resulted in large amounts of sewage flowing into the Vistula River and strained relations with the surrounding communities. By 1943 teams of engineers and planners were fully engaged in designing a sewage treatment facility for Auschwitz. While none of the civil servants who worked on the sewage problem directly killed anyone, the camp's continued operation required their complicity (Van Pelt, 1994, 135–136).

In discussing the role of the railroad administration in the Holocaust, Hilberg points out that its heavy participation in activities that supported the genocide of the Jews should command our attention because neither the railroad administration nor most other public agencies in Nazi Germany conformed to any common definition or characteristics of an ideological vanguard or movement (Hilberg, 1989, 126): "If nothing else, their history should tell us that if Hitler and the Nazi Movement . . . were essential for the Holocaust to occur, so was at least in equal measure the readiness of ordinary agencies to engage in extraordinary tasks inherent in the Final Solution."

Does this mean that German public servants were "willing executioners" (Goldhagen, 1996), or banal functionaries who merely followed orders (Arendt, 1963)? The answer, as in the intentionalist versus functionalist debate, is both. Genocide became public policy after the massive increase in Jews under Nazi rule following the invasions of Poland and the Soviet Union and was not simply the result of carrying out well-defined orders from the center or of spontaneous killing. It evolved through a series of steps—from seeking solutions to successive problems—including how to get the most slave labor out of prisoners while systematically killing them, how to make the killing easier (than shooting) for the executioners, and how to dispose of the thousands of bodies "produced" by the killing process. The death and slave labor camps, gas chambers, and crematoria were the final solution to these and other aspects of the Jewish problem, and were relatively short steps to take after traveling a long road toward this horrific, unmasked administrative evil (Bauman, 1989; Browning, 1992).

## Adolf Eichmann and the Banality of Evil

Perhaps more than any other historical event, the Holocaust gave new life to the concept of evil. The atrocities committed by the Nazis against the Jews of Europe and the other perceived enemies of the racial state added new dimensions and horror to humanity's repertoire of murder and human degradation: millions of innocents were killed in the name of the racial state. Yet one of the most enduring and influential conceptions of evil that emerged from the study of the Holocaust stands in stark contrast, apparently, to the enormity of the event: Hannah Arendt's (1963) notion of the banality of evil. When confronted with one of the central actors of the Holocaust, Arendt saw not the homicidal monster or psychopath that one might expect, but an everyday bureaucratic functionary. At his trial in 1961, Adolph Eichmann looked like an ordinary employee of a large organization and spoke of mass murder as if it were a typical industrial and bureaucratic process. The banality of evil challenges the assumption that the perpetrators of radical evil must be exceptional departures from normal, civilized behavior, and raises the possibility that anyone engaged in organizational routines can be complicit in humanity's worst crimes.

Eichmann's career is almost a microcosm of the development of the Nazi regime. Before joining the Nazi Party, Eichmann made his way through post–World War I Austrian society by taking the advice and accepting the help of others, including Jews, who were in positions to advance his interests. In his biography of Eichmann, David Cesarani (2006) chronicles Eichmann's transition from being a reasonably successful salesman of petroleum products to becoming a Nazi Party member and officer in the security service (SD) division of the SS. The record suggests that, at least in his first few years in the Nazi Party, he was motivated less by anti-Semitism than by the nationalistic political and economic platform of the Nazis and the modest prosperity, security, and opportunity for professional advancement the party afforded during the tough economic times of the 1930s. In 1934, Eichmann joined the SD when it had no executive functions and relatively little influence in the Nazi Party, including on Jewish matters. He fit in well with the men who came to form the core of the Nazi security apparatus: energetic, confident young men in their thirties and forties, university educated, intelligent, rational, neither misfits nor mindless conformists who "developed a generational lifestyle that was cold, hard, and objective, rooted in the all-embracing ideology of radical volkisch nationalism" (Cesarani, 2006, 46).

As Cesarani tells it, Eichmann's Nazi superiors recognized in him the "right objective, problem-solving and managerial outlook combined with fierce German nationalism grounded in racial pride" (47). As the SD emerged as "one of the most dynamic and innovative organizations within the Party and . . . the state apparatus" (39) and eventually the driving force of anti-Jewish policy in Nazi Germany, Eichmann embraced its mission without hesitation. The SD cultivated in its members a rational, professional anti-Semitism. It was their duty to rid the nation of what they believed to be a growing, existential menace. In the 1930s, the mission did not entail mass murder, but focused on the all-out effort at Jewish emigration from Germany and Austria to other lands, including Palestine. This policy relied on systematic discrimination to induce emigration and became increasingly coercive and destructive. Yet Eichmann never wavered in his belief that he was doing what was necessary and right for Germany, a classic moral inversion.

From 1935 to 1941, Eichmann built his career on the backs of German and Austrian Jews by designing means to induce and eventually force them to emigrate (all the while fleecing them of their wealth). Based on his success in directing forced emigration of Jews from Austria, he became a relatively powerful bureaucrat: Someone who could be relied upon to get an important job done. As more responsibility and promotion came his way, he reveled in his newfound power, behaving like "a 'young god' in a shiny black uniform," and "his appetite for power and promotion (meshed) with the dynamic of the SD and the Nazi regime" (71).

War presented Eichmann with new, hitherto unimagined possibilities. Following the lead of Himmler and Heydrich, he spearheaded grand schemes for relocating populations inspired by the fantasy of a greater Reich free of supposedly inferior races. Jews, Poles, and other Slavic peoples were deported to make room—living space—for German settlers. Such actions began almost immediately following the invasion and occupation of Poland, with thousands of Poles and Jews forcibly removed from their homes and replaced by German settlers. Eichmann focused on creating plans aimed at moving (in a way that would assure their eventual demise) as many as 5.8 million Jews from Germany and their temporary domicile in the squalor of Poland's ghettos to places such as Nisko (an almost uninhabitable swampy region in eastern Poland), then to Madagascar, and finally to somewhere in the east once the Soviet Union was defeated (Bloxham, 2009). These plans were aborted (although several thousand Jews were deported to Nisko) or came to naught as the German war machine ground to a halt in the Russian winter. By late 1941, forced relocation was replaced by the policy of mass murder as the next logical step in the effort to rid Europe of Jews and other "undesirables" (Aly, 1999; Friedlander, 2007). Eichmann at first showed little enthusiasm for the new policy direction, not because he thought it wrong to kill Jews but because it meant the end of the emigration programs and plans that he had devised and directed.

The Wannsee Conference in January 1942, with which he is so notoriously associated, signaled a new phase of Eichmann's career as he became directly involved in the new policy of extermination. He went on to play a critical role in the genocide, managing the complex process of transporting victims to concentration and death camps, culminating in his work in Hungary, organizing the last major deportation of Jews to Auschwitz in 1944. Cesarani (2006, 157) summarizes Eichmann's role in genocide this way:

> Eichmann's attitude towards the Jews had assumed a cold inhumanity. . . . [He] managed genocide in the way that the director of a multi-national corporation manages production and distribution of product: calibrating the supply of raw material to the capacity of plant, monitoring output and quality controls and assuring prompt delivery.

It was in this capacity that Eichmann gained his reputation as a "desk murderer."

## Eichmann: Exceptional or Banal?

Recognizing the banal side of Eichmann and other perpetrators does not require accepting their defense of just following orders or being mere cogs in a larger system. Anti-Semitism was a necessary yet insufficient basis for explaining perpetrator behavior in the Holocaust. Eichmann and others made themselves indispensable to their leaders at the expense of the Jews. Most joined the Nazi Party at a time when they felt cast off by society and found in the party a sense of belonging among other marginalized and like-minded men. They later became part of and socialized into bureaucratic organizations in a totalitarian regime where the individual is subordinate to the position and the needs of the regime and can be eliminated at any time (Westermann, 2010). They helped to *institutionalize* mass murder and dehumanization, making them routine and banal, and providing "important" positions and careers for the Nazi faithful. Plans were in place to continue this process well beyond eliminating the Jews by extending the society of total domination to millions of conquered Slavs in Poland and Russia, giving permanence to the society of total domination that was "perfected" in Auschwitz. Eichmann and others like him would never become superfluous as long as there was a massive population of "surplus people" to be enslaved and dehumanized (Rhodes, 2002, Rubenstein, 1975).

Cesarani (2006) correctly points out that Arendt overemphasized Eichmann's apparent banality in 1961; Eichmann's behavior was hardly common-place while sending Jews to their deaths in 1942–44. Nevertheless, Arendt's analysis of Eichmann's trial and testimony opened up a whole line of inquiry into the Holocaust as to how, not just why, a crime of such magnitude could occur. The concept of the banality of evil stemmed from Arendt's (and Hilberg's) frightening observation that ordinary men implementing bureaucratic norms and procedures, which are part and parcel of every modern organization, managed the deportations, concentration camps, and killing centers. Conventional conceptions of evil or wrongdoing tempt us to view the Holocaust as the product of a singular time and culture. But the trial of Eichmann suggested that he and other perpetrators were more ordinary—their behaviors and attitudes less uniquely German and more typically modern—than we might care to admit. Eichmann became a *genocidaire* within an organization and system where he and others learned and embraced a cold-hearted hatred as part of a job (Lozowick, 2000; Westermann, 2010). Eichmann and many thousands of others were enlisted in such a horrible and far-reaching enterprise through the medium of bureaucratic organization, which provided countless connections, both direct and indirect, between ordinary jobs and genocide. At a minimum, the Eichmann trial helped to reveal the banal side of evil, if not that evil IS banal.

In another study, Michael Mann shows that the Holocaust was indeed perpetrated by a core population of dedicated Nazis who hated Jews, but not only by them (2000, 357):

> These "real Nazis" operated amid a much broader range of perpetrators, many of whom were likely to be rather more "ordinary." . . . Among the lower administrators in the transport and other agencies smoothing the flow

of victims, we would doubtless find many Germans with virtually no prior history of Nazism or violence, exhibiting the whole range of prejudices, equivocations, and moral evasions that studies have suggested characterized the German population as a whole. Germans turned a blind eye, thought about matters of more personal concern, cared nothing for disliked Jews, and facilitated the trajectory of the victims, with practiced and entirely normal human moral weakness.

The banality of evil was symptomatic of a process whereby the perpetrators destroyed and then disposed of their victims as objects or refuse by employing what closely resembled "normal" administrative procedures. This was not the only method of mass murder in the Holocaust, but it does set it apart from premodern mass murders and challenges our confidence in modern political/administrative institutions and processes. Administrative evil is masked, in part, because it occurs at the heart of modern civilization, perpetrated by the servants of the nation-state. The facts of the Holocaust show that the same procedures, and, more important, the same mental map that created and ran the concentration and death camps are part and parcel of every modern organization. Thus we can see Eichmann as both exceptional and banal. Exceptional in that he became a cold-hearted anti-Semite at the center of the circle of perpetrators, and banal in that he wore the mask of administrative evil, embodying the persona of the desk murderer that so many others could comfortably adopt. What frustrates all who would seek justice for the victims and prevent future genocides is that the motives of so many perpetrators were superficial and uninspiring (Osiel, 2001); there is no greatness, only waste and loss. They mistook duty for morality, destruction for production. They only managed to set the bar low enough so that many could pretend to have accomplished much at the expense of the innocent.

**Perfectly Safe Ground?**

More than seventy years later, what is the meaning of the Holocaust for public life? There is no single, satisfactory answer to this question. However, given what we now know about the Holocaust and how it was implemented, we would pose an imperative that all professionals involved in public life continually raise this question and make administrative evil a central ethical concept in their practice. For example, the role of the professional civil service and public bureaucracy in the Holocaust should give us pause when we consider the following statement by Woodrow Wilson from his classic essay on the study of administration, a work that continues to influence conventional views of public management and administration (1887, 221):

> When we study the administrative systems of France and Germany, knowing that we are not in search of *political* principles, we need not care a peppercorn for the constitutional or political reasons which Frenchmen or Germans give for their practices. . . . If I see a murderous fellow sharpening a knife cleverly, I can borrow his way of sharpening the knife without borrowing his probable intention to commit murder with it; and so, if I see a monarchist dyed in the wool managing a public bureau well, I can learn his business methods without changing one of my republican spots. . . . By keeping this distinction in view, that is, by studying administration as a means of putting our own politics into convenient practice . . . we are on perfectly safe ground.

Wilson wrote at the end of the nineteenth century and in the heyday of Progressivism, before the horrors of the World Wars.

At the dawn of the twenty-first century, it is difficult, standing in the long shadow of the Holocaust, to conclude that public servants, in whatever political or administrative context, can find anything resembling safe ground anywhere. The historical record shows that the Holocaust was not the result of a departure from the practice of modern, technical-rational administration, but represents one of its inherent and now demonstrated possibilities (Bauman, 1989; Rubenstein, 1975). The public service facilitated every stage of the killing process. As the final solution evolved, there was nothing that is normally considered part of modern professionalism, education, and expertise, ethical standards, scientific methods, bureaucratic procedures, accountability to elected officials, and so on that could prevent or resist the genocide of the Jews. Public servants were both willing and helpless in the face of great evil. Today, they remain just so because administrative evil wears a mask.

While there is little in the way of solace or comfort to be found in the history of public service and the Holocaust, it does tell us that all professionals in public life—scholars, students, and practitioners alike—would do well to reflect on the possibility that their systems and actions can contribute to the worst kinds of human behavior, and that our ethical standards and professional training do not adequately address the potential for administrative evil. In this era of increasingly ideological and polarized politics (Hacker and Pierson, 2011; Hunter, 1991; Lowi, 1995) and unwanted, surplus populations (Fritz, 1999; Rubenstein, 1983), no profession should be taught, practiced, or theorized about without considering the psychological, organizational, and societal dynamics that can lead those in public service to confound the public interest with acts of dehumanization and destruction.

# Administrative Evil Masked

## From Mittelbau-Dora and Peenemünde to the Marshall Space Flight Center

> I could not watch the *Apollo* mission without remembering that that triumphant walk was made possible by our initiation to inconceivable horror.
>
> —*Jean Michel, Mittelbau-Dora survivor,* 1979 (247)

In this chapter, we tell the story of the von Braun team of German rocket scientists and engineers who were brought to the United States after World War II. They became the premier rocket development team in this country, and in the 1960s they designed and built the Saturn rockets that propelled *Apollo* to the moon. While rumors about their past apparently followed the von Braun team from their first stop at Fort Bliss, Texas, to their eventual American home of Huntsville, Alabama, and the Marshall Space Flight Center, the version of history they told had rather tenuous connections with the administrative evil that they tried to leave behind at Peenemünde and Dora.

Of the 118 members of the von Braun team who came to the United States in 1945 (many hundreds of Germans, some connected to von Braun and others not, came later), about half had been members of the Nazi party—most were so-called nominal members, and therefore not barred by policy from entering the United States. But at least a handful, including Wernher von Braun himself, had been actively engaged first in the decision to use, and then in using, SS-provided slave labor in weapons production—an act that led directly to a war crimes conviction against Albert Speer, Hitler's Minister of Armaments, among others. In the end, we are left with the reality that a handful of America's most competent and successful public managers in NASA, the government agency that was lionized in the 1960s as the paradigmatic high-performing organization, had been either "committed Nazis," or had been directly engaged in actions for which others in post-war Germany were convicted of war crimes. This story begins at Mittelbau-Dora, where administrative evil wore no mask.

## Mittelbau-Dora

Although Mittelbau-Dora was not one of most notorious concentration camps of the Holocaust, it does merit a special place in the history of the twentieth century. Dora was not among the infamous death camps, such as Birkenau—the part of Auschwitz that became essentially a factory for killing, with gas chambers that could destroy 2,000 of the doomed at one time. Rather, Dora was a slave labor camp—and even in this it was far from unique—for large German corporations invested heavily in the concentration camp industry, such as IG Farben at Auschwitz (Hayes, 1989). Indeed, Heinrich Himmler, head of the SS, expressly created the Economic and Administrative Office for this purpose (Neufeld, 1996, 186):

> The SS began, in effect, a rent-a-slave service to firms and government enterprises at a typical rate of four marks a day for unskilled workers and six marks for skilled ones. In return, the SS supplied guards, food, clothing, and shelter, usually in a manner that led to a heavy death toll from starvation, disease and overwork. The lives of camp inmates were, by definition, expendable.

Dora was unique for other reasons. Mittelbau-Dora, the last SS concentration camp to be established, was the only one exclusively formed for the purpose of weapons production. It was one of the first camps liberated by advancing American troops, and some of the first images of corpses stacked like cordwood and the thin ranks of emaciated survivors came from there. Dora was the site of the huge, underground Mittelwerk factory that built the V-2 rockets for the Reich. Mittelwerk produced just about 6,000 rockets and 20,000 dead slave laborers in its less than two years of operation (Neufeld, 1996). Each V-2 rocket thus carried, at least symbolically, three corpses with it to its final destination. During two periods of its short life, it became arguably among the worst of the living hells produced by the SS concentration camps.

Dora was initially a minor appendage of the better-known Buchenwald concentration camp. Only in 1943, when Hitler decided to make V-2 rocket production the top armament priority, did Dora mushroom. In August 1943, after the extensive British air raid on Peenemünde, the Nazi rocket development facility on the Baltic Sea, V-2 production had to be moved to a place as secure from air attack as possible. An underground location had become the preferred choice for all of German armament and industrial production at this time. The original Nazi plan for the Mittelwerk mining complex near Nordhausen in the province of Thuringia was to house a large petroleum reserve there. Mittelwerk had two huge tunnels, each about a mile long and large enough to accommodate two rail lines. These two main tunnels were connected at regular intervals by smaller tunnels of 500 feet apiece; there were 46 of these. All told, Mittelwerk incorporated about 35 million cubic feet of space. At its peak, 10,000 slave laborers at a time lived and toiled in this massive complex.

### The Beginning

Unfortunately for those who would work and perish there, SS General Hans Kammler was placed in charge of the construction necessary to make Mittelwerk operational. He had also overseen the construction of the F-1 production facility at Peenemünde. An architect and civil engineer who joined the Nazi Party in 1933 and in 1942 became commander of the SS Economic and Administrative Office, Kammler's resume included the razing of the Warsaw ghetto and the construction of the death camps at Maidenek and Belzec, as well as the later phases of the Auschwitz death camp. He had a well-earned reputation as among the most vicious and inhuman in the entire SS pantheon (Hilberg, 1989).

   During the early phase at Mittelwerk, detainees were housed in several of the cross tunnels immediately adjacent to the final mining operations in Tunnel A, which was being punched through to the south side of the mountain. This meant that after working twelve-hour shifts, detainees were crammed into bunks (sometimes two at a time) where they could get little or no sleep because of continuous mining noise, which included frequent explosions (Piszkiewicz, 1995, 134):

> In the tunnels of the Mittelwerk, the conditions which were initially intolerable got worse. Two shifts alternated sleeping in bunks, which were stacked four deep. There was no heat, no ventilation, no sinks, no tubs to bathe in. The food was often soup, usually vile and always insufficient. There was no water. The prisoners found themselves drinking the water that oozed from the rock walls and condensed from the cold, damp air; it collected in muddy puddles on the tunnel floor. The latrines were half barrels with planks laid across their open tops. Not surprisingly, disease ran rampant amid the inescapable filth. Scabies, ulcers, abscesses, gangrene, anemia and dysentery were the common lot.

These conditions led inexorably to a remarkable death rate: in October 1943, 18; in November, 172; in December, 670; in January 1944, 719; in February, 536; and in March, 767. Until a crematorium could be built at Dora, the dead were stacked at the railhead for shipment to the crematorium at Buchenwald. Dora quickly developed a considerable reputation at Buchenwald. Additional transports brought the seriously ill or otherwise "useless" detainees to death camps such as Bergen-Belsen. Dora's death toll during this early construction phase was estimated at 6,000 in six months (Piszkiewicz, 1995, 135):

> Dr. A. Poschmann, medical supervisor of the Armaments Ministry, visited the Mittelwerk at this time. A few years later at the Nuremburg war crimes trials, he would describe what he had seen, confirming the reports of inmates who had survived. The slaves, Dr. Poschmann said, "worked a minimum of 72 hours a week, they were fed 1,100 calories a day. Lung and heart disease were epidemic because of the dampness and intense air pressure. Deaths averaged 160 a day. When a deputation of prisoners petitioned for improved conditions, SS Brigadefuehrer Hans Kammler responded by turning machine guns on them, killing 80."

As Kammler knew only too well, there was a virtually inexhaustible supply of slave labor available to the SS.

### The Mittelwerk Factory

For a six-month period in 1944, conditions got better—at least, relatively—at the Mittelwerk. SS General Kammler's lowest priority had been the construction of the Dora camp itself, but when this was completed and the 10,000 workers were moved out of the tunnels, sleep became at least a possibility. Now that the factory was primarily devoted to the production of V-2 missiles, workers were somewhat better treated, at least until acts of sabotage and resistance began to appear. The warm weather months helped as well. During this half-year period, the death rate was under 1,000, although this figure does not count transports to death camps of detainees who were ill or otherwise unable to work.

In September 1944, the SS formally created Mittelbau-Dora as a separate administrative entity from Buchenwald—the last of the SS concentration camps. At that time, the total camp population was over 32,000, with nearly 14,000 in Dora itself. Initially, there were few Jews at Dora. About a quarter of the Dora detainees were Russian, another quarter were Polish, and a seventh were French. There were also about 1,000 Germans, 500 Czechs, and smaller numbers of Gypsies, Belgians, Italians, and Hungarian Jews. The first

Jews arrived at Mittelbau-Dora in May 1944 during the massive transports of Hungarian Jews, the large majority of whom went straight to the gas chambers of Auschwitz. Dora's low population of Jews would grow somewhat as the war's end drew nearer.

### The Catastrophic End

By the end of 1944 and the first two months of 1945, the detainee population began to grow, and conditions deteriorated quickly. As the Russians advanced from the east, the concentration camps located in Poland began to be overrun, and the SS instituted the practice of shipping the remaining inmates to other camps and then attempting to destroy the empty camps—and with them, the evidence of their horrors. Large numbers of Jews from Auschwitz in particular, but also from Gross Rosen and Mauthausen, were shipped to Mittelbau-Dora, with the overall prisoner population reaching a peak of over 40,000 and Dora itself housing nearly 20,000.

This period of time also saw the SS response to acts of sabotage and resistance among the Dora detainees. A series of public hangings using the large crane (which hoisted the V-2s upright for a final check) in one of Mittelwerk's main tunnels were instituted; these escalated when Richard Baer, who had been Auschwitz's last commander, succeeded Otto Forschner as the Mittelbau-Dora commandant (Forschner moved on to Dachau). After a rebellion and breakout of fifty-three Russian detainees (nearly all of whom were captured and killed), Baer simply executed all the remaining Russians and Poles who lived in that particular barracks—nearly 200 detainees. While production of the V-2 continued into March, the camp was finally evacuated in April 1945, with most detainees shipped to Bergen-Belsen where survivors were liberated. These last, frantic transports became horrific death marches and train rides where half and more of the prisoners perished along the way. On one of these marches of detainees from Mittelbau-Dora, the SS and Luftwaffe guards herded 1,000 prisoners into a barn at Gardelagen and set it on fire (Beon, 1997). They shot those who tried to escape.

One of the early visitors to the just liberated Dora happened to be the famous American aviator Charles Lindbergh, who wrote the following (Lindbergh, 1978, 348–349):

> "Twenty-five thousand in a year and a half," he said. He was seventeen years old, Polish. . . ."Twenty-five thousand in a year and a half. And from each there is only so much." The boy cupped his hands together to show the measure. I followed his glance downward. We were standing at the edge of what had once been a large pit, about eight feet long, six feet wide, and I guessed at six feet

deep. It was filled to the overflowing with ashes from the furnaces—small chips of human bone—nothing else. Apparently bucketsful had been thrown from a distance, as one might get rid of the ashes in a coal scuttle on a rainy day.

Of the 60,000 detainees who came to Mittelbau-Dora, approximately 20,000 perished, and about 10,000 of those died directly from work on the V-2. The V-2 was thus a highly unusual weapon (Neufeld, 1996, 264):

> More people died producing it than died from being hit by it. In round numbers, 5,000 people were killed by the 3,200 V-2s that the Germans fired at English and Continental targets. . . . By that measure, at least two-thirds of all Allied victims of the ballistic missile came from the people who produced it, rather than from those who endured its descent.

This result was not what the German rocket scientists and engineers, who worked diligently during the war years at a weapons development and production facility on the Baltic coast, had had in mind.

## Von Braun and Peenemünde

The German rocket program originated in the early 1930s. While the Luft-waffe (the German air force) would also become interested in rockets, it was army ordnance officers Karl Becker and Walter Dornberger who saw in the rocket a potentially fearsome weapon, and, importantly, a weapon system not banned by the Treaty of Versailles, which ended World War I. Dornberger discovered the young Wernher von Braun, who became one of the world's pioneers of rocket science. Von Braun was born in 1912, the second of three sons of Baron Magnus von Braun and his wife, Emmy. At the age of eighteen, von Braun graduated from high school and enrolled in the Charlottenburg Institute of Technology. He became active in the Verein für Raumschiffarhrt (VfR—Society for Space Travel), which was essentially a rocket club. The club and von Braun attracted Dornberger's attention.

Sufficiently impressed with von Braun's talents, Dornberger made him a civilian employee of the army and financed his education, including the completion of his undergraduate degree and his Ph.D. in physics in 1934 from the University of Berlin, which he completed in a remarkable two years. In the mid-1930s, von Braun and a staff of eighty worked on rocket develop-ment at Kummersdorf West, near Berlin, which was Germany's first facility for the development of rocketry.

In 1937, the new rocket development facility, Heeresversuchsstelle (Army Research Station) Peenemünde, opened and the entire team moved north to the

Baltic coast (McElheran, 1995). It was here that the design and testing of the V-1 cruise missile and V-2 rocket were accomplished (Kennedy, 1983). Many other projects were pursued during Peenemünde's eight-year life, among them the conceptual design of an intercontinental ballistic missile (ICBM), which included the calculation of distance trajectories for New York, Pittsburgh, and Washington, D.C. (Klee and Merk, 1965; Wegener, 1996). Dornberger, who became a major general by the end of the war, commanded the facility, and von Braun was the technical director. The group of engineers and scientists later to be known as the von Braun team, and who would follow von Braun to the United States, first assembled at Peenemünde.

As the rockets grew more successful and the Luftwaffe lost effectiveness through continual attrition, attention at Peenemünde began to shift from development to production (Garlinski, 1978). However, as early as 1939, Dornberger insisted that Peenemünde must incorporate full production facilities on site, and this was in fact accomplished by 1941. The first V-2 (or A-4, as it was known in Peenemünde) launch was in 1942, but numerous problems delayed its readiness for full production. However, the "A-4 Special Committee" was formed to ensure that full production could get under way when the rocket was ready. The Peenemünde production facilities had used prisoner-of-war (POW) labor from two camps in the immediate area, Karlshagen and Trassenheide. These prisoners were primarily Polish and Russian POWs. Ironically, the bulk of the casualties of the initial British air raid on Peenemünde in August 1943 were in these two camps, which of course had no underground bunkers as protection against air raids. In a further irony, it was two Polish POWs from the Trassenheide camp who got word through the Resistance to the British about the existence of Peenemünde; they both perished in the air raid.

Throughout the war, German industry experienced severe labor shortages, and after 1941 the Russian front demanded more and more manpower for the German army. In such difficult circumstances, the use of forced labor—although lamentable—seems predictable enough. This was the initial choice at Peenemünde for rocket production. The use of civilian slave labor constituted an entirely different issue. These were concentration camp detainees (*Häftlinge*) under the control of the SS. Wernher von Braun was fully aware during this time of the use of SS-provided slave labor in the production of rockets; indeed, the management team led by Dornberger and von Braun explicitly discussed and adopted as policy the use of SS-provided slave labor in rocket production (Neufeld, 1996, 187). Slave labor had been investigated, promoted, and then requisitioned by Arthur Rudolph (Piszkiewicz, 1995, 96–97):

> Slave laborers not only worked at Peenemünde, they were requisitioned from the SS by the army's rocket development group. In a note dated April 16, 1943,

Arthur Rudolph, who headed the Development and Fabrication Laboratory, reported on his observations of the exploitation of prisoners at the Heinkel aircraft works in Oranienburg. He wrote, "The employment of detainees (*Häftlinge*) in general has had considerable advantages over the earlier employment of foreigners, especially because all non-work-related tasks are taken over by the SS and the detainees offer greater protection for security." Rudolph concluded, "Production in the F-1 (the main assembly building in Peenemünde) can be carried out by detainees." On June 2, 1943, Rudolph formally requested 1,400 slave laborers from the SS. The first 200 members of this group arrived on June 17.

Based on this policy decision, slave labor was also requisitioned for the other V-2 production facilities at Friedrichshafen, Wiener Neustadt, and later, at Zement. Walter Dornberger was fully aware of this decision (Neufeld, 1996, 195):

Dornberger's minutes from August 4 read: "As a basic principle, production in all four assembly plants will be carried out by convicts" . . . Rocket assembly would be done primarily by slave labor, a concept Dornberger fully accepted. In a draft of a letter to Saur that he wrote in advance of the meeting, he said: "Production by convicts—no objections." To him they were merely factors of production.

Later, after V-2 production was shifted to Mittelwerk, Dornberger, Rudolph, and von Braun were all present at a May 1944 meeting in which the use of additional slave labor because of labor shortages was discussed and agreed upon. Wernher von Braun traveled a number of times from Peenemünde to Mittelwerk, as did Dornberger and other members of the von Braun team. Arthur Rudolph was among a number of personnel who moved full time to Mittelwerk; he became the chief production engineer, with an office on one of the main tunnels. Magnus von Braun, Wernher's brother, worked under Rudolph on site. Another dozen members of the von Braun team who eventually came to the United States also staffed Mittelwerk. No one could have any illusions about a factory whose production mode during most of its existence was quite simply to work its labor force to death, although their roles may not have involved some of them directly in decisions about, or relationships with, *Häftlinge*. Von Braun's substantial involvement, however, is quite clear (Neufeld, 1996, 228):

[T]here is no doubt that he remained deeply involved with the concentration camps. On August 15, 1944, he wrote to Sawatski (director of Mittelwerk) regarding a special laboratory he wanted to set up in the tunnels. . . . The letter begins:

"During my last visit to the Mittelwerk, you proposed to me that we use the good technical education of detainees available to you and Buchenwald to tackle . . . additional development jobs. You mentioned in particular a detainee working until now in your mixing device quality control, who was a French physics professor and who is especially qualified for the technical direction of such a workshop."

I immediately looked into your proposal by going to Buchenwald, together with Dr. Simon, to seek out more qualified detainees. I have arranged their transfer to the Mittelwerk with Colonel Pister [Buchenwald camp commandant], as per your proposal.

The coming end of the war brought disaster to Mittelbau-Dora, as we have seen, but it was to become a new beginning for the von Braun team of rocket scientists and engineers.

## Operations Overcast and Paperclip

The von Braun team was brought to the United States as a part of Operations Overcast and Paperclip (Bower, 1987; McGovern, 1964). How this happened has two rather distinct story lines. Wernher von Braun clearly relished telling one version of this story; it appears in several publications, most of them sanctioned by NASA or penned by members of the von Braun team. This "official" version usually follows a story line much like this (Graham, 1995, 159–160):

Knowing that Germany was doomed, von Braun, upon arriving back at Peen-emünde, immediately assembled his rocket team and asked them to decide to whom did they want to surrender. The Russians frightened most of the scientists; the French would treat them like slaves; the British did not have enough money for a rocket program; that left the Americans. After stealing a train with forged papers, von Braun led 500 people through war-torn Germany to surrender to the Americans. Additionally, the SS had orders to kill the German engineers who built the V-2. Hiding their notes in a mine shaft, the German scientists evaded their own army searching for the Americans. Finally, the entire German rocket team found an American private and surrendered to him. The Americans imme-diately went to Peenemünde and Nordhausen and captured all of the remaining V-2s and V-2 parts before the Russians. After they had picked the places clean, the American Army destroyed both places with explosives, leaving the remains to the Russians. The Americans brought over 300 train car loads of spare V-2 parts to the United States.

This "official" story has some tenuous connections to what actually happened, and in this, it resembles virtually all of the von Braun team's disingenuous and self-serving accounts of their wartime experiences.

The more accurate historical account of events reads as follows: In January 1945, both the Russians from the east and the Allies from the west were advancing well into the German homeland. There was considerable confusion, with many parties issuing orders. Military commanders closest to Peenemünde issued orders to remain and defend the homeland. Two engineers who attempted to flee were captured and shot (this appears to be the source of the "order" to shoot the engineers who built the V-2). However, it was precisely an SS order, described later, from none other than General Hans Kammler, that von Braun and his team followed.

Also, it was a much smaller group (about ten), that decided that surrendering to the Americans was the best bet, but this decision was not made until months later. Kammler's order was to move nearly all Peenemünde operations—personnel and records—to the Mittelwerk, where von Braun and his team spent nearly three months. Mittelwerk remained in full production at this time with rapidly deteriorating conditions. The thousands of Peenemünde personnel did not all move at once, but over a period of about a month and about three-quarters relocated to the Mittelwerk. They hid the Peenemünde records in a deserted mine shaft in the area, for use as a bargaining chip with the Americans. As it happened, the rocketeers had no need for such a bargaining chip.

In April 1945, Kammler issued another evacuation order; this time the von Braun team was ordered to move to Oberammagau, a small village in the Bavarian mountains of southern Germany. Of the 3,000 who had moved to the Mittelwerk, only 400 went to Bavaria. One can speculate that von Braun and the others may have welcomed this order, since it had the effect of putting considerable distance between them and Mittelwerk and the Dora camp. Within a week of von Braun's departure, the U.S. Third Army liberated Mittelbau-Dora and the Mittelwerk. The von Braun team made contact with the Americans on May 2, 1945. The unconditional surrender of Germany came five days later.

### Post-War Chaos

Chaos reigned during the summer of 1945 in post-war Germany. Ordinary Germans faced desperate living conditions. The Allies established a number of Displaced Persons (DP) camps for Holocaust survivors and many others who had been imprisoned or otherwise uprooted by the Nazis. Conditions in these camps, though an infinite improvement over concentration camps, were difficult. As the war wound down, a large number of technical teams were formed under the auspices of the Combined Intelligence Objectives Committee (CIOS); these teams had a three-part mission (Gimbel, 1986, 436):

> First, they were to find out what the Germans knew about weapons, radar, synthetic rubber, torpedoes, rockets, jet engines, infrared, communications, and other such things. . . . Secondly, they were to gather information that could help shorten the war against Japan. . . . Finally, the CIOS teams were to locate and detain—even intern—German scientists and technicians to interrogate them for information . . . and to prevent them from slipping away to seek safe haven in another country and continue their wartime research and development programs and projects.

These CIOS technical teams represented a developing U.S. policy toward German scientific and technical knowledge in the post-war world. This emerging policy was, unsurprisingly in wartime, under the jurisdiction of the U.S. military, in particular, the Joint Chiefs of Staff. Several principles were advocated, some in at least partial conflict with others. One was not to repeat the mistake of leaving the German nation with the scientific and technical capacity to rearm, as was done after World War I. This principle gained added weight from the demonstrated Nazi superiority in several areas, including rocketry. Another principle was to prevent any intact groups of scientists or technicians from escaping to another country and simply continuing their research. The focus here was on South America—already known to be a destination of choice for escaping Nazis. The principle that became paramount, at least after the fact, was the idea of denying this expertise to the cold war adversary-to-be, Russia.

## Denazification

At the same time, the Allies had a policy of denazification, and of bringing Nazi war criminals to justice (Lippman, 1995). The Joint Chiefs of Staff addressed denazification in Paragraph Six of Directive 1067 (FitzGibbon, 1969, 432):

> All members of the Nazi Party who have been more than nominal participants in its activities, all active supporters of Nazism or militarism and all other persons hostile to Allied purposes will be removed and excluded from public office and from positions of importance in quasi-public and private enterprises. . . . Persons are to be treated as more than nominal participants in Party activities and as active supporters of Nazism or militarism when they have

(1) held office or otherwise been active at any level from local to national in the party . . . (2) authorized or participated affirmatively in any Nazi crimes, racial persecution or discriminations. . . . No such persons shall be retained in any of the categories of employment listed above because of administrative necessity, convenience or expediency.

Denazification was carried out first by the military government until May 1946, and then under the German Law for Liberation from National Socialism and Militarism (Gimbel, 1990, 443). The earliest definition of a "committed Nazi" (that is, more than a "nominal Nazi") came in 1944, and included anyone who joined the Nazi Party before Hitler came to power in 1933. A later, July 1945, policy listed 136 mandatory removal and exclusion categories, and indicated that Nazi Party membership prior to May 1937 was cause for mandatory removal and exclusion. The centerpiece for denazification policy was a widely distributed questionnaire, *Fragebogen*. Later, when denazification had been turned over to the German authorities, a new questionnaire (*Meldebogen*) was used, and officials utilized five categories for respondents: major offenders, offenders, lesser offenders, followers or nominal Nazis, and persons exonerated. Denazification policy under the Germans became progressively weaker, and after 1948, only the more obvious cases were pursued.

One of the more revealing juxtapositions of these competing U.S. policies thus became evident in and around Mittelwerk and Dora. While two of the CIOS technical teams were rounding up all of the V-2 components from the Mittelwerk and interviewing people to find the rocket scientists and engineers, other teams were interviewing Dora survivors and others for the coming war crimes trials and as part of the larger effort at denazification. In a number of instances, these teams were directed to the same people.

Certainly, war criminals and committed Nazis were not going to be welcome in the United States. During the war, the Office of Special Services (OSS, the precursor to the CIA) had actively recruited SS members and other Germans as intelligence agents—American spies. However, when OSS director William Sullivan asked President Roosevelt in December 1944 if these agents could be permitted to enter the United States after the war, Roosevelt's replied (Hunt, 1991, 10):

I do not believe that we should offer any guarantees of protection in the post-hostilities period to Germans who are working for your organization. I think that the carrying out of any such guarantees would be difficult and probably be widely misunderstood both in this country and abroad. We may expect that the number of Germans who are anxious to save their skins and property will rapidly increase. Among them may be some who should properly be tried for war crimes or at least arrested for active participation in Nazi activities. Even with the necessary controls you mention, I am not prepared to authorize the giving of guarantees.

We will, of course, never know whether Roosevelt might have had a different answer for German scientists and engineers needed by the United States to achieve technological superiority.

### Bringing Them Over

As noted, two of the CIOS technical teams targeted the Peenemünders, because the chief of the Rocket Branch in the Ordnance Department at the Pentagon was very interested in the V-2 rocket. It was well known that the Germans had advanced rocketry far beyond the Americans and the Russians. Colonel Holger Toftoy was in charge of the two army ordnance technical teams in Europe. One team focused on locating and interrogating rocket personnel, and was headed by Major Robert Staver. Wernher von Braun, regarded as the world's premiere rocket scientist, was at the top of Staver's list. In summer 1945, some 400 rocket scientists and engineers from Peenemünde and Mittelwerk were gathered together in Garmisch-Partenkirchen for interrogation. Soon, Operations Overcast and Paperclip would bring hundreds of German scientists, engineers, and technical experts to the United States. The actual task of moving all of the available V-2 rockets and spare parts fell to a second technical team, headed by Major James Hamill. His team essentially cleaned out the Mittelwerk (which was located in the soon-to-be Russian zone) and shipped everything they could by rail to Antwerp, Belgium, where it filled 16 Liberty ships for passage to the United States.

In August 1945, the United States initiated Operation Overcast, which aimed to bring selected Germans over to participate in the production of German-inspired weapons, including V-2s, to be used against the Japanese. Overcast gained final approval in August 1945, and of course, the Japanese surrendered later that month. Overcast included an assurance that if any committed Nazis were inadvertently brought to the United States, they would be returned to Europe for trial.

In September 1945, Wernher von Braun and 118 members of the von Braun team came to the United States under Operation Overcast, which was revised and renamed Operation Paperclip in March 1946. Under Overcast, Colonel Toftoy succeeded in obtaining early permission to bring over this key group of rocket scientists and engineers. Their first stop was Fort Bliss, Texas, and the nearby White Sands, New Mexico, proving grounds. Here, they supervised a large number of V-2 launches. By the end of the 1940s, they moved on to the Redstone Arsenal at Huntsville, Alabama, which later became the Marshall Space Flight Center.

Although Paperclip was publicly terminated in 1952, it apparently continued covertly at least until 1973 (Hunt, 1991). The Paperclip policy, as proposed by Secretary of State Dean Acheson and approved by President Truman, increased the number of German personnel that could be brought to the United States to 1,000 (Hunt, 1991, 39):

> The specialists would be under military custody, since they would enter the United States without visas. The War Department would screen their backgrounds and assure that "the best possible information" about their qualifications was submitted to the State and Justice Departments for visa consideration. Employment contracts would provide for their return to Germany if they were found not to be qualified or acceptable for permanent residence. While war criminals were obviously excluded, one clause in the policy banned those active in nazism or militarism as well: "No person found by the commanding general . . . to have been a member of the Nazi party and more than a nominal participant in its activities, or an active supporter of Nazism or militarism shall be brought to the U.S. hereunder."

The impetus for Operation Paperclip clearly came from the War Department, and as it happened, the State Department, which was responsible for approving the Germans' entry into the United States and ultimately for granting citizenship, created numerous obstacles for Paperclip (Gimbel, 1990, 443): "In the state department, Spruille Braden, the assistant secretary of state for American republic affairs, protested to Acheson that Project Paperclip would permit military research by Germans in this country which they were prohibited by Allied Control Council (ACC) Law No. 25 from doing in Germany." Subsequently, the State Department kicked back the first ten dossiers submitted for visas for Germans who were already in the United States, signaling their intent to require extensive documentation and investigation of these specialists. State Department recalcitrance and other complicating factors eventually caused changes in Paperclip policies.

One of these factors was the fact that a number of Paperclip candidates in Germany refused to sign contracts until their future status was clarified. The other, more difficult factor was that some of the von Braun team (and some others) who were in the United States under Overcast contracts that were due to expire in September 1946, threatened not to renew their contracts unless their families could join them and unless their status was clarified. The real difficulty was that the Overcast group could not easily be allowed to leave the United States because they already were privy to top secret knowledge about the projects they had been working on.

Thus, the original, practical goals of obtaining as much scientific and technical personnel and information as possible for national security purposes simply superseded other considerations, including legal and ethical ones. The Paperclip logjam broke from the eventual shift of emphasis away from whether denazification procedures had been followed to the satisfaction of two new criteria: whether the individual's entry was in the national interest and whether the individual was likely to become a security threat to the United States in the future. Michael Neufeld (1996, 271) notes that:

> Security reports for a number of individuals, including von Braun, had to be revised or fudged to circumvent the restrictions that still existed. Some writers have seen those actions as evidence of a conspiracy in the Pentagon to violate a policy signed by President Harry Truman, but it really reflected a conscious choice by the U.S. government, approved up to the level of the Cabinet at least, to put expediency above principle. The Cold War provided ample opportunity after 1947 to rationalize that policy on anti-Communist grounds, but the circumvention of restrictions on Nazis and war criminals would have gone ahead at some level anyway, because the Germans' technical expertise was seen as indispensable.

Gimbel summarizes the outcome of the shifts in Paperclip policy as follows (1990, 462–463):

> [T]here is no question that the using agencies portrayed their candidates in the best possible light. Engaging in practices that should hardly be a surprise to academicians familiar with personnel evaluations for purposes of reappointment, tenure and promotion, they dissembled, equivocated, fudged and cheated to accomplish their purposes. But they also made effective use of the shift in policy: the shift from consideration of the candidates' activities under the Nazi regime to judgments about their value to the United States and whether their presence constituted a threat to national security.

Von Braun's mentor and boss, Walter Dornberger, was not among those brought over with the von Braun team. As it happened, the British wanted Dornberger as a potential war criminal, since they had been the primary target of the V-2 missiles. After holding Dornberger in custody for nearly two years, until 1947, the British released him when they realized that trying someone responsible for so few deaths—at least relatively speaking—was probably not feasible. Still, Dornberger made an impression on the British (Neufeld, 1996, 269): "According to a U.K. interrogator, the former rocket general had extreme views on German domination, and wishes for a Third World War."

Dornberger was immediately thereafter brought to the United States by the Air Force under Operation Paperclip to work as a consultant at Wright Field in Ohio on missiles. He subsequently applied for and received U.S. citizenship. In 1950, he took a position with Bell Aerospace Corporation of Buffalo, New York, where he spent the remainder of his career. He rose to become vice president and chief scientist for Bell, and retired in 1965. He never forgot his protégé, von Braun, and wrote the following for a von Braun *Festschrift,* published in 1963 (Stuhlinger et al., 1963, 364):

> Dr. von Braun is a unique person with outstanding ability. I doubt that one could find in the world another human being of the same ability in his field. It is my opinion that he is the first representative of a totally new class of modern creative man, combining in one person outstanding qualities of the scientist, the engineer, the manager, and the true leader.

If the last sentence of the above quotation appears to resonate with the philosophy of Nazism, perhaps that is because Dornberger, although a member of the regular army officer corps, was also a committed Nazi (Neufeld, 1996, 182–183):

> In his notebooks one can find a draft of the pep talk he gave to his senior subordinates on assuming the commander's post on May 12, 1942. He states: "My National Socialist beliefs should be widely known." He goes on to say that his sole aim was to " . . . put in the hands of the Fuhrer sufficient numbers of this weapon [the A-4, or V-2], which—it is my conviction and unshakable belief—will decide the war."

Walter Dornberger, who achieved great success as a manager both in Nazi Germany and in the United States, died in West Germany in 1980.

### The Von Braun Team

Within a few years of the end of World War II, the uncomfortable moments for the von Braun team had largely passed. The army clearly had a vested interest in them, and had shielded a few of them from testifying at the Mittelbau-Dora war crimes trial, held at Dachau in 1947. Von Braun himself and other members of the team successfully maintained the fiction that the use of slave labor had been the exclusive province of the SS, and that they were rocket scientists interested in space flight, who had been forced to take a temporary detour into wartime weapons development on the way to their real goal. They enjoyed a better than half-hearted acceptance, after a time, by their adopted community of Huntsville, Alabama, and their colleagues within NASA. Still later, they were rewarded for their great achievements in the *Apollo* program. Huntsville now has a Wernher von Braun civic center, and several of the Germans, including Arthur Rudolph, received NASA's highest civilian honor, the Distinguished Service Award.

While stories and rumors circulated about the past of some members of the von Braun team, it was only after most of them had left government service in the early 1970s that the facts about their past began to emerge. Survivors of the French Resistance who had been imprisoned at Dora knew and spoke the truth all along (Michel, 1979). Americans were much slower to recognize the unsavory past of some of these Germans. Still, based on the information we now have, it would be equally mistaken to issue a blanket condemnation of all of the Germans who came over with von Braun. Of the 118 who originally came with von Braun, somewhere between half and three-quarters had been members of the Nazi Party (Piszkiewicz, 1995). Certainly, most of these were only nominal members. Most also had no direct involvement with slave labor and the policy decision to use it. Only four were known to have joined the SS, although there may have been more (Neufeld, 1996). Von Braun himself was one of these, receiving his commission in 1941, although this is not an early membership, which ordinarily would mark a "committed Nazi." He is reported to have worn his SS uniform only once; however, it was clearly to his advantage to do so on the day that Heinrich Himmler, the head of the SS, visited Peenemünde to see for himself how rocket development was going. Himmler rewarded von Braun with a promotion to major. In this action and in many others, von Braun appears as more an opportunist than a hardcore Nazi. Another SS member, Kurt Debus, was an earlier adherent and apparently more committed. Debus reportedly wore his SS uniform regularly at Peenemünde and at one point, denounced a colleague as anti-Nazi to the Gestapo (effectively sentencing that person to death) (Piszkiewicz, 1995, 237). After working for some time with von Braun in Huntsville, Debus became the first director of the Kennedy Space Flight Center in Florida. Arthur Rudolph was a seriously committed Nazi who joined the party in June 1931 and had other early Nazi affiliations.

### Huntsville, Redstone, and the Marshall Space Flight Center

By 1950, the von Braun team had moved from Texas to Huntsville, Alabama. While their condition as "prisoners of peace" had already eased somewhat at Fort Bliss, the move to Alabama marked the real beginning of their new American life. The facility in Huntsville that became the Marshall Space Flight Center was an arsenal developed during World War II as part of the American war effort. After the war, production was shut down and the site slated for closure. However, the army was looking for a facility to house its budding missile program, and thus the Redstone Arsenal came into being. From 1950 to 1960, the Redstone Arsenal was the home of the Army Ballistic Missile Agency (ABMA). The ABMA facility at Redstone was run by Wernher von Braun and staffed by members of his team.

During the 1950s the United States pursued both military ballistic missile development and space applications for those missiles. The air force took the lead in ballistic missile development, while the navy and the army had competing satellite programs. The navy's Vanguard project was given the nod to launch America's first satellite into space. Apparently, this was in part because President Eisenhower balked at the idea of having the army's team of German rocket scientists responsible for the first American satellite. However, when the navy program sputtered and failed, and the Russians successfully launched *Sputnik* in 1957, the United States turned to the von Braun team, which successfully launched *Explorer* in 1958. The von Braun team thereby established itself as the premier rocket team in the United States, and it would remain so through the coming decade of space exploration.

After NASA's legislative creation in 1958, the ABMA was one of the existing organizations transferred over as NASA became operational in 1959–60 (Rosholt, 1966). The Marshall Space Flight Center was created in 1960, with Wernher von Braun as its first director. The German team formed at Peenemünde had developed the "everything-under-one-roof" approach to rocket development. As it turned out, this approach—having all of the scientific and technical expertise for all of the subsystems in one location—was consistent with the existing approach in the army's arsenals (Neufeld, 1996, 271):

> At Huntsville, one of the keys to the Germans' success was the "everything-under-one-roof" approach developed at Kummersdorf and Peenemünde under the direction of Becker and Dornberger. It proved very compatible with the U.S. Army's "arsenal system" of in-house development. Under von Braun's leadership, the German-dominated group successfully developed the nuclear-tipped Redstone and Jupiter missiles in the 1950s. The Redstone—which was really just a much-improved A-4 [V-2]—then became the vehicle that put the first American satellite and first American man into space. Finally, under NASA aegis after 1960, the Peenemünders crowned their success with the phenomenally reliable Saturn vehicles, which launched *Apollo* spacecraft into orbit and put humans on the moon.

### Saturn and Apollo

The National Aeronautics and Space Administration was widely regarded in the 1960s as the paradigmatic example of a successful, high-performing organization, particularly for one in the public sector (McCurdy, 1993, 2; see also, Anna, 1976; Delbecq and Filley, 1974; Levine, 1982). The *Apollo* program and its great success, punctuated by the moon landing, was clearly the principal reason. The von Braun team at the Marshall Space Flight Center was an integral part of this success; their Saturn rockets boosted all of the crews into orbit and on to the moon. The management strategy first developed by von Braun at Peenemünde worked exceptionally well at Redstone and then at Marshall. As NASA grew at a very rapid pace, and as more and more work was contracted out, it became impossible to retain the "everything-under-one-roof" approach, but von Braun surrendered this ground slowly and never eliminated the philosophy altogether.

For example, Marshall built the first of the Saturn I vehicles as well as the first few Saturn I-C first stages (Bilstein, 1980). While they did not construct subsequent versions of the Saturn, they doggedly maintained the in-house technical expertise to duplicate component testing and even some of the hardware. They thus had the technical expertise to understand from the inside out exactly how prime contractors were designing and building the rockets, and thus to see behind unacceptable design compromises. Wernher von Braun described this approach as follows (von Braun, 1963, 250):

> At Marshall we still can carry an idea for a space-launch vehicle and its guidance system from the concept through the entire development cycle of design, development, fabrication and static testing; we have every intention to preserve and nurture a limited in-house capability. . . . In order for us to use the best possible judgment in spending the taxpayer's money intelligently, we just have to do a certain amount of this research and development work ourselves. We have to keep our own hands dirty to command the professional respect of the contractor personnel.

The von Braun team's philosophy of management was widely known as the "dirty hands" approach. Whether this was some sort of "Freudian slip"— based on their history at the Mittelwerk and Peenemünde—is unknown, but at a minimum, the irony is striking.

The project manager in charge of the Saturn V Program Office was none other than Arthur Rudolph. Much as Wernher von Braun established himself as an outstanding manager and leader in the United States, Arthur Rudolph achieved impressive results with his management of the Saturn Program Office. He developed the concept of the Program Control Center (PCC), which essentially gathered relevant information about all of the Saturn subsystems in one large conference room, and made them visually accessible. The Saturn Program Office became a premier example of the matrix and project forms

of management for which NASA was nationally famous during this period
of time (Chapman, 1973, vii):

> The extraordinary success of . . . [NASA] in leading the United States from a
> position of relative inferiority to one of world leadership in astronautics during
> the 1960s has stimulated wide interest in the organizational and management
> systems which contributed to this feat . . . especially project management, be-
> cause of the public visibility of its projects [including] the moon landing.

James Webb, the NASA administrator during the *Apollo* years, was given
a tour and briefing on the PCC in 1965 and commented that: "I saw here . . .
one of the most sophisticated forms of organized human effort that I have ever
seen anywhere" (Bilstein, 1980, 291). The Saturn Program Office was used as
a model for the Apollo Program Office at NASA headquarters in Washington,
as well as for other NASA centers and for prime contractors. Webb was so
impressed by the PCC that he sent a procession of academics and executives
from business and government to Huntsville to see the operation that Arthur
Rudolph put together (Bilstein, 1980, 291).

A look at the organization chart from the Marshall Space Flight Center
from 1960 shows that former Peenemünders held about three-quarters of the
management and laboratory director positions. This remained the case during von Braun's entire ten-year tenure at Marshall. The von Braun team was
obviously a very tightly knit group, and it makes sense that they would be, if
for no other reason than the fact that they came as a group to a new country
(Stuhlinger and Ordway, 1994). They also shared a past, part of which needed
to be kept secret. While most of them were no more than nominal Nazis, nor
had they engaged directly in utilizing slave labor or other SS-related activities,
their leader and several of the other key members of the team had a past that
needed to be hidden, or at a minimum, whitewashed, for the group to be successful in their new country. Keeping this secret, which required widespread
collusion, was clearly another factor in the Germans' insularity.

Thus the von Braun team and Marshall actually developed a kind of siege
mentality, and a feeling that they had to do better work than anyone else in
order to overcome what they perceived as unfair treatment (Piszkiewicz,
1995). The von Braun team knew that President Eisenhower had chosen the
navy rocket program to launch America's first satellite, and they knew it was
because the army missile program was run by a "bunch of Germans." The
von Braun team felt misunderstood, slighted, and even attacked, and, quite
naturally, they fostered a kind of "fortress Marshall" mentality over the years.
Even in the glory years of *Apollo*, they never felt they received the degree of
credit they deserved, and all because they were Germans. The organizational

culture developed first at Redstone and then at Marshall was thus a defensive one. Their "dirty hands" approach to management, apart from both its logic and its success, was at least in part a manifestation of their need to maintain a kind of "deep control" over all aspects of their programs—and their past as well (McCurdy, 1993, 19).

Not surprisingly, the hold of the von Braun team over Marshall caused some misunderstanding and resentment among American employees at Marshall, at the other centers—particularly the Johnson Space Flight Center—and at NASA headquarters in Washington. At Marshall, there was resentment about the Germans being the favored group of employees (Hunt, 1991, 221):

> A longtime administrator at Marshall said they complained about [Operation] Paperclip because Germans were being hired instead of Americans. . . . Furthermore, Paperclip recruits received preferential treatment over Americans at Marshall because the top officials were themselves German.

And there were other concerns expressed as well (Lasby, 1971, 215):

> In 1960, a Jewish scientist who had been working with the specialists [von Braun team] for fifteen years revealed his personal impressions in a letter to a close friend. He distinctly remembered the initial shock that an enemy would be imported and placed in a security-conscious atmosphere and, as younger men arrived in large numbers, the discomfort of many Jews in a German atmosphere where English seem to be a secondary language. . . . He believed that on the surface, at least, the specialists had fit into the "American way of life," and he expressed understanding about their tendency to "gravitate into a clique." But he could not entirely accept their claim that they were as unaware of the atrocities as the average American was of the true conditions in Sing Sing. "I don't know," he concluded, "I kind of yet see blood on their hands."

This was not the sort of "dirty hands" image the von Braun team had in mind to evoke.

Later, as *Apollo* began to wind down after 1970, the von Braun team began to retire. Some were forced out by the reductions in force that swept NASA during this time. The Germans, of course, did not enjoy veteran's preference, and some retired or left rather than take a reduction in rank and a reduced role. Even in the end, the von Braun team felt victimized; they referred to this period at Marshall as the "Great Massacre." Here also, there was probably no intent to resurrect the experience of about a dozen members of the von Braun team at Mittelbau-Dora, but again, the irony is striking.

Arthur Rudolph, a clearly outstanding public manager in the most successful American public organization in modern times and earlier at the Mittelwerk
in the Third Reich, retired from NASA with its highest civilian award. He was
living quietly in retirement in San Jose, California, collecting his government
pension, when he was confronted in the early 1980s by the Office of Special
Investigations (OSI), the Justice Department unit created by Congress in 1979
for the express purpose of pursuing Nazi war criminals living in the United
States. Unsurprisingly, surviving members of the von Braun team were early
subjects of OSI investigations, and some still were as of 1997 (Rosenbaum,
1997). In 1984, at the age of seventy-seven, Arthur Rudolph renounced his
U.S. citizenship voluntarily and left the country, after signing an admission
that he could not contest the OSI charges in court. In effect, he admitted his
guilt. He did not lose his federal pension, however. During the OSI interrogation, Rudolph was shown photographs of the crematorium at Dora, and the
following dialogue ensued (Hunt, 1991, 243):

> "Did you ever see it?" asked Sher, referring to the crematorium.
> "From the distance, yes."
> "And you knew that prisoners who died at Mittelwerk were cremated at
> the crematorium. You knew that, didn't you?" (Rudolph nodded his head in
> agreement). "Turn to the next page, Mr. Rudolph. You'll see pictures of pris-
> oners who worked at Mittelwerk when they were liberated by the Allies." The
> photograph showed a truckload of dead prisoners whose bodies were nothing
> more than skeletons. "Do those people look like they were working under
> good conditions?"
> "No, certainly not."
> "You know the figures are that nearly twenty thousand people died during
> your service at this facility?"
> "No."
> "Twenty thousand. Did that—would that surprise you?"
> "To me, yes."
> "You knew people were dying?"
> "Oh, yeah. I knew that."

Wernher von Braun died in 1977, so he never had to suffer the final in-
dignity of a war crimes investigation by OSI. However, in 1985, a fortieth-
anniversary reunion and celebration of the von Braun team's arrival in the
United States was held in Huntsville. Arthur Rudolph was invited back,
and attempts were made to obtain a temporary visa for him. These efforts
failed. Rudolph died on January 1, 1996, in Hamburg, Germany, at the age
of eighty-nine.

## Administrative Evil

As discussed in the preceding chapter, in the Holocaust administrative evil went unmasked for all to see, and certainly evil went unmasked at Mittelbau-Dora, where Arthur Rudolph completed the first leg of his highly successful career as a manager. However, American public policy and our own public servants placed the mask on this administrative evil, under Operations Overcast and Paperclip, and brought it to the United States in the form of some of the members of the von Braun team, where that history now tarnishes the singular achievements of the space program. Colonel Toftoy and the other technicians representing army ordnance may or may not have been truly aware of the evil that was Dora, but their single-minded pursuit of their narrow technical goal blinded them to larger issues that mattered a great deal, at a minimum to Dora's survivors. Or perhaps they simply failed to notice at all. It is the height of irony that, in the narrow pursuit of technical superiority, NASA in essence made a Faustian bargain with administrative evil, only to find that evil sullying America's most remarkable technical achievement, the moon landing.

# Organizational Dynamics and Administrative Evil

## The Marshall Space Flight Center, NASA, and the Space Shuttles Challenger and Columbia

We expected NASA leadership would set high standards for post-Columbia work. We expected upfront standards of validation, verification, and certification. We expected rigorous and integrated risk management processes. We expected involved and insightful leadership from NASA Headquarters. We were, overall, disappointed . . . the return to flight effort taken as a whole, was not effectively led or managed.

—*Final Report of the Return to Flight Task Group,* 2005 (196)

This chapter examines the role of the Marshall Space Flight Center (MSFC) in the space shuttle *Challenger* disaster with a focus on how less visible dynamics of organizational culture can lead to administrative evil. The discussion also covers the space shuttle *Columbia* tragedy, which sadly echoes many of the *Challenger* issues. Neither the *Challenger* nor the subsequent *Columbia* disasters were cases of intentional evil activity. In fact, doubt has been cast on interpretations of the *Challenger* incident that portray those involved as deliberately evil (Vaughan, 1996). Thus, we view the case of Marshall, NASA, and the shuttle disasters not as simple and clear-cut cases of administrative evil, but as opaque and complex—and therefore typical—

cases in which administrative evil is not only difficult to pinpoint, but in which its very presence is subject to varying interpretations and conclusions. Such opacity and complexity is a hallmark of administrative evil in our own time and culture.

We are able to identify destructive organizational dynamics within the MSFC, and within NASA more generally, that represent a typical organizational pathway that can lead to administrative evil *when no one intends evil.* The absence of evil intentions is another hallmark of administrative evil as it manifests in organizations. The defensive organizational culture at the MSFC, which was quite functional under the leadership of Wernher von Braun, became destructive as the environment surrounding it became less favorable and its leadership turned in a punitive direction.

When dealing with inherently risky technology, like an experimental aircraft or a space shuttle, both test pilots and astronauts understand that, say, one in a hundred flights represents the probability of an accident with loss of life—a "normal" accident, if you will. In the space shuttle program, the organizational dynamics at Marshall, and to a lesser extent those within NASA as an organization, led to a much greater degree of risk, such that, even if the *Challenger* launch had been stopped, the likelihood of a shuttle disaster was far greater than it should have been, and a disaster would have likely happened anyway—most likely sooner rather than later.

Unfortunately, the space shuttle *Columbia* disaster of 2003 shows that these dynamics continued within NASA, even after the lessons of *Challenger* (Columbia Accident Investigation Board, 2003). It is a brute fact that NASA lost 40 percent of the shuttle fleet (fully 50 percent of the original four shuttles—the *Endeavour* was built in 1992 as a replacement for *Challenger* at a cost of $2.1 billion), and the lives of fourteen astronauts. Marshall's and NASA's environment, especially the political and budgetary climate, made those decisions that escalated risks substantially appear to be good ones, particularly from the perspective of technical rationality. Those same dynamics persisted throughout the program's history. Even in the absence of evil intentions, organizational dynamics that escalate the chances of disastrous outcomes can be termed administrative evil (albeit with considerable caution), if the members of an organization could reasonably have been expected to do better. This was the case with the space shuttle program. Indeed, we agree with those in Congress and elsewhere who have argued that the time has come to end manned space flight—at least on the space shuttles, which ended in 2011. However, even those who disagree with our interpretation can still see how ordinary—though in most cases less visible—organizational dynamics can create a pathway leading to administrative evil.

## Organizational Dynamics and the Pathway to Administrative Evil

Modern organizations, as we have already noted, can be the locus of both wrong-doing and evil (Darley, 1992, 1995, 1996). Indeed, they are the home base of administrative evil. Organizations can engage in such activities both internally and externally. Internally, evil acts may be inflicted on members of the organization, while externally, customers, clients, or citizens in various combinations become the victims. And of course, organizations may commit wrongdoing or evil activities that impact both those outside and inside the organization.

As we have said, modern organizations are characterized by the diffusion of information and the fragmentation of responsibility (Adams and Ingersoll, 1990). With diffuse and scattered information, literally no one in the organization may have a complete enough picture to know about the destructive activity. Those who might have enough of a picture to infer a problem may well assume that higher management must be aware of the problem and choose to do nothing about it. With regard to responsibility, those in operational units may note a problem, or a part of a problem, but are more often than not inclined to understate it so as not to bring negative news to superiors. Not knowing may be replaced by "strategic ignorance," which organizational actors may decide is the safer approach.

The longer wrongdoing or evil activity persists in an organization, the more difficult it becomes to acknowledge it. The notion of "sunk costs," borrowed from economics, is descriptively helpful here. Each step along the way in which such activity is not halted becomes an additional commitment to that trajectory. This dynamic can be described as "successive ratification." As a consequence, bringing such activity to a halt (recalling a product, grounding a fleet, etc.) requires extraordinarily decisive action. One needs clear and overwhelming evidence to do so, for one can be certain that no thanks will initially be forthcoming, if at all. Allowing normal processes (the status quo) to continue requires no action at all—momentum alone becomes a very powerful social force.

In some cases, a turning point is reached at which administrative evil turns into evil, and those actively participating in it become evildoers (Darley, 1992). The mask falls from administrative evil at this turning point. This is the moment at which people in the organization realize or discover that the organization has been engaged in acts of administrative evil—in the more egregious cases, for example, those involving the deaths of innocent others. Occasionally one can find cases of organizations in which people have knowingly engaged in harmful, destructive acts—that is, evil plain and simple—the unmasked version. More often, the activities that constitute the wrongdoing are thought by the participants (or at least some of the participants) to be benign or even beneficial. However, at the turning point, the painful truth is seen.

At this point, personal guilt and shame—and organizational liability—are immediately present, because in hindsight, most reasonable observers would say that someone should have known what was occurring. Since it is readily apparent that others are likely to react as though those involved should have known, relevant actors are likely to feel a level of guilt and shame commensurate with "knowingly" doing harm or evil. This in turn becomes a powerful psychological incentive to deny the harm or evil. If the wrongdoing or evil stems from management, such denial may be read by those lower in the organization as sufficient direction to collude in a cover-up or lie. Apprehension over the potential loss of one's job is often sufficient incentive for such collusion.

While the psychological incentives to deny and cover up are clearly powerful, individuals in the organization have made a fundamental shift at the turning point from engaging in harmful or evil activities unknowingly to doing so knowingly. This is the "evil turn" (Darley, 1996). It is evident that the incentives to cover up are socially powerful, if not overwhelming, because we also know that cover-ups rarely succeed, and usually result in the complete disclosure of the harmful or evil activities. Perpetrators persist in choosing denial and cover-up in the face of knowing they are unlikely to work. We see these dynamics at work in the case of the space shuttle *Challenger* disaster, to which we now turn.

### The Marshall Space Flight Center, *Challenger*, and the Pathway to Administrative Evil

The space shuttle *Challenger* disaster can be explained and understood from a technical standpoint (O-ring failure, etc.), but the underlying factors that led to the disaster have more to do with organizational dynamics (Ingersoll and Adams, 1992) than with a technological failure or flaw. As we have said, these dynamics represent a typical organizational pathway that can lead to administrative evil when no one intends evil. Despite, and in part because of, its reputation as a high-performance organization, the National Aeronautic and Space Administration, and more specifically, the Marshall Space Flight Center (MSFC), developed organizational dynamics that tacitly endorsed covering up mistakes and denying the existence of persistent problems. By openly punishing the bearers of bad news, or those who caused shuttle launches to be delayed for any reason, the leadership at MSFC enacted an atmosphere of defensiveness and intimidation that produced the conditions under which warnings of an O-ring failure could be dismissed as misguided or trivial, and where the espoused value of putting safety first could be replaced with a primary concern for meeting unrealistic launch schedules. This case illustrates how an organization can lapse into administrative evil (in this case, bringing about the loss of life that could have been, and should have been, prevented).

For the leadership of MSFC, concern for safety gradually became more wish than reality in a tacit effort to preserve the agency's status, funding, and image of high performance.

On January 28, 1986, the space shuttle *Challenger* was launched at 11:38 a.m. Just over a minute later, it exploded, killing all seven people on board (Macidull and Blattner, 2002; Trento, 1987). Among the seven on board was Christa McAuliffe, the "Teacher in Space," who was also the first civilian to participate in a manned space flight. The Presidential Commission, which examined the incident, called the event an "accident" (Rogers, 1986). Others refer to it as a disaster, because there was prior knowledge of the O-ring problem (the cause of the explosion) and because two of NASA's contractors actually recommended against launching during the sequence of events leading up to the launch (Committee, 1986; Romzek and Dubnick, 1987). In other words, this event could have been prevented.

If an individual had used a gun to kill the seven astronauts or had detonated a hidden bomb on the *Challenger* or the *Columbia*, we would almost certainly call such action evil. Identifying a single, individual perpetrator helps us name an action as evil. From the victims' perspective, and in this case the surviving victims were the families of the astronauts, there might be an inclination, if it was believed that the disaster was preventable, to call at least some of the activities "evil." Still, neither the Presidential Commission on Challenger nor the Columbia Accident Investigation Board made any mention of evil; rather, they termed each event an "accident" that virtually no one would call evil. Whether or not some of the actions in these two disasters can be termed as evil is arguable, but the organizational dynamics evident in these cases illustrate how administrative evil can and does emerge within organizations and help us to understand how normal organizational interaction, overlaid with technical rationality, can mask administrative evil.

## *A Flawed Design*

We know that it was the failure of an O-ring (a rubber seal—a larger version of the O-ring used in a faucet) that caused the *Challenger* to explode. We also know that the space shuttle, like any complex mechanical system, inherently involved risk. In complex systems, risk is always present and accidents are "normal" (Perrow, 1984). Cars, airplanes, experimental aircraft, and space shuttles have accidents, some of which are catastrophic and lead to loss of life. Some have argued that thinking of such accidents in terms of causation, let alone blame or culpability, may be misguided. They suggest that accidents are simply an inherent result of the risk that is present in all of the technological systems that pervade modern society.

This argument has validity in the sense that, when launching space shuttles a crash is bound to happen. Perfection in technical systems (really, sociotechnical systems) is not possible, because of both flaws in materials and human error. Indeed, in the early 1980s, the air force did its own risk assessment of a shuttle crash and calculated a 1 in 35 probability of such a crash. Prompted by that assessment, they removed their satellites from the shuttle's payload roster, reasoning that they could achieve better reliability with ordinary rockets. NASA management by contrast assessed the probability of a shuttle crash at an astonishing 1 in 100,000. Such an estimate, it turned out, was symptomatic of some of the problems that NASA developed as an organization and which contributed materially to the risk of a disaster. Nobel Prize–winning physicist Richard Feynman, a member of the Presidential Commission on Challenger, conducted his own investigation into NASA's inflated failure estimates. He reached the following conclusions (Rogers, 1986, F-1):

> If a reasonable launch schedule is to be maintained, engineering often cannot be done fast enough to keep up with the expectations of originally conservative certification criteria designed to guarantee a very safe vehicle. In these situations, subtly, and often with apparently logical arguments, the criteria are altered so that flights may still be certified in time. They therefore fly in a relatively unsafe condition; with a chance for failure of the order of a percent (it is difficult to be more accurate). Official management, on the other hand, claims to believe the probability of failure is a thousand times less. One reason for this may be an attempt to assure the government of NASA perfection and success in order to ensure the supply of funds. The other may be that they sincerely believe it to be true, demonstrating an almost incredible lack of communication between themselves and their working engineers.

The case of Marshall and NASA contains a series of organizational decisions and reactions that, over time, created a far greater likelihood of disaster than should have been the case (Vaughan, 1996, 406). Similar decisions and reactions continued following the *Challenger* disaster, at least after a time, and culminated in the loss of a second shuttle, the *Columbia,* in 2003. Unfortunately, these dynamics still pervade the organizational culture of NASA (Report of the RTFTG, 2005).

### NASA's History as an Organization

As we have seen, NASA was created in 1958 largely as a response to the sense of emergency that arose from the Soviet Union's launching of the *Sputnik I* satellite in 1957. America's self-image of technological and military superiority was fundamentally challenged by its global, cold war competitor. What NASA as an organization subsequently accomplished in ten short years—landing people on the moon—has few parallels in either the public or private sectors; it met the challenge issued by President Kennedy to win the race to the moon. Its early success, however, set the stage for later travails (Schwartz, 1990).

NASA began with about 4,000 employees, doubled by 1960, and reached a peak of 36,000 employees in 1966 (McCurdy, 1993). In the same time period, the NASA budget increased eightfold, peaking at about $5 billion dollars in 1965; this was 0.8 percent of the U.S. gross national product for that year. This is stunning growth, and whatever else may be said about NASA, it deserves much credit for successfully achieving its goals in the midst of such growth.

This growth, however, was short-lived, and NASA, like many organizations more recently, experienced real challenges in downsizing (McCurdy, 1993). NASA actually began to contract in 1967, before the *Apollo* moon landing. The NASA budget shrank each year until 1975, and as a percent of GNP fell to 0.2 percent by 1975. NASA employment likewise fell from its peak of 36,000 to 22,000 in 1975. And the number of contractor employees funded by NASA shrank from more than 300,000 in 1966 to 100,000 by 1972. Both budget levels and number of employees remained roughly the same through 1990 (although for the budget, this represented a decline in real dollars for nearly a decade, until a couple of spikes in the 1980s). In 1965, NASA's budget of $5.2 billion represented about 5.3 percent of the entire federal budget. If NASA had had the same share of the 1992 federal budget, its budget would have been $65 billion, and for the 2004 federal budget, their budget would have been $100 billion. However, the agency's actual 1992 budget was $15 billion, and the budget request for NASA for the 2004 fiscal year was $15.5 billion. Today, the NASA budget hovers around $17 billion, and continues to lose ground in purchasing power, even as the agency has been given a new and expensive mandate to return to the moon by the president.

During NASA's first ten years, it earned a reputation as a high-performing organization with a "can do" attitude. Since that time, it has settled into a performance level consistent with older, more stable private and public sector organizations. However, as we shall see, NASA developed several idiosyncrasies that made matters worse. For one thing, NASA had what might be termed a "mission crisis" after the successful moon shot. What could any organization do for an encore after "one small step for man, one giant leap for mankind"? For another, NASA used a management system fully consonant with the narrow perspective of technical rationality—that is, what NASA called "project management"—which faltered under the stress of resource stability and decline. Also, NASA pursued a system of decentralized management for the shuttle program, as opposed to the more centralized system of the Apollo program. This may seem benign on the surface, but a decentralized system renewed and considerably exacerbated competition and division between the three space centers: Johnson, Marshall, and Kennedy. This became particularly significant because it was a key factor, along with leadership changes, in shifting the organizational dynamics of Marshall from defensive but relatively benign under Wernher von Braun, to dysfunctional and destructive in the 1970s and 1980s.

### The Space Shuttle Program

For the space shuttle program, the NASA management challenge was to balance cost, schedule, and weight, while maintaining reliability. In the case of the shuttle, cost considerations were paramount from the very beginning. Conceived first by Wernher von Braun in the 1950s and then advanced by NASA not long after the moon shot, the shuttle itself was a relatively minor appendage to a grander design for a space station. NASA's new dream, conceived by von Braun, entailed an elaborate space station in earth orbit, serviced by a fleet of space shuttles. Federal budget constraints during the Nixon administration dictated putting the space station on indefinite hold, and selling the shuttle as a valuable project in its own right.

The shuttle program was grossly oversold and underbudgeted from the beginning. In 1972, NASA promised sixty shuttle flights per year. In 1983 and 1984, as the shuttle became "operational," there were four and five flights respectively, with a peak of nine in 1985. (It is interesting to note that one of the recommendations of the Columbia Accident Investigation Board [2003] was to remove the "operational" designation from the shuttle fleet—acknowledging that the uncertainties and complexities of space flight can never be other than "experimental.") Budgetary cost constraints were program-wide, but most vivid in retrospect was NASA's choice of Morton Thiokol's design for the solid rocket booster (SRB) used to rocket the shuttle into space. While NASA engineers at the MSFC in the early 1970s referred to Morton Thiokol's design as "unacceptable," NASA management cited Thiokol's "substantial cost advantage" as the chief reason for awarding them the contract for the SRB. In 1977 and 1978, NASA engineers at Marshall again raised concerns over this fatal design flaw.

With the shuttle, NASA's scheduling woes were self-inflicted. They sold the shuttle to Congress as a kind of "space truck," with airliner-like reliability (sixty flights per year). In part, this was done because the political and budgetary climate effectively demanded it. As Vaughan (1996, 389) stated, NASA's leadership "made decisions and took actions that compromised both the shuttle design and the environment of technical decision making for work groups throughout the NASA-contractor system. Congress and the White House established goals and made resource decisions that transformed the R&D space agency into a quasi-competitive business operation, complete with repeating production cycles, deadlines, and cost and efficiency goals."

While NASA scaled back these early flight estimates, in 1983 they promised twenty-four flights per year by the mid-1980s; and then in 1986, just before *Challenger*, they again promised the same twenty-four flights by 1988. President Reagan had declared the shuttle "fully operational" (using language provided by NASA) in 1982 after only four flights. This meant that fewer funds would be available for any still-needed design work (such as redesigning the flawed field joint and its O-rings), and that expectations for the number of flights would escalate.

NASA engineers had flagged an unacceptable space shuttle design even before the contract was awarded. When the O-ring design (using a clevis and tang approach) turned out even worse than expected in flight, concern mounted. As shuttle flights continued, the O-rings did not "seat" (that is, provide a good seal) as expected, and compounding the problem, hot gases from inside the rocket "blew by," eroding not only the primary seal, but the secondary seal as well. In 1982, NASA officially reclassified the Thiokol SRB joints from "criticality 1R" (meaning that a failure would be catastrophic, but that it was a redundant system by having a second, backup O-ring) to "criticality 1" (meaning that the backup did not work and could not be counted on—no redundancy). As the Presidential Commission noted (Rogers, 1986, 148): "The space shuttle's Solid Rocket Booster problem began with the faulty design of its joint and increased as both NASA and contractor management (Thiokol) first failed to recognize it as a problem, then failed to fix it, and finally treated it as an acceptable flight risk."

In August 1985, a briefing was held at NASA headquarters on the O-ring problem, in which resiliency, or the ability of the O-ring to return to a normal shape from an oval shape (which was negatively impacted by colder temperatures, that is, the colder the temperature, the longer it took for the seal to return to its round shape), was highlighted as the number-one concern. Marshall management insisted on recommending that flights continue as attempts were made to rectify the field joint problem. This decision provided what NASA headquarters wanted to hear, but it effectively escalated the risk of disaster to the point that it was only a matter of time before one occurred; the decision itself was conditioned by the destructive organizational culture that had developed at Marshall.

## The *Challenger* Disaster

A wild card was introduced into the equation when it became apparent that record low temperatures were forecast the night before the *Challenger* launch. The coldest prior launch (January 1985) had been at a seal temperature of 53 degrees; this launch looked like it would take off at below-freezing temperatures. Since cold temperatures, which seriously impacted resiliency, had been flagged as the number-one concern on O-ring erosion, this news could not have been more unwelcome at Morton Thiokol, where a meeting of engineers rather quickly agreed that this launch should be stopped if the expected low temperatures materialized.

A teleconference on the evening before the launch was convened between Thiokol, the MSFC, and the Kennedy Space Center to present the Thiokol engineers' concerns. They recommended against launching at a temperature below 53 degrees. To put this recommendation in context, throughout NASA's history the practice had always been that a contractor's role was to show NASA that its system was safe and ready to launch. That is, the contractor had an affirmative responsibility to show NASA it was safe to "go." In this particular instance, something completely different happened. NASA managers, affiliated with the MSFC, now put Thiokol management in the position of proving that it was *unsafe* to launch—a complete reversal of standard NASA practice. Thiokol managers got the picture that they were not telling NASA what it wanted to hear, namely, that it was OK to launch. After a recess, Thiokol management, in disregard of their engineers' best thinking, then used the same data charts to "conclude" that launching was OK.

The next day, when it a significant ice accumulation on the launch pad was discovered, Rocco Petrone (who, incidentally, had managed the Apollo program for NASA) of Rockwell International (the prime contractor on the shuttle vehicle itself) directed his representative at the Kennedy Space Center to inform NASA that "Rockwell cannot assure that it is safe to fly." This was the second contractor to recommend against launching. In this case, Arne Aldrich of the Johnson Space Flight Center, and the NASA manager in charge of the shuttle program, suggested that since Rockwell had not insisted against launching, that the launch should proceed. The Presidential Commission noted (Rogers, 1986, 148): "NASA appeared to be requiring Rockwell to prove that it was not safe to launch rather than proving it was safe." Once again, this was in complete reversal of standard NASA pre-launch practice for its entire history. NASA had never had a contractor recommend against a launch. Not only did NASA find a way to ignore one contractor's initial recommendation not to launch, it ignored two contractors' recommendations against launching.

### An Extraordinary Launch

*Challenger* was truly an extraordinary launch, given that NASA had never had a contractor recommend against a launch before and given the reversal of its standard practice of asking contractors to demonstrate that it was safe to launch. Three reasons have been advanced for the extraordinary pressure to launch *Challenger* on January 28 (Cook, 1986, 20):

1.  The scientific satellite *Ulysses*, scheduled for launch on *Challenger*'s next mission, faced a thirteen-month delay (due to planetary positioning) if flight 51L did not launch by January 29, the next day.
2.  It was generally known, both by NASA and contractors, that President Reagan intended to comment upon the lift-off of the first private citizen in space, teacher Christa McAuliffe, and report on his conversation with her in space, in his nationally televised, State of the Union address on the night of January 28.
3.  The previous shuttle flight, the *Columbia*, launched on January 12, had earned the record as the most delayed lift-off ever, after seven nonstarts. In addition, flight 51L's postponements had already received extensive press coverage.

In fact, the *Ulysses* launch had a two-week window beyond January 29, so that issue was not as pressing as it might have been. The latter two reasons surely had some impact, but something even beyond these was at work. Richard Cook, one of the two chief whistleblowers during the *Challenger* investigation, who subsequently devoted considerable time to his own investigation of the incident, made the following statement after speaking with a former Reagan aide in March 1991 (Meier, 1992, 50):

> I have been told by one eyewitness source that the decision was made by the President of the United States to proceed with the launch in the face of what the President was told were cold weather concerns, because they wanted to get the Shuttle in the air in connection with the publicity for the Teacher-in-Space program. That is where the impetus came from.

Moreover, a phone call from or on behalf of the president (if indeed it was made) would have been made to William Graham, then acting administrator of NASA, who had just recently been brought into the organization as James Beggs's deputy. Beggs fought the appointment of Graham, whose role was essentially to manage the shuttle's planned involvement with the Star Wars program, because Graham had no space program experience. Graham was subsequently appointed as the president's science advisor. As acting NASA administrator, Graham would not have been in the normal decision loop for a launch, and it seems reasonable that he may not have known about Thiokol's or Rockwell's recommendations not to launch. He was certainly well aware that the "Teacher in Space" was an important public relations initiative for NASA, and that delays in the shuttle's flight schedule were exacting a heavy toll on the agency. And he, above all, would have been likely to be quite responsive to a phone call from the president himself.

If indeed President Reagan himself made a phone call to NASA ordering a *Challenger* launch, with the knowledge that there were cold-weather concerns, would it be too great a stretch to call that action evil? Perhaps. Of course, we are unlikely to ever know for sure if the president made such a telephone call, or just how much he knew about or understood the potential risk. If William Graham received such a phone call from the president or even a presidential aide, and subsequently ordered his subordinates to go forward with the launch, would that action too be fairly called evil? Perhaps. It becomes more difficult to label as evil the actions of those farther down the organizational hierarchy. Many of them were simply being obedient to duly constituted authority, much like the subjects in the Milgram experiments discussed in Chapter 2. It is precisely this sort of ordinary behavior within the MSFC that we want to focus on more closely, because it is just such ordinary organizational dynamics that enable administrative evil to surface. Indeed, even if the *Challenger* launch had been stopped on that cold January day in 1986, the destructive organizational culture of Marshall and NASA had practically ensured a shuttle disaster—it was just a matter of time. Tragically, those same dynamics resulted in the loss of a second shuttle, the *Columbia* in 2003, and to this day appear to remain entrenched in NASA's organizational culture.

## The Marshall Space Flight Center

Both Morton Thiokol, as the prime contractor on the solid rocket booster, and Marshall, as the project manager for the SRB, were responsible for the field joints and their O-rings, which were a growing problem as shuttle flights continued. The predominant problem was not that the O-rings were slow to seal; rather, it was that the hot gas "blow-by" eroded the rings. Once the seal took effect, hot gas no longer got through. But because the O-rings did not seat as quickly as their designers had predicted, there was a longer period of time for the hot gas to escape. This resulted in a potentially deadly race against time during each launch. Hot gas erosion was evident on the second shuttle mission in 1982, but then disappeared for the next seven missions. Then, on the tenth shuttle mission, in 1984, it reappeared. On the subsequent missions (11 through 24), erosion occurred on all but three. The damage was particularly dramatic on mission 15 in January 1985, with the coldest launch to date—53 degrees seal temperature. On that flight, hot gas blow-by and erosion had occurred through nearly one-third of the circumference of the primary seal, but was stopped when the secondary seal functioned properly. Then, on mission 17, the primary seal in a nozzle joint was completely destroyed, and the secondary seal was damaged. If that had occurred in an SRB field joint, that mission would have been lost.

At this time, in mid-1985, Larry Mulloy, the SRB project manager at Marshall, placed a "launch constraint" on the SRB field joints; however, he subsequently waived the constraint for all of the missions to follow, including *Challenger*. A pattern of censoring problematic or negative information for higher-ups within NASA became evident on Mulloy's part and on Marshall's part more generally. A similar pattern was noted at the Hubble Space Telescope Program, which also had its program office at Marshall (Smith, 1989, 302). As the Presidential Commission noted (Rogers, 1986, 84), "neither the launch constraint, the reason for it, or the six consecutive waivers prior to 51–L (*Challenger*) were known to Moore (Level I) or Aldrich (Level II) or Thomas (the Launch Director at Kennedy)."

A NASA headquarters briefing was held on August 19, 1985 (five months before *Challenger*), at which O-rings were presented as the chief concern in shuttle safety, and resiliency (that is, the reduced seating capacity of the O-rings as temperatures got colder). Marshall staff, however, deleted the following statement from the conclusions chart: "Data obtained on resiliency of the O-rings indicate that lower temperatures aggravate this problem." More seriously, they concluded: "It is safe to continue flying." Jesse Moore, the NASA Associate Administrator for Space Flight, was briefed on this meeting by his deputy and followed up by phoning George Hardy, the Deputy Director of Science and Engineering at Marshall, to confirm that, indeed, the fleet did not need to be grounded until this problem was fixed. Hardy indicated it was safe to fly.

This decision became just the latest in a series of decisions made within NASA, Marshall, and Thiokol that, as they accumulated, communicated an acceptance of the safety of the O-rings. This consensus led to a false sense of security. Interestingly, Larry Mulloy, the SRB project manager, notes that more time and concern was spent on the parachutes, which were not functioning properly in returning the spent boosters safely back to the ocean surface so they could be picked up and reused (Vaughan, 1996). The parachutes were so prominent a concern because they had immediate and considerable *cost* implications. Put another way, cost considerations eroded over time the necessary level of attention to safety issues.

The Presidential Commission included among its findings (Rogers, 1986, 104):

> 1. The Commission concluded that there was a serious flaw in the decision-making process leading up to the launch of flight 51–L. A well-structured and managed system emphasizing safety would have flagged the rising doubts about the SRB joint seal. Had these matters been clearly stated and emphasized in the flight readiness process in terms reflecting the views of most of the Thiokol engineers and at least some of the Marshall engineers, it seems likely that the launch of 51–L might not have occurred when it did.
>
> . . .
>
> 3. The Commission is troubled by what appears to be a propensity of management at Marshall to contain potentially serious problems and to attempt to resolve them internally rather than communicate them forward. This tendency is altogether at odds with the need for Marshall to function as part of a system working toward successful flight missions, interfacing and communicating with the other parts of the system that work to the same end.

This tendency within Marshall was fostered by its director, Dr. William Lucas, a veteran of the Apollo program and Marshall's director since 1974, following von Braun and the brief three-year tenure of Eberhard Rees, a former von Braun deputy and the last of the top Germans. In the 1970s and 1980s, Marshall was run like a Teutonic empire (ironically, this was after nearly all the Germans were gone), and Lucas was its dictator (McConnell, 1987, 108):

> [T]his autocratic leadership style grew over the years to create an atmosphere of rigid, often fearful conformity among Marshall managers. Unlike other senior NASA officials, who reprimanded subordinates in private, Lucas reportedly used open meetings to scornfully criticize lax performance. And like many demanding task masters, he demanded absolute personal loyalty.

Essentially, the three centers, Marshall, Johnson, and Kennedy, but particularly the former two, engaged in a competitive rivalry, and the least favored center would be the one that slowed the launch schedule. Lucas was determined that Marshall should win that competition (Vaughan, 1996, 218):

> Lucas' management style, combined with the production pressure the center was experiencing, not only exacerbated the intercenter rivalry but resulted in competition between the three Marshall projects. Each Project Manager vied with the

> others to conform to the cultural imperatives of the original technical culture. . . .
> They competed to meet deadlines, be on top of every technical detail, solve their
> technical problems, conform to rules and requirements, be cost-efficient, and, of
> course, contribute to safe, successful space-flight. . . . No Project Manager wanted
> his hardware or people to be responsible for a technical failure. To describe the
> pressure at Marshall simply as production pressure is to underestimate it. It was,
> in fact, performance pressure . . . that permeated the workplace culture.

Lucas let it be known that under no circumstances would Marshall be responsible for delaying a launch (McConnell, 1987, 109). And indeed, in the twenty-five Flight Readiness Reviews in the shuttle program's history, not a single time had Marshall indicated that a launch should not go forward as planned, although it was responsible for a number of the technical glitches that delayed launches.

## The Evolution of a Destructive Organizational Culture at Marshall

Wernher von Braun's subordinates, by all accounts, ranked him very high as a manager and leader (Bilstein, 1980). Among members of the von Braun team, this is perhaps not surprising, since his leadership rescued the group from the dead end of post-war Germany, brought them to a new land, and led them forward to great accomplishments. His leadership inspired a *Festschrift,* originally including forty papers done primarily by his subordinates, in honor of his fiftieth birthday in 1962. Von Braun was known to practice his "dirty hands" approach to management by dropping in on one of his prized laboratories unannounced, and asking about a detail that most agency directors would not be unaware of. His knowledge of technical detail was legendary, and he successfully negotiated the boundary between Marshall and NASA headquarters, and more generally, society at large. From his mid-twenties until his retirement in 1972, von Braun held increasingly responsible management positions and exercised clear leadership in all of them.

Von Braun's leadership style was expansive, as manifested by an attempt (Allcorn and Diamond, 1997, 27) "to master and control events and people in order to allay anxiety." He exhibited clear tendencies toward a narcissistic approach to management, defined here by Allcorn and Diamond (31): "Projects an image of self-confidence and demands admiration and loyalty from others. Dreamer and risk taker. . . . Develops big ideas and plans which are accompanied by boundless energy." Von Braun's "dirty hands" approach, while quite functional in the context of developing the Saturn and other rockets, was also very controlling.

Von Braun showed his narcissistic bent in a number of other ways. He accepted large numbers of public speaking engagements during the 1950s and 1960s; during the latter decade, the number of engagements was in apparent violation of NASA regulations. James Webb, the NASA administrator at the time, is said to have told von Braun to limit these engagements (McConnell, 1987, 17). During the 1950s, von Braun developed a relationship with Walt Disney and even served as a consultant on three space-related Disney films from those years. He clearly saw himself as a visionary for space and its exploration, and acted in ways that asked—or demanded—that others view him that way as well. When narcissistic tendencies are carried too far, however, it becomes easy to denigrate subordinates, as von Braun does subtly in the beginning of a paper written in 1962 (von Braun, 1963, 248):

> It is a rare opportunity for me to have an audience of such experienced and distinguished managers. I appreciate the privilege of telling you the same thing everybody else does; namely, that no matter *how* you are running your organization, you are doing it *all* wrong and you should do it *our* way. . . . It takes a manager with a rare sort of ability to get much work out of people and still keep them happy, or at least keep them from fighting in the halls. . . . It is the same rare manager who can pass out the money, assign functions, allot office space, authorize carpets and reorganize the entire outfit without anyone losing face, quitting, or getting drunk on the job. It also takes real managerial talent to pacify employees who often are harassed by headquarters, sometimes outwitted by industry. . . . But it is the greatest manager of all who can keep reasonable peace in the family after he has split all the annual resources among all the department heads.

This introduction was surely written—and probably delivered—with humorous intent by von Braun, yet it reveals his narcissistic bent as a leader.

While there were problems during von Braun's tenure, Marshall was clearly not only a functional organization, but arguably a high-performing one through the 1960s (McCurdy, 1993). Still, as discussed in Chapter 4, Marshall developed a siege mentality during those years, with the von Braun team always feeling slighted and, at times, even attacked. At the same time, there were divisions and occasional conflict between the Germans and subordinate Americans at Marshall, as well as between the Germans and their American superiors at NASA headquarters in Washington. Why did these factors not lead to a destructive culture during von Braun's tenure at Marshall?

Apart from von Braun's and other team members' talents as managers and leaders, which may well have been considerable, one factor in Marshall's (and NASA's) success was a clear sense of mission: this was a *race* to the moon. And the resources were there. This was largely a period of rapid expansion, which, as we have noted, represents a serious managerial challenge in itself (a good problem, if you will, but a problem nonetheless). Also, the "everything under one roof" approach in which Marshall sought to maintain the necessary technical expertise to design and construct in-house, was far stronger in the 1960s than in the 1970s and 1980s. However, when a defensive organizational culture exists, change in the surrounding environment or change in the organization—particularly in leadership—can trigger this potential into destructive dynamics. This appears to have occurred at Marshall.

NASA began to contract as an organization even before the moon landing in 1969. Recall that the budget began to shrink in 1967, and personnel levels shortly before, in 1966. However, this trajectory increased dramatically as it became clear that the Apollo program was going to wind down in the early 1970s. Remember that this was a period of time that the von Braun team referred to as the "Great Massacre." Marshall's technical culture gradually became more illusion than reality. And recall, too, that NASA underwent a "mission crisis" at this time. While Marshall had many projects under way during the 1970s, these were all pale shadows of Apollo. No one was in a race anymore, and NASA was no longer favored with large budgets. As Vaughan notes, NASA top management made decisions that were significant compromises for the agency (1996, 390):

> [T]hey made bargains that altered the organization's goals, structure and culture. These changes had enormous repercussions. They altered the consciousness and actions of technical decision makers, ultimately affecting the Challenger launch deliberations. Also, NASA top administrators responded to an environment of scarcity by promulgating the myth of routine, operational space flight.

This was the context in which Dr. William Lucas assumed leadership at Marshall in 1974. Lucas had spent his entire career at Marshall (and earlier at Redstone)—nearly twenty-five years at that time. In 1960, the Marshall organization chart shows Lucas in charge of the Engineering Materials Branch, within the Structures and Mechanics Division under the direction of William Mrazek, a member of the von Braun team (Bilstein, 1980, 446). As Marshall's director, Lucas had von Braun's expansive shoes to fill, and also, by comparison, a much less propitious situation in terms of projects, personnel, and budget. We have no way of knowing whether Lucas may have thought he was emulating von Braun's management style, but we do know that his own became quickly apparent (McConnell, 1987, 107):

[M]any observers saw Lucas' leadership style as the exact opposite of von Braun. Where von Braun had been a charismatic visionary who instilled loyalty through personal magnetism, Lucas was a coldly distant (and often rigid) master bureaucrat. He believed in doing things by the regulations. Interpreting the regulations was his prerogative.

Vaughan sheds further light on Lucas's management style (1996, 218):

Saddled with a vastly more complex Marshall organizational structure and apparently lacking von Braun's charisma and skill at maintaining personal contact with people at different levels in the Marshall hierarchy, Lucas relied on hierarchy and formal mechanisms to transfer information. He insisted on bureaucratic accountability for monitoring and controlling internal operations.

As it happens, this leadership style is closer to von Braun's than one might at first imagine. It shares with von Braun an expansive approach; however, rather than a narcissistic style, Lucas manifested an arrogant-vindictive style, defined by Allcorn and Diamond as: "Highly competitive and must win all encounters at any cost, intent upon defeating and humiliating others who harm arrogant pride. Paralyzes others with fear by being intimidating" (1997, 30).

Under the arrogant-vindictive leadership of William Lucas and no longer in the exalted (but also defensive) position as the world's premier rocket facility, Marshall developed a persecutory organizational identity. The concept of "organizational identity" is defined by Diamond (1988, 169) as "the totality of repetitive patterns of individual behavior and interpersonal relationships that taken together comprise the unacknowledged meaning of organizational life." These patterns include both conscious and unconscious interaction, are an important constituent of an organization's identity, and represent a fruitful avenue into the implicit dimension of organization culture, particularly at the level of interpersonal and group relations (Adams, 1993; Diamond, 1993). At Marshall, the defensiveness characteristic of the von Braun years escalated under Lucas into a persecutory organizational identity in which "workers feel powerless and disrespected" (Allcorn and Diamond, 1997, 241–242):

They experience their conflict with the organization and its leadership in a manner that is passive . . . things (decisions and actions) are done to them. They have little say and often feel they have little recourse. . . . The lack of mutual respect between the leadership and the workforce is signified by unilateral . . . top-down executive . . . decisions and actions of an oppressive organizational culture.

Lucas was notorious for publicly reprimanding—or more accurately, verbally tearing apart—subordinates who made mistakes (Boisjoly, 1997). This meant that the preferred choice for Marshall employees was to avoid making mistakes. And as perfection is difficult to produce at all times, camouflaging mistakes would be the next best bet. Lucas and other managers were quite predictably told what they wanted to hear (no mistakes, no delays, no problems), not what they needed to know (Smith, 1989). While there were several levels of Flight Readiness Review (FRR) within Marshall, the highest level, the Marshall Center Board, was notorious (Vaughan, 1996, 219):

> The Marshall Center Board FRR was the quintessential embodiment of Marshall culture. Although Marshall's Level IV and III FRRs were adversarial and rigorous, they paled in comparison to the Lucas-embellished culture of the more formal, large-audience Center Board review. The Center Board was the final in-house review before Marshall Level III Project Managers made their assessments of flight readiness at Level II and Level I before Johnson and NASA top administrators respectively. Lucas presided. Here we see the distinctive Marshall performance pressure.

Vaughan quotes more extensively from a personal interview with Larry Wear, one of Marshall's program managers (1996, 219–220):

> The Center Board would be held in a humongous conference room that looks like an auditorium. It's an open meeting. There might be one hundred—one hundred fifty people there. . . . It's great drama. . . . And it's an adversarial process. I think there are some people who have, what's the word, there is a word for when you enjoy somebody else's punishment . . . masochistic, they are masochistic. You know, come in and watch Larry Wear or Larry Mulloy or Thiokol take a whipping from the Board.

The decentralization of the Space Shuttle Program Office in the early 1970s to the Johnson Space Flight Center in Houston (the Apollo Program Office had been at NASA headquarters in Washington) had the added effect of escalating the competition and conflict between the centers—a conflict that had existed as well during the von Braun years. This led to Lucas's disastrous insistence that Marshall not be responsible for any launch delays on the shuttle flight program. As Vaughan observes (1996, 220):

> Marshall's concerns about looking good among other centers translated into competition between the SRB, Main Engine, and External Tank Projects at the Center Board FRR. Impression management was the name of the game.

Performance pressure resulted in managing impressions by *leaving no stone unturned*. This thoroughness created intense preoccupation with procedural conformity and "going by the book." [italics in original]

Quite apart from the *Challenger* disaster, Marshall's unwillingness to "fail" or "lose" by grounding the fleet until the fatal design flaw could be fixed, and its increasingly rigid and pressurized approach to the Flight Readiness Review process, essentially guaranteed that a shuttle disaster would occur sometime soon.

### The Space Shuttle *Columbia* Disaster

The mantra of NASA's post-*Challenger* safety program was "never again." Knowing that space flight is inherently risky, was the *Columbia* disaster just a "normal" event? Or do we see similar organizational dynamics at work in NASA and the shuttle program that once again acted to escalate that risk to unacceptable levels? The Columbia Accident Investigation Board's report (2003) clearly states that the organizational dynamics at NASA—most of them disturbingly similar to *Challenger*—made the *Columbia* mission a disaster waiting to happen (again).

In the aftermath of *Challenger*, the shuttle budget, and especially the safety budget, saw rather dramatic increases. In 1988, 49 percent of the shuttle program budget was spent on safety and performance upgrades. However, by 1999 that number had dropped to 19 percent of the budget. During the Clinton years, budget declines and policy shifts brought dramatic changes to the shuttle program. Touting the apparent success of these moves, NASA proudly noted that the shuttle budget had been cut by 40 percent, but that malfunctions had been reduced by 70 percent.

Following the most popular trajectory in the federal government during the 1990s, NASA escalated its long-standing practice of contracting out more and more of its programs, including the space shuttle. In recent years, 92 percent of the shuttle budget has gone to NASA contractors, most notably the United Space Alliance, a cooperative, private organization made up of Lockheed Martin and Boeing (mostly former Rockwell International) units that work on the shuttle. NASA, of course, has always depended on contractors. However, when one contrasts the current state of affairs at NASA to both the old, military arsenal system of "everything under one roof" and the von Braun team's "dirty hands" approach to rockets and space flight, one finds almost the direct opposite of the old philosophy. "Everything under one roof" and "dirty hands" meant at a minimum the in-house capacity to both design and build a component—for example, an entire Delta rocket. Von Braun actually preferred to design and build the most critical rocket components in-house. Even by the time of the Apollo program, the capacity to build had eroded, and virtually the entire shuttle system was built by various contractors. The most striking thing about NASA in the years preceding the *Columbia* disaster is not the loss of the last vestiges of design capacity, but the erosion, if not loss, of sufficient technical capacity even to oversee contractors' work (see Chapter 8 for a detailed discussion of this problem in relation to ethics and administrative evil). NASA appears to us to be a poster child of the "hollowed out" federal agency.

Arguably, NASA eroded its scientific and engineering capacity to make sound judgments about the myriad technical decisions and choices made by contractors. NASA touted the tagline that they moved from "oversight" of contractors to "insight," although it is not clear exactly what NASA had "insight" into. NASA's critical loss of capacity was nowhere more evident than in its safety program, which became in effect a paper tiger with "no there there" (Columbia Accident Investigation Board's Report, 2003). In the shuttle launch process, redesigned after *Challenger*, the chief shuttle safety officer sat right beside the shuttle chief administrator, who made the final launch decision. However, as the Columbia Accident Investigation Board chair, Admiral Gehman, said, "The safety organization sits right beside the person making the decisions. But behind the safety organization, there is nothing back there. There is no people, money, engineering expertise, analysis."

Both NASA and United Space Alliance placed heavy emphasis on safety. However, when the shuttle funds devoted to safety fell by 60 percent (and fell even further in effective purchasing power), shuttle safety once again became an empty shell of rhetoric. To be sure, there were contract incentives for safety; these were at work in reducing "malfunctions" by 70 percent in the 1990s. However, there were greater incentives for performance, and perhaps most tellingly, the federal government indemnifies—that is, holds harmless—United Space Alliance in the event of loss of a shuttle. We have already noted the decline in budget dollars, and especially those resources devoted to safety and performance upgrades. There were other factors at work here as well.

It is clear that the technical cause of the *Columbia* disaster was a large piece of foam (about the size of an average suitcase) that separated from the launch pivot arm and struck the vulnerable reinforced carbon-carbon (RCC)–coated edge of the shuttle's left wing with considerable force (Covault, 2003). This strike created a seam or hole in the wing's front edge, ultimately allowing superheated gas to destroy the shuttle during re-entry on February 1, 2003. Like many other aspects of the shuttle, NASA and the United Space Alliance were working on the problems of foam strikes and the wing edge. Indeed, a 2000 report from a Marshall engineer listed thirty "high risk" problems related to the foam. Foam strikes had been declared "criticality 1" in the 1980s, but that problem was thought to have been fixed until it reappeared in STS-112, a *Discovery* flight in 1999. However, for reasons that are unclear, this foam strike was not given criticality 1 status.

The foam problem was clearly not going to be solved by the contractor unit responsible for it—namely, the Michoud Assembly Facility in Louisiana, operated by Lockheed (United Space Alliance). Prior to the *Challenger* tragedy in 1986, Michoud had a workforce of 4,800, which was cut to 3,800 by December of that year. In 2002, Michoud laid off 15 percent of their workforce of 2,400. Like NASA and many of the contractor organizations, Michoud had a core workforce of employees with twenty-plus years of experience, and then the remainder with only a few years of experience. As those at the bottom gained some years of experience, they were hit with one wave of layoffs after another. The NASA organization had similar issues: in 1993, 28 percent of NASA's workforce was under age thirty-five; ten years later, only 11 percent were under age thirty-five. NASA lost its reputation as an attractive employment opportunity by the nation's best young engineers and scientists. While there are still a few pockets of excellence within NASA, such as Goddard and the Jet Propulsion Laboratory, the organization has deteriorated to the point where its ability to conduct manned space flight is—or should be—in question.

## Return to Flight

The *Challenger* disaster grounded the shuttle fleet from January 1986 through August 1988. Following the *Columbia* disaster, the shuttle fleet was grounded for about two and half years, from January 2003 through July 2005. During this second interval, NASA formed an independent team of experts, which came to be known as the Return to Flight Task Group (RTFTG). This was done in part to avoid some of the mistakes that were made in the return to flight after *Challenger*. The Columbia Accident Investigation Board's report presented fifteen recommendations that it believed were necessary to implement before the shuttle fleet returned to flight; the job of the RTFTG was to monitor this process from an independent perspective. The RTFTG's final report in 2005 indeed verified that NASA had addressed these recommendations; however, the report included a set of annexes that were reports and observations of various members of the RTFTG. Annex Two, twenty-eight pages in length and signed by seven members of the task group, is particularly noteworthy. Among the signees was a prominent public administration scholar, Rosemary O'Leary of Syracuse University; she describes in her book, *The Ethics of Dissent*, how these dissenting reports came about. The two astronaut co-chairs of the RTFTG (O'Leary, 2006, 117): "were insisting that only positive insights, analyses and observations about NASA be included in the task group's final report." Faced with a number of members of the task group vowing to publish a dissenting report separately from the final report, the compromise was the annexes.

The "observations" of the seven task group members in Annex Two, while taking pains to acknowledge the real progress made on engineering, technical, and organizational aspects of the return-to-flight process, provide a distressing critique of NASA (Return to Flight Task Group Report, 2005, 188):

> The Rogers Commission and the Columbia Accident Investigation Board (CAIB) reports are both rich in explanation of factors that have weakened NASA's ability to effectively manage a high-risk program. Yet while NASA leadership was focused on the 15 CAIB return-to-flight recommendations, they missed opportunities to address the enduring themes of dysfunctional organizational behavior that the CAIB and other external evaluators have repeatedly found. As a result, in our view, many fundamental concerns persist.

Their observations are organized around concerns in the four areas of rigor, risk, requirements, and leadership. The linchpin is of course leadership (194):

> What our concerns about rigor, risk and requirements point to are a lack of focused, consistent leadership and management. What we observed, during the return-to-flight effort, was that NASA leadership often did not set the proper tone, establish achievable expectations, or hold people accountable for meeting them. On many occasions, we observed weak understanding of basic program management and systems engineering principles, an abandonment of traditional processes, and a lack of rigor in execution. Many of the leaders and managers . . . lack the crucial ability to accurately evaluate how much or how little risk is associated with their decisions, particularly decisions to sidestep or abbreviate any given procedure or process.

These observations also took note of NASA's attitude of continuing arrogance, even in the face of quite spectacular failures.

Both President Bush and President Obama announced new visions for space flight within NASA. Neither vision has been funded or implemented, nor are they likely to happen in the future. While the dream of space exploration is alive for many, the dynamics of the federal budget are such that the prospects for funding any new, very expensive programs in any federal agency are very low, bordering on nonexistent. Given that NASA appears to be deeply entrenched in systemic organizational dysfunction, with repeating patterns of defensive and even arrogant senior management, perhaps NASA's likely absence from future space flight and exploration may well be positive.

## The Pathway to Administrative Evil

Should we then infer from the discussion in this chapter that NASA as an organization has been evil? Or should we conclude that the von Braun team was somehow responsible for the *Challenger* disaster? Of course not—neither would be a reasonable conclusion; but we can identify dynamics present at Marshall and NASA in both the *Challenger* and *Columbia* disasters and their aftermaths that strongly suggest—although not conclusively—that both tragedies could have been, and should have been, prevented.

William Lucas's leadership placed Marshall at an escalated level of risk because, even if *Challenger* had not been launched, the destructive organizational dynamics virtually assured a shuttle disaster resulting in the loss of astronauts' lives in the near term. Nobody at the MSFC, Lucas surely included, set out to make mistakes or to do wrong, but the organizational dynamics that manifested before, during, and after *Challenger* put lives at unnecessary risk and therefore suggest a case of administrative evil. It would be unfair and unwarranted to connect *Challenger* or *Columbia* with the unmasked and essentially transparent administrative evil demonstrated at Mittelbau-Dora and Peenemünde. Operations Overcast and Paperclip, policies of our own government, each abetting administrative evil, represent only an ironic connection to later events at the MSFC and with *Challenger* and *Columbia*. However, we can see how many different groups of professionals—most of whom would think of themselves as embodying professional ethics—were nonetheless drawn into actions and nonactions that led first to unacceptable risks and finally to the tragedy of fourteen unnecessary deaths. When NASA, Marshall, and Morton Thiokol each responded independently and spontaneously to the explosion of *Challenger* with a cover-up, administrative evil was nearly unmasked via their "evil turn." These attempted cover-ups did not last very long and were largely unsuccessful because of the high-profile investigation and two whistleblowers. NASA did better after the *Columbia* tragedy, according to Robert Hotz, a member of the Presidential Commission on Challenger: "At least they are better than with the *Challenger*, when they didn't want to say anything, and when they did, they lied." All of the dynamics leading to these earlier tragedies remain in place within NASA, making it difficult not to expect tragic outcomes in the future. Whatever administrative evil can be legitimately attributed to Marshall and NASA as a result of these twin tragedies is of the typical organizational variety in our time and in our culture. It is opaque and complex, and no one can be identified with evil intentions. It is well masked.

> NASA needs to learn the lessons of its past . . . lessons provided at the cost of the lives of seventeen astronauts.
> —*Final Report of the RTFTG*, 2005 (197)

# Public Policy and Administrative Evil

Racism is a policy first, ideology second. Like all politics,
it needs organization, managers and experts.

*—Zygmunt Bauman,* 1989 (74)

In the preceding chapters, we have examined how the Holocaust and other, more masked instances of administrative evil, which have exemplified the technical-rational approach to administration, encourage professionals and citizens alike to equate or replace substantive values with procedural ones. Doing things the right way, and protecting organizational interests, can define or supersede doing the right things, and make it easier to commit or contribute to destructive acts by separating—mentally—the doer from the deed (Keeley, 1983). While certainly not inherently evil, the values of procedural correctness and efficiency can mask both the context in which they are applied and the human consequences of administrative action. The purpose of this chapter is to explore the contemporary context in which public policy is made and implemented, with a focus on how the tacit assumptions that undergird technical-rational solutions to messy, intractable social problems can unwittingly contribute to the breakdown of community, the creation of "surplus populations," and—through moral inversions and administrative evil—even public policies of destruction.

## Public Policy and Problem Solving

The modern approach to public policy and planning is summarized best, and most commonly, in terms of the process of problem solving. That is, the stated purpose of public policy is to identify, develop, and implement solutions to an array of discrete social problems (Schon, 1993). Doing so requires a confluence of scientific method or technology (means) and political will or consensus (ends). However, this image of public policy as problem solving is realized only in those rather uncommon instances when the technology for addressing the problem is known and a political consensus exists on the goals of the policy. In such rare contexts, public administrators can rationally predict outcomes, focus on optimizing the efficiency and effectiveness of their processes and programs, and be held accountable for their performance (Christensen, 1985). In effect, they can solve policy problems by following scientifically or rationally established procedures. In most social policy arenas, this image of public policy as problem solving is largely a fiction.

Public policy as problem solving has its roots in the modern, scientific worldview that seeks to bend nature and society to the will of scientific method and technology (Bauman, 1989; Keller, 1985). As a conceptual framework for thinking about public policy, problem solving implies—and creates the expectation—that a satisfactory end point, a solution, or, ideally, the elimination of a social problem can be achieved through the application of modern scientific methods. We are reminded of the common question: Why is it that we can put a man on the moon but can't find a solution to homelessness (or some other intractable social problem)?

But sending astronauts to the moon was far from the discrete, programmable project with a clear end point or goal that our popular understanding implies. And as we have seen, it was connected to a public policy—and its implementation—that represented administrative evil, at least in part. Still, the image of engineering and scientific methods as able to assume predictable and stable cause-and-effect relationships endures: that specific problems could be identified and addressed according to known procedures by a dedicated workforce. Further, the space program was undertaken in a context of considerable political and social consensus—perhaps an all-too-facile consensus. Thus, our social fantasy was that this was a project that could be programmed, implemented, and completed more or less according to plan (Christensen, 1985).

In contrast, poverty, crime, terrorism, drug abuse, illegal immigration, racism, discrimination, and so forth transparently do not fit this image of discrete problems that can be solved once and for all with analytic methods. They are complex, lived situations, where cause-and-effect relations, when they exist at all, are chaotic, shifting, and unpredictable. It is both puzzling and ironic that the technical-rational, problem-solving approach to public policy appears to have more than the cat's nine lives, even as the most recent "solution" is disparaged as too narrow, or insufficiently understood, or becomes the new problem to be solved. The problem-solving approach has been continually frustrated by the vagaries of human behavior and societal dynamics, yet it endures. Programmed solutions to such "problems" are partial, temporary, and largely ineffective, and political consensus is often elusive (Blanco, 1994). Further, these solutions often produce unintended consequences, "which come to be perceived as problems in their own right (as public housing, conceived initially as a solution to the problem of housing the temporarily poor, came later to be perceived as a concentration of social pathology)" (Schon, 1993, 144). As tempting as it has been to use the moon shot or other technological achievements as putative models for solving public policy problems, social problems continue to resist attempts to solve them with specific, rational programs.

### Critiques of the Problem-Solving Approach to Public Policy

A number of authors (Bauman, 1989; Blanco, 1994; Saul, 1992; Schon, 1993; Stone, 1988; Yanow, 1995) have questioned whether problem solving itself is an appropriate conceptual framework for public policy, especially in the realm of social policy (more than forty years ago, essentially the same arguments were made by Sir Geoffrey Vickers in *The Art of Judgment*, 1995, orig. 1965). In their view, problem solving is a metaphorical, and not a literal, way of thinking about governmental responses to undesirable social and economic circumstances; or, more specifically, it is the basis for generating specific metaphors and concepts for understanding social problems. What they see as especially problematic is the extent to which problem solving has attained an unquestioned dominance in the policy arena with little or no reflection on the possible consequences of addressing social issues in this way (Schon, 1993, 148): "In order to dissolve the obviousness of diagnosis and prescription in the field of social policy, we need to become aware of, and to focus attention upon, the generative metaphors which underlie our problem-setting stories. Often we are unaware of the metaphors that shape our perception and understanding of social situations."

Authors such as Saul (1992), Schon (1993), and Bauman (1989) argue that western society has placed all its faith and energies at the service of a "single, all purpose elite using a single all purpose methodology" (Saul, 1992, 135). Or, as Bauman (1989, 12) puts it, "the chorus of experts who assure us that human problems are matters of wrong policies, and the right policies mean elimination of problems." These technical-rational experts and their scientific methodology work to systematically reduce the fundamental contradictions and ambiguities that characterize social life into formulas, models, and programs. This preintegrated logic, systematically taught at the leading institutions of higher learning as policy analysis, seeks to drive out contradiction and pursues efficient solutions to messy social problems. Saul (1992) argues that Western civilization appears unable to deal with its social problems, largely because the "dictatorship of reason," that is, technical rationality, has left its leaders with little memory of their history and the social processes and institutions that contributed to contemporary problems. Hence, the most common responses to the inability to achieve solutions are to either redouble the uncritical application of technical-rational methods, or to abandon and discredit public policy in frustration, all the while overlooking or denying more fundamental issues.

We recognize that technical rationality has brought many benefits to humankind. However, we also maintain that the dominance of technical rationality has created a more impermeable mask for administrative evil. Saul (1992) finds the fundamental flaw of technical-rational management in its lack of historical consciousness and dismissal of the past as an uncontrolled variable. For the technocrat, past failures cannot be due to the application of rational methods, but to having been insufficiently rational. If events did not turn out as planned, the problem is not with the policy, but a result of uncontrolled deviations from it. Hence, we need more and better planning, and more efficient, controlled systems that will preclude messy aberration. While the past confronts us with the complexities of a socially constructed reality, the future represents a pristine canvas on which to impose new rational plans and systems, with the present always subject to technical control. The lack of historical consciousness is virtually an open invitation to administrative evil.

The linking of technical rationality and morality not only leads to frustration with failed solutions to social problems; it can also set the stage for administrative evil because rational programming in human affairs inevitably entails some degree of dehumanization and often restrictions on the political rights of those affected (Bauman, 1989; Rubenstein, 1975, 1983). To the extent that "good" is expected to result from rational solutions to perceived problems, obstacles to these programs cannot be tolerated—invoking metaphors of removal or elimination—like pulling weeds from a carefully cultivated garden (Bauman, 1989, 18) or ridding an organism of a disease (Schon, 1993). In cases of moral inversion, when something evil is repackaged or otherwise redefined as good, great eruptions of administrative evil may occur.

Engineered or programmed solutions to social problems can achieve only limited success in eliminating a problem when programs are constrained by concerns about the political rights and humanity of the target population. For example, the "crime problem" could perhaps be solved if police were allowed to conduct investigations without regard for the civil rights of suspects, as they are in some countries. Illegal drug trafficking could perhaps be reduced to near zero if property could be searched and seized without warrants, and suspected dealers could be tortured or shot on the spot. Illegal immigration could be greatly reduced by barricading the borders of Texas, New Mexico, Arizona, and California (a reverse Berlin Wall staffed by special forces with orders to shoot to kill), and by incarcerating captured violators in concentration camps, thus discouraging prospective violators by making failure too costly. Public policy appears to be moving in these directions, but not dramatically—only in successive, small increments.

In the United States, many such social problems remain unsolved in part because the polity maintains an "uneasy equilibrium" (Berlin, 1991) between competing values rather than pursue unambiguous, final, and potentially inhumane technical solutions to social problems. Social problems can be ameliorated, but not solved, while at the same time preserving human rights and civil liberties. The drive to solve social problems has thus been balanced with concern for political and human rights. But this equilibrium becomes most tenuous when the problem involves potential "surplus populations" (Rubenstein, 1975, 1983), that is, a defined group of people who are made to appear "useless," or worse, who are viewed as detrimental to the well-being of everyone else. When the objects of public policy programs are rendered "socially dead" (Goldhagen, 1996), and portrayed as unwanted vermin or disease in the midst of society (Bauman, 1989), the resulting moral inversion may unleash tendencies toward administrative evil and policies of elimination or even extermination.

## Surplus Populations and Public Policy Metaphors

It is easy to think of extermination as an extreme measure. But it may not be perceived as such an extreme act when the object of extermination is considered dangerous, out of place, or unwanted, and when it is preceded by a series of successively more aggressive measures, each of which—relatively innocuous by itself—extends the boundary of the acceptable toward a moral inversion. We routinely exterminate vermin from buildings, spray chemical pesticides on destructive insects or plants that invade our crops, and euthanize animals in pounds and shelters. Such actions are perceived as routine and justifiable (by those doing the exterminating) because the object of extermination is not human and not perceived as belonging to anyone, or alternatively, is seen as a threat to the well-being of society. Eliminating the smallpox virus has been of great benefit to humankind, bringing an end to one of the most lethal and widespread contagions in human history. In these cases, extermination represents an efficient and effective solution to difficult problems.

Successful application of modern scientific methods to eliminate or control agricultural and medical problems has contributed to the introduction of agricultural and medical metaphors into public policy discourse. Eliminating blight, contagion, or cancerous growths in the body politic through the application of expert knowledge and methods has become a common means of understanding how to solve many difficult policy problems (e.g., urban decay, illicit drugs, illegal immigration). The desire to eliminate such problems, and, more specifically, the potential surplus populations with which they are associated, often forms the hidden metaphorical subtext of the search for solutions.

Rubenstein (1983, 1) defines a surplus population as "one that for any reason can find no viable role in the society in which it is domiciled." He argues that the overproduction of people and concomitant programs for their elimination are central features of modern civilization. Governments have pursued a variety of eliminationist programs throughout the world during the modern period (e.g., the Irish famine, U.S. policy toward Native Americans, the Armenian Genocide, forced collectivization and starvation in the Soviet Union, the Great Leap Forward in China, the Holocaust). Rubenstein (1975, 9–10) views them as

> [a]lternative attempts to solve a common problem, one of getting rid of people whom governments perceive to be without function or otherwise undesirable. . . . The history of the twentieth century has taught us that people who are rendered permanently superfluous are eventually condemned to segregated precincts of the living dead or are exterminated outright.

In contrast, many of the social policies of the post–World War II era represented a proactive effort by government to include formerly unwanted or marginal people in the mainstream of society. The present willingness to abandon such policies without seeking alternative approaches may lead to the creation of new surplus populations in the United States.

Again, the Holocaust is instructive here because it provides the clearest historical link between the search for permanent solutions to problems and eliminationist public policies. The policies of separation (definition and concentration) and elimination of the Jews from German and European society were often expressed through metaphors of disease and blight (Glass, 1997; Bauman, 1989). The poverty and misery of the Jewish ghettos in Poland intensified and gave meaning to German anti-Semitism and to the association of Jews with vermin. Descriptions of ghettos (conditions that were forced on the Jews by the Germans) suggested that the whole of Polish Jewry was one large diseased entity. For example, a government-sponsored magazine commented in 1944 about the conditions in German-administered Poland (Dwork and Van Pelt, 1996, 37):

> Millions of Jews lived amidst other ethnic groups in the territory of today's
> Government General. Here, in the breeding ground of modern World Jewry, the
> Jewish Problem reached its zenith. . . . We had a moral obligation to wipe out
> the breeding places of the most horrendous, the most inhuman, and the most
> beastly vice that, arising from Poland, infested the whole world. It was a task
> that, in its fulfillment, was meant to bring salvation to the whole of humanity.

The metaphors of disease and vermin thus provided the conceptual framework that guided the search for a final solution to the "Jewish problem."

Contemporary social problems are often framed in similar terms. Consider
the metaphorical language used to describe urban slums and the problem of
urban decay in the United States (Bellush and Hausknecht, 1967, 62):

> The experts concluded that if the community were to be healthy, if it were not to
> revert again to a blighted or slum area, as though possessed of a congenital disease,
> the area must be planned as a whole. It was not enough, they believed, to remove
> existing buildings that were unsanitary or unsightly. It was important to redesign
> the whole area so as to eliminate the conditions that cause slums. . . . In this way
> it was hoped that the cycle of decay of the area could be controlled and the birth
> of future slums prevented.

Eliminating the "blighted" conditions that cause slums entailed the dis-
mantling and displacement of entire communities. While downtown areas
were "renewed," many of those who were displaced were only shifted to
other slums (Katz, 1989, 136), keeping the surplus populations out of sight
and mind of newly gentrified neighborhoods and commercial/entertainment
districts. Fortunately, what many came to call "Negro removal" did not escalate to eliminationist policies.

The dominance of the metaphor of blight and disease limits the consideration of other approaches to urban policy. Little room exists for alternatives to
eliminating the so-called slums when action is driven by tacit concepts that are,
at best, poor descriptors of the actual conditions to be addressed by the policy
(Schon, 1993, 150): "It is precisely because neighborhoods are not literally
diseased that one can *see* them *as* diseased. It is because urban communities
are not literally natural that one can see them as natural. In this 'seeing-as' we
construct what is wrong and what needs fixing" [italics in original].

Other dangerous, contemporary metaphors of public policy tend to identify
the cause of social disease or decay as residing in individual behaviors and
environmental conditions. The job of the policy expert is conceived of as
ridding society of the behaviors and conditions that are deemed inconsistent
with dominant norms and visions of the good life. Nevertheless, even while

decrying racism rhetorically, the effect can be to marginalize groups that do not conform to definitions of normality and social health.

## Welfare Policy and Illicit Drug Policy

Two problem areas around which a considerable societal consensus has developed in recent times are welfare dependence and illicit drug use. Both are seen as threats to the very fabric of society and as meriting vigorous efforts to achieve a lasting solution. Long-term welfare recipients have been characterized as moral degenerates who avoid or disdain work and take advantage of the tax dollars of hard-working citizens. The concept of the "underclass" has given expression to the notion that an undeserving and possibly genetically inferior, poor population undermines the moral order of society (e.g., Herrnstein and Murray, 1994; Murray, 1984). "They" have all but become a surplus population.

The "solution" to this problem as enacted in 1990s welfare reform legislation entailed work requirements and strict time limits on the receipt of benefits. The belief that virtually any work builds character and fulfills social obligations was the basis for these programs (Katz, 1989). Minimal consideration was given to the possibility that the economy might not provide the needed jobs. The fact that the majority of those affected by punitive welfare policy were children did not seem to matter, unless it became a political issue (Edelman, 1977). Empirical evidence that contradicts such assumptions has done little to dissuade those who would force welfare recipients to work (Jencks, 1992; Katz, 1989). That welfare dependence is a problem of "their" moral deficiency, to be solved by compulsory work, has become the conventional wisdom. Welfare recipients are required to work for their benefits and can receive those benefits only for a limited time period (arbitrarily set at two years in most states). During that time, they are carefully monitored for proper behavior and, in a growing number of jurisdictions, even fingerprinted to ensure they do not collect extra benefits. Once that period is up, benefits end. Welfare dependency is replaced by the hard lessons of the marketplace: Learn to work, or face the consequences. In a classic instance of moral inversion, some call this "empowerment."

Thus, poverty ceased to be a legitimate reason for entitlement to government benefits. In fact, welfare, not poverty, became the problem to be solved. The measure of success became the reductions in the welfare rolls, not a reduction in the number of people living in poverty. While "welfare queens" and others dependent on welfare are now "freed" from their bondage to the system through the medium of work, the number of working poor, increasingly concentrated in both central city and urban areas, increased dramatically between 1999 and 2005

(Kneebone and Berube, 2008): "Now a large number of low-income people live among the circumstances that we need to be concerned about that high poverty brings, which includes: lack of investment, lack of local job opportunities; poorer performing schools, higher crime rates; and the poor physical and mental health that goes along with all of those problems." At the bottom of this group are the growing numbers of the "disconnected," low-income single mothers who tend to be very poor and face serious barriers to achieving economic self-sufficiency for their families, including long-term welfare recipients and those who left welfare without stable employment (Blank and Kovak, 2008). This problem has only become worse in the wake of the Great Recession of 2008, with millions facing long-term unemployment and increasing poverty with a shrinking and porous social safety net (Lawler, 2012).

Looking at this approach to welfare reform, as Bauman (1989) would suggest, through the window of the Holocaust, we can see, with chilling effect, similarities between it and Nazi beliefs and policies toward the Jews. The Nazis, consistent with a long heritage of anti-Semitism, portrayed the Jews as parasites (Goldhagen, 1996, 285): "whose working lives were devoted to feeding on the blood of the industrious German people." This belief was not to be shaken by contrary evidence. Nor did it matter whether the work was productive or not. The Jew must work. Even as they planned and carried out their destruction, the Nazis felt it necessary to put the Jews to work in ghettos and concentration camps: To punish them for their supposed slothfulness and to demonstrate German mastery over the Jewish race. The infamous sign hanging over the entrance to Auschwitz and other concentration camps expressed this moral inversion to perfection—WORK MAKES FREEDOM (*Arbeit Macht Frei*).

The point of this discussion is not to say that those who advocate a particular approach to welfare reform are Nazis or have genocidal intent, but to highlight the dangers, and the possibility of a moral inversion, inherent in an approach to public policy that tacitly defines people as inferior and forces them to take jobs that do not pay enough to lift them out of poverty.

To use Schon's (1993) terms, the welfare problem has been framed in a way that relieves society of responsibility for those who do not succeed. Undoubtedly some will make their way out of poverty, but others will not. What will happen in the midst of a serious economic downturn to those who cannot find adequate employment after their benefits run out? Who will ensure that their children are educated and healthy? Is society willing to invest sufficient resources to ensure that everyone who wants to work has a job? What solution will society employ if confronted with growing numbers of unemployed people who are deemed unworthy of public support? Rubenstein raises a chilling possibility (1975, 85–86):

In a multiethnic society the dominant ethnic majority might retain scarce jobs and resources for itself and eliminate competing minorities. That, in effect, is what the Germans did. We know to what extremes men with power can be driven under conditions of stress. . . . There could come a time when bureaucrats might attempt to eliminate all of the ills associated with urban blight, such as crime, drugs, and unsafe streets, by eliminating those segments of the population that are regarded as prone to social pathology. The Germans had such a program in mind when they planned to eliminate "asocials" from German society by exterminating them. Is it possible, for example, that some future American administration might solve the problem of non-white "welfare loafers" who are "too lazy to work" by such measures?

To some extent, one answer can be seen in policies toward the sale and use of illegal drugs.

Prisons have been overflowing throughout the country, and corrections budgets have mushroomed in an effort to incarcerate the large numbers of drug users and dealers that have been sentenced to long terms in state and federal prisons. This has occurred despite the tenuous relationship between the legality of drugs and the harm that each may cause (Schlosser, 1994). The "war on drugs" is waged against substances at least some of which arguably cause much less harm to society as a whole than legal narcotics such as tobacco and alcohol. As the incarceration "solution" inexorably unfolds to its logical conclusion, governments, under the leadership of those who would "get government off our backs," enthusiastically invest huge sums of public money in the building and maintenance of prisons. This policy reminds us of the propensity of modern governments and societies to define and then concentrate a surplus population. Proposals to expand the death penalty for drug dealers suggest that the limits for how to dispose of this growing surplus population have not yet been reached.

Again, the argument here is not that drugs ought to be legalized, that their abuse is not a problem, or that we are (presently) a genocidal society. The difficulty stems not from the problem itself, but from the way in which it is framed or defined (Schon, 1993). It has been difficult for politicians to ask whether our current approach to drug policies is worth pursuing, even as costs mount and drug use continues unabated. Policies of "zero tolerance" and the search for a final solution to the drug problem have led us to support ineffective polices, to tolerate police practices that at times infringe basic constitutional protections, and to crowd more and more people into the largest prison population in the "civilized" world (only Russia is our equal in the rate of incarceration—no one else is even close). Put another way, the incarceration rate in the United States is four times the world average. The national economy has become increasingly dependent on the massive "prison-industrial complex" that provides thousands of jobs in the public and private sectors while keeping hundreds of thousands of working-age men and women convicted of nonviolent drug offenses in prison and out of the job market (Marie, 2012; Schlosser, 1994, 1998; Shelden and Brown, 2000). Given the recent policy developments, it is not difficult to imagine both welfare and drug policies evolving to the point where the routine acts of administrators could be directed at eliminating an unwanted population.

### Immigration Policy

We can see in the debate over U.S. immigration policy a similar, and equally serious, tendency to frame public policies in a way that creates surplus populations. For the most part, the problem is defined in terms of the impact of immigration on the economy and culture of the United States (Borjas, 1996; Kennedy, 1996). Those who support more open immigration policies point out how past immigrants have contributed to the economic and cultural development of the nation, and how the nation's future depends upon our ability to fashion new ways to make immigrants part of our polity. Proponents of cracking down on illegal immigrants and limiting legal immigration maintain that immigrants will, at best, take jobs away from deserving Americans or, at worst, become parasites dependent on welfare or crime. Thus it is argued (and made policy, for example, in California's Proposition 187) that public education, health benefits, and welfare should be denied to illegal and even to legal immigrants, with less consideration given to the nation's role in providing safe haven for political refugees. The specter of a surplus population looms as unwanted peoples, including and even especially, children and the elderly, are denied any legitimate role in society. Few policy makers seem to want to consider looking at the problem in a different way—for example, as one that stems from the structure of the world economy and the practices of corporations that maximize profits by using low-wage labor and maintaining high unemployment in Third World countries.

Efforts to crack down on illegal immigration from Mexico to the United States have reduced the flow of illegal immigrants across key border areas (Thompson, 2008) but have also had some disturbing unintended consequences. Corruption increased as the Department of Homeland Security hired thousands of new border agents, many of whom were not properly vetted and had many opportunities to work both sides of the fence, so to speak (Archibold and Becker, 2008). Intensified security in the most heavily traveled border areas, including those with the newly constructed border fence, has pushed many illegal migrants to try more dangerous routes across wide swaths of desert, causing a marked increase in fatalities (Archibold, 2007). From 2000 to 2008, more than 1,000 people died trying to enter the United States through the Arizona desert, some 700 more than all those who died attempting to cross the Berlin Wall in its twenty-eight-year history (*Economist*, 2008). The policy to try to reverse this trend by hiring more border agents and extending the fence belies the Statue of Liberty (*Economist*, 2008, 27): "A truly impregnable border . . . would involve two layers of fencing 2,000 miles long, with a large no-man's land . . . and plenty of watchtowers. [It] would have to look as it does near San Diego, or as it used to in Berlin."

## A Shameful Historical Precedent

Any debate over immigration policy should consider the historical record and the tragic consequences of past restrictions on immigration. The unwilling-ness of Congress to expand immigration of Jews from Europe in the 1930s stranded thousands of Jews who wanted to escape from Nazi Germany. Many of those denied entry to the United States and other countries eventually died in the Holocaust (Wyman, 1984). The ill-fated voyage of the *St. Louis* is a case in point.

On May 13, 1939, the German liner *St. Louis* left Hamburg with 930 Jewish refugees. Of these, 734 held United States quota numbers, permitting entry into the United States within three years. All of the refugees had Cuban landing certificates. En route to Havana, those onboard the ship learned that Cuban authorities might be questioning the "authenticity" of the landing certificates. On May 27, the *St. Louis* landed at Havana, but only twenty-two refugees were allowed off the ship. Five days later, Cuban authorities ordered the *St. Louis* to leave Cuban territorial waters. On June 3, the U.S. State Department rejected a proposal that the 734 refugees holding U.S. quota numbers be al-lowed to land in our country. The *St. Louis* sailed slowly along the coast of Florida, while efforts were made by U.S. Jews to offer the Cubans "financial guarantees" (bribes, really) of one million dollars; the Cubans rejected this and other overtures. On June 6, President Roosevelt received a telegram beg-ging the United States to reconsider its refusal to provide a haven for these refugees. He failed to respond. After Chile, Paraguay, Argentina, and Colombia all refused asylum, the *St. Louis* returned to Europe. On June 11, the captain of the *St. Louis* considered beaching his ship on the English coast to prevent a return to Hamburg. The next day, Britain, Holland, and Belgium agreed to take the refugees, and they landed at Antwerp. The 620 who remained in Holland and Belgium came under Nazi occupation within a year; nearly all were transported to concentration camps. The 288 refugees who were accepted by Britain were interned as "enemy aliens" for a year after their admission;

however, they survived the war. If the story of the *St. Louis* reminds one of the more recent voyage of the garbage barge that was refused entry at every port of call on several continents, recall that the cargo of the *St. Louis* were human beings, but ones the Nazis had redefined as vermin.

The failure to provide leadership in this area, to send a message to Hitler that these people were valued members of the world community, confirmed in Hitler's mind the notion that the world did not care what happened to the Jews. By denying entry to Jewish refugees, the United States contributed to a world order in which the Jews were a surplus population and to their destruction by the Nazis. In light of our poor performance in earlier times, we should be able to raise the question today: To what extent does our immigration policy contribute to a world order that impoverishes and exploits the very people who long to emigrate to our nation?

### Operations Overcast and Paperclip

In stark contrast to the restrictions on Jewish immigration to the United States, the von Braun team of German rocket scientists and engineers, over one hundred strong, were in the United States within a few months of the war's end. Under Operation Overcast, they easily entered our country. This should not be surprising, since both Overcast and Paperclip were policies based on the goal of technical superiority. Achieving and maintaining superior technical expertise was simply a paramount goal for the United States, which as a country is certainly an exemplar of modernity. Nor should it be surprising that this end justified highly questionable means—we have been arguing all along that that is precisely a consequence of technical rationality. In spite of the fact that the Paperclip policy explicitly barred committed Nazis and, even more obviously, war criminals, the end of technical superiority was all the justification needed by military intelligence officers and other public servants (Gimbel, 1990, 442):

> German scientists and technicians were brought to the United States under a national policy that was developed and implemented by duly authorized, responsible agents of the U.S. government, including cabinet officers who consulted with and received the approval of the president. Under that national policy, the scientists were brought from Germany—either in disregard of or in violation of denazification procedures that the United States insisted on for other Germans.

Eli Pollach represents an interesting contrast to Arthur Rudolph and the rest of the von Braun team. While Rudolph was included in the first Overcast wave in September 1945, Eli Pollach found himself in a displaced persons (DP) camp at that time. Still, the DP camp was a great improvement over what had preceded it. Pollach was a Hungarian Jew who was seventeen when his entire family was transported to Auschwitz in late 1944. Pollach was the only one of his family to leave Auschwitz; he was transported to Dora, where he may well have seen, if only from a distance, Arthur Rudolph. Pollach spent those last months of the war on the V-2 assembly line at the Mittelwerk factory. After Pollach was liberated, it took him four years to get to the United States, in spite of the fact that he had relatives there (Hunt, 1991, 225). By that time, Arthur Rudolph and the von Braun team were moving to Huntsville, Alabama, and were settling into their new country quite nicely. Eli Pollach did not think that the treatment afforded to the von Braun team was just; however, he was still remarkably understanding in this quotation (Hunt, 1991, 226): "They have a saying in Hebrew, if you need the thief, then you cut him off the gallows. But even if the United States needed these scientists, they should have reckoned a little bit for what they did." Operations Overcast and Paperclip make an interesting contrast with the benighted policy of forcible relocation and internment of Japanese Americans during World War II.

## The Evacuation and Relocation of "All Persons of Japanese Ancestry"

Between March 1942 and December 1945, about 120,000 Japanese Americans and Japanese citizens in the United States were subjected to a process of evacuation and relocation in which they were removed from their homes and businesses in the western United States and placed in a number of "relocation centers" (Smith, 1995). About 35,000 were successfully "resettled" outside the military exclusion zone (roughly, east of the Rocky Mountains). This episode has been widely castigated as among the most dismal in all of American history, with frequent references to "America's concentration camps" (Grodzins, 1949).

The forcible evacuation and internment of Japanese Americans was a deeply flawed policy and certainly qualifies as an example of administrative evil (Guterson, 1995). While in no way attempting to defend a policy and program that are fundamentally indefensible, this episode is nonetheless instructive for its differences with Operations Overcast and Paperclip, a policy and program that arose within the same administration (although both overlapped the Roosevelt and Truman administrations) but has been remembered very differently. It also serves as an interesting contrast with similar processes in the Holocaust that led to far different results.

### *"The Decision Nobody Made"*

While the Japanese attack on Pearl Harbor on December 7, 1941, was certainly the immediate precipitant of the relocation, the context requires a look at events both before and after Pearl Harbor. For most of the twentieth century, there was growing American anxiety about Japanese aggression and militarism. Certainly, the western United States in particular was characterized by racism toward all Asian Americans, but perhaps most notably toward Japanese. The Immigration Act of 1924 excluded Japanese as "aliens ineligible to citizenship." Feelings ran sufficiently high so that in the fall of 1941, well before Pearl Harbor, President Sproul of the University of California initiated the Northern California Committee for Fair Play for Citizens and Aliens of Japanese Ancestry, a group that was widely subscribed to by academics and other community leaders.

The attack on Pearl Harbor escalated existing anxieties exponentially. It was followed in short order by successful attacks on Guam and Wake Island. Hong Kong fell by Christmas, and on January 2, 1942, Manila in the Philippines was overrun. Americans on the west coast were genuinely fearful of an imminent Japanese invasion. In hindsight, we know this fear was unwarranted, but it was widely shared across military and civilian boundaries. Even the most responsible and cautious elements were honestly concerned. Thus, we can probably safely say in hindsight that the relocation policy was justified by a perceived military necessity that arguably never existed in reality. But it most certainly existed in perception at the time. Other factors, such as racism and deep cultural differences between Americans and Japanese, doubtless made their contribution as well.

One author (Smith, 1995) calls the relocation of Japanese Americans the "decision nobody made," and this characterization is apt. The sequence of events resembles quite closely a functionalist interpretation of the Holocaust, as well as the evolution of Operations Overcast and Paperclip. As we have observed, no one sets out to do administrative evil. There was certainly a debate within the Roosevelt administration concerning this policy. As often happens, the War Department had a quite different perspective on this issue than the Justice Department. Attorney General Francis Biddle, of the "blue blood" Philadelphia family, was initially very resistant to the notion of evacuation (Smith, 1995, 99):

> War threatens all civil rights and although we have fought wars before, and our personal freedoms have survived, there have been periods of gross abuse, when hysteria and hate and fear ran high, and when minorities were unlawfully and cruelly abused. . . . If we care about democracy, we must care about it as a reality for others, for Germans, for Italians, for Japanese, for those who are with us as those who are against us. For the Bill of Rights protects not only American

citizens but all human beings who live on our American soil, under our American flag . . . all are alike under the law. And this we must remember and sustain—that is if we really love justice, and really hate the bayonet and the whip and the gun, and the whole Gestapo method as a way of handling human beings.

President Roosevelt responded in a similar manner (Smith, 1995, 100):

It is one thing to safeguard American industry, and particularly the defense industry, against sabotage; but it is very much another to throw out of work honest and loyal people who, except for the accident of birth, are sincerely patriotic. . . . Remember the Nazi technique: "Pit race against race, religion against religion, prejudice against prejudice. Divide and Conquer." We must not let that happen here. We must not forget what we are defending: Liberty, decency, justice.

Church organizations, the governor of California, and the California attorney general, Earl Warren, echoed these sentiments. With this level and quality of opposition, how could the policy of evacuation and relocation have carried the day?

### The Military Trump Card in Wartime

John DeWitt, by all accounts a rather undistinguished and punctilious sixty-one-year-old general, was commanding officer of the Western Defense Command, and was thus charged with defending American soil on the west coast from potential—and widely feared—Japanese invasion. The rapid succession of Japanese military victories following hard on the heels of Pearl Harbor, along with sporadic incidents such as a Japanese submarine shelling a shore installation in Oregon, escalated tensions. West coast cities were under a blackout at night, and there were occasions of sporadic anti-aircraft fire, even if there were never any actual Japanese planes. There was widespread concern that those of Japanese ancestry, some of whom happened to live in close proximity to sensitive military installations, would use shortwave radios or other signals to guide a Japanese attack to its target.

Quite apart from the military issues, concern grew about the safety of both Japanese aliens and Japanese-American citizens when they and their property were subject to increasing levels of harassment and violent attacks. This concern was shared to some extent within the various Japanese communities. Thus, part of the momentum for evacuation came from genuine concern for the safety of Japanese citizens.

General DeWitt was rebuffed at first when he sought the evacuation of the Japanese. His initial response was to request mass raids without warrants in Japanese communities that were close to the most sensitive defense and military areas; his primary objective was uncovering and confiscating short-wave radios, but he also wanted to identify and remove those who genuinely posed a national security threat. Attorney General Biddle stonewalled this initiative. Ironically, if these mass raids had gone forward, it is possible that the momentum for a total evacuation might have slowed or even stopped.

Gradually, the call for at least some form of exclusion grew. Biddle asked three prominent New Deal attorneys for an opinion about the legality of exclusion. Their reply was (Smith, 1995, 117): "So long as a classification of persons is reasonably related to a genuine war need and does not under the guise of national defense discriminate against any class of citizens for a purpose unrelated to the national defense, no constitutional guarantee is infringed." Symbolic of the change in climate was a Walter Lippmann column, entitled "The Fifth Column on the Coast," in which Lippmann warned of the west coast being in imminent danger of attack from within and without. He opined that the entire west coast should be treated as a war zone under special rules.

As the climate continued to change, Attorney General Biddle essentially ceded authority for any evacuation to the War Department. Secretary of War Henry Stimson proposed to President Roosevelt that the most sensitive military areas be evacuated, and was told to go ahead but "be as reasonable as you can," a response that would have been somewhat surprising in wartime only if it had been otherwise. On February 19, 1942, a little over two months after Pearl Harbor, Executive Order 9066 initiated the official policy of evacuation of Japanese aliens and Japanese-American citizens from certain military exclusion zones. The words "concentration" and "internment" were deliberately dropped from usage; instead the initial collection points, run by the military, were euphemistically called Assembly Centers, and were most typically at racetracks and fairgrounds (Smith, 1995). The eventual destinations, which had to be built hurriedly, were called Relocation Centers, and as it turned out, they had some significant differences from both internment and concentration camps.

## Implementation

The initial evacuation from military exclusion zones was voluntary, and was an unmitigated disaster (U.S. Department of War, 1943). Those in the Japanese communities were horribly conflicted as to whether or when they should leave, and the obvious opportunities for exploitation by outsiders were rapidly and chillingly taken advantage of. "Fire sales," for pennies on the dollar, of personal and real property were rampant (U.S. House of Representatives, 1942). The movement to forced evacuation, in this context, was in many ways positive in that it meant a "controlled" evacuation under government protection and with at least some certainty of expectation.

Perhaps not so surprising given the centrality of property rights in our culture, there was immediate attention to protecting the property of those who were evacuated. Interestingly, the Federal Reserve Bank was initially given responsibility for recording and storing evacuees' property through a hastily created Evacuee Property Department. So far as we know, virtually all property that entered this system—about $200 million worth—was eventually restored to its owners. The policy, which remained intact when responsibility was passed to the newly created War Relocation Authority, was to ship property free of charge to the Relocation Centers, if requested. Alternatively, property was held until evacuees returned to their old—or new—homes, and then shipped to that location free of charge. It is important to note that the property of most evacuees did not enter this federal system, and thus was not as well safeguarded, or was lost altogether. Much property was entrusted to friends, to churches, and others. Still more was sold off at pennies on the dollar. The substantial losses of property and income, possibly $100 million or more, were clearly among the worst outcomes of this unfortunate policy.

Overall authority for the evacuation and relocation was transferred from the Wartime Civil Control Administration to the War Relocation Authority (WRA) created by Executive Order 9102 in March 1942. The WRA developed into a very interesting agency. Its first director, Milton Eisenhower (Dwight's youngest brother), described its mission as:

> (1) aiding the army in carrying out the evacuation of military areas, (2) developing and supervising a planned, orderly program of relocation for evacuees, (3) providing evacuees with work opportunities so that they may contribute to their own maintenance and to the national production program, and (4) protecting evacuees from harm in the areas where they are relocated. The first specific task of the authority is to relocate some 100,000 alien and American-born Japanese from the military areas of the far Western states. (Eisenhower, 1974, 145)

The agency drew its personnel largely from the Department of Agriculture (including both of its directors, Eisenhower and, later, Dillon Myer), and it developed its own culture as a New Deal agency that was going to create communities (the Relocation Centers) that were "schools of democracy," as overtly contrasted with the concentration camps of the Germans (Leighton, 1945).

By June 1942, Military Area 1 (coastal California, Oregon, and Washington) was evacuated, and Military Area 2 (most of the rest of the Western Defense Command) was evacuated by August 1942. The initial destinations of evacuees were the Assembly Centers. Church organizations were present and visible at all of the Assembly Centers, organized primarily by the Protestant Church Commission for Japanese Service (Suzuki, 1979). They assisted in a variety of ways, one of which included acting as an informal watchdog for mistreatment. There were fourteen Assembly Centers in California, Oregon, Washington, and Arizona. Their populations peaked in May and June of 1942, and by mid-November 1942, the last Assembly Center closed down. (Manzanar in California and Poston in Arizona began as Assembly Centers and were converted to Relocation Centers.)

Milton Eisenhower, who idolized Woodrow Wilson, was determined to put a human face on the relocation policy. He met and consulted regularly with an advisory council made up of members of the Japanese-American Citizens League (JACL), which was headed by Mike Masaoka. While quite capable of representing the evacuees, Masaoka was a very young man (he was only twenty-four), which was insulting to the Issei, the Japanese nationals who were older men and thus in positions of greater respect in Japanese culture (Kitigawa, 1967). This kind of cultural misunderstanding was rampant during the entire episode. So was the genuine attempt to implement this policy in a uniquely American, democratic, and humane manner. Eisenhower went into a meeting with the inter-mountain governors looking for cooperation with the WRA's primary policy initiative of resettling evacuees into new homes and jobs outside the exclusion areas. With the exception of the governor of Colorado, the governors excoriated Eisenhower for attempting to dump the nation's enemies into their towns and cities. Eventually, resettlement was most successful in midwestern and eastern metropolitan areas.

Milton Eisenhower left the WRA after only three months, sending a final memorandum to President Roosevelt, which said in part (Eisenhower, 1974, 145):

> I cannot help expressing the hope that the American people will grow toward a broader appreciation of the essential Americanism of a great majority of the evacuees and the difficult sacrifice they are making. Only when the prevailing attitudes of unreasoning bitterness have been replaced by tolerance and understanding will it be possible to carry forward a genuinely successful relocation program and to plan intelligently for re-assimilation of the evacuees into American life when the war is over. I wish to give you my considered judgment that fully 80 to 85 percent of the Nisei [Japanese Americans born in the U.S.—citizens] are loyal to the United States, perhaps 50 percent of the Issei are passively loyal; but a large portion of the Kibei (American citizens educated in Japan and about 9,000 in number) have a strong cultural attachment to Japan.

Eisenhower's hopes were largely unrealized, although arguably Japanese Americans are today well assimilated into American culture.

Dillon Myer, who succeeded Eisenhower as director of WRA, shared most of his predecessor's aspirations and goals (Myer, 1971). He fully supported the notion of making the Relocation Centers into "little democracies," largely self-governing, with their own community councils. Here again, cultural misunderstandings were an obstacle, as the Issei were initially excluded from the councils; this policy was rescinded in April 1943. While the Relocation Centers may indeed have superficially resembled concentration camps, surrounded as they were by barbed wire fences and with a military presence of guards, there were important differences (Spicer, 1969). Both the fencing and the guards were largely symbolic; each Center had a detachment of about three officers and 125 troops to "guard" communities of between eight and twelve thousand inhabitants. Many residents came and went freely from the centers, and increasingly large numbers came to be "on leave" from them. The leave policy included three types: short-term, work, and indefinite leave. Indefinite leave was granted to those who were successfully resettled, and while this policy never succeeded as planned, about 35,000 individuals and families were eventually resettled. Ironically, many residents initially denounced the leave program, and resettlement more generally, as an abdication of the government's responsibility to care for them (Tateishi, 1984).

In yet another irony, the Battle of Midway in June 1942 effectively canceled out the whole premise of the evacuation. The Japanese defeat at Midway eliminated any realistic chance for a Japanese invasion of the west coast of the United States. This was before very many of the evacuees had left the Assembly Centers for the Relocation Centers. It was probably too much to hope for any sort of rapid about-face in policy. The population of the Relocation Centers peaked in January 1943 at 110,240, and had dropped through resettlement by July 1943 to 103,282 and went on to decline further at a rate of about 10,000 per month (Smith, 1995). As mentioned, eventually some 35,000 Japanese-American citizens were resettled.

### Denouement

The threat of Japanese invasion had long since passed, and by mid-1944, a consensus in the government had formed that the centers could be closed. However, there was concern in the administration that the electoral votes of California could be jeopardized in the presidential election of 1944 if the centers were closed before the election. The decision to terminate the centers was made in December 1944, and all of them, with the exception of Tule Lake in California, were closed by December 1945 (Houston and Houston, 1966). Initial resistance to leaving the centers abated and evacuees successfully returned to old and new homes in the former exclusion zones.

The population dynamics of the Japanese communities were quite different after the return. Nearly 35,000 of just over 50,000 who resettled to the east of the exclusionary areas remained in their new homes. Chicago, Denver, Salt Lake City, Detroit, and New York City were the metropolitan areas that became the new homes of thousands of Japanese Americans. California had about 93,000 Japanese and Japanese Americans before the relocation; as of March 1946 about 49,000 had returned. Only about 30 percent of Washington State's Japanese community returned, about 4,000 (Daniels, Taylor, and Kitano, 1986). For good reasons, those who returned were much more likely to settle in urban areas. The WRA had centers in the large urban areas, and these provided assistance to returning evacuees. Church organizations, an important source of support and aid throughout the process, were also more likely to have a presence in the cities. Likewise, law enforcement agencies in urban centers were more likely to treat Japanese and Japanese Americans equitably.

It is worth noting that more than 25,000 Japanese Americans served in the U.S. armed forces from 1940 to 1945. About 20 percent of the total number became casualties (killed, wounded, or missing in action). The Japanese Americans from the mainland formed into the 442nd Combat Team, and served with great distinction in the European theater. In fact, the Nisei 442nd became the most decorated unit in the U.S. Army (Shirey, 1946). In an ironic turn of events, a part of the 442nd, soldiers of the 622nd Field Artillery Battalion, were among the Allied troops that liberated Dachau. The heroic exploits of the all-Nisei 442nd were widely reported in the press and played a part in turning public opinion toward closing the Relocation Centers.

In perhaps the final irony in a tragic episode that had many such ironies, the Japanese-American Citizens' League held a dinner at a New York hotel in Dillon Myer's honor in May 1946. At the dinner, he was presented with a scroll that commended him as a "champion of human rights and common decency whose courageous and inspired leadership . . . aided materially in restoring faith and conviction in the American way to . . . Americans of Japanese ancestry and their resident alien parents" (Smith, 1995, 43).

## Surplus Populations, Moral Inversion, and Administrative Evil

Operations Overcast and Paperclip and the internment of Japanese Americans provide insight into the processes that lead to administrative evil. While not extreme cases, both are examples of "[administrative] behavior that deprives innocent people of their humanity . . . where the behavior of one person, or an aggregate of persons is destructive to others" (Katz, 1993, 5). Both cases involve moral inversion, where administrators set out believing that what they were doing was in the best interests of the country. Despite these similarities, the two cases have been treated very differently.

In hindsight, it has been easier to discern administrative evil at work in the case of the internment of Japanese Americans due to the specter of barbed wire internment camps and thousands of citizens unjustly deprived of their rights. And the implementation of the internment camp policy resembled Nazi concentration camps in more subtle ways. The policy evolved gradually, from "reasonable" wartime concern about the loyalty and safety of Japanese Americans, to "voluntary" relocation, then to forced relocation to internment camps and a policy that continued well beyond any practical justification for it. Further, each step was cloaked with euphemism and legalities, and buttressed by the long-standing prejudice against Asian immigrants to the United States. Administrators in multiple agencies and levels of government helped to implement the policy without ever believing that they were doing anything wrong, and, in fact, believing that they were doing good.

Despite procedural resemblances to the Holocaust, the internment camp policy did not progress to the extremes of exploitation and extermination found at Mittlebau-Dora. The key difference consists in how the victims of the Holocaust, including those forced to build the V-2 rockets, were treated as a "surplus population" by the Nazis and their collaborators. They became subject to dehumanization and extermination when they ceased to belong to a polity and lost all rights and connections to a protective state (Rubenstein, 1975). The Nazis had no intention of returning these concentration camp inmates to society. They did not fit into the Nazi vision of a community and country, and essentially ceased to exist once they entered the camps.

The tragedy of the Japanese-American internment case was mitigated because key administrators, such as Dillon Myer, managed to view the internees as citizens and kept in mind their eventual return to society. For the most part, government officials were able to recognize the internees as belonging to the polity and deserving of protection, a fact worth remembering. While this may provide little solace to the victims of the policy, and certainly does not justify the violations of their rights, administrators managed to curtail administrative evil and avoid its worst consequences. This was not the case in Operation Paperclip, where the victims of Mittlebau-Dora were not considered in the process of building the U.S. space program, and remain unrecognized more than fifty years later as we celebrate the achievements that they unwillingly contributed to with their lives.

The willingness to at least acknowledge the administrative evil of the internment camps, even though it took forty years to legislate small reparations, stands in stark contrast to the utter blindness toward the administrative evil of the von Braun case. Decades after the fact there is still no recognition of the sad background of our premier rocket development team for the space program. The von Braun case thus illustrates the power of technical rationality to strengthen the mask of administrative evil. We will probably never know the extent to which those who crafted Operation Paperclip knew of the slave labor and mass murder at Dora when they initiated our space program's reliance on von Braun and his compatriots. Regardless of what they knew, once the program was under way, administrative processes and technical achievements progressively placed layer after layer of masking on the wartime activities of von Braun, Rudolf, and others, thereby obscuring the effect their values (or lack of them) and concerns about their past had on the organizational culture at Marshall, and later at NASA.

With the benefit of hindsight, Operations Overcast and Paperclip appear to be examples of administrative evil. While technical superiority has not disappeared as a paramount American goal, even today, and while national security has been a valid rationale for many actions, a justification for bringing committed Nazis and some individuals who were directly implicated in the use of SS slave labor (a war crime) to the United States is not easily provided. While the cold war provided an after-the-fact rationale for Paperclip, at the time this was primarily an affirmative exercise—we wanted this technical expertise for ourselves. The principle of denying this expertise to others could have easily been met in other ways. Rocket scientists who are incarcerated are not lending their expertise to anyone else. There were plenty of "clean" Germans to work on our rockets, and their lives would not have been sullied by the knowledge and continuous anxiety of keeping the past secret. Arguably, we could have done without the Germans altogether. For example, there was a budding group of rocketeers at the Jet Propulsion Laboratory in California (Neufeld, 1996). Granted, they were years behind the Germans, but would it really have mattered in the greater scheme of things if the moon landing had occurred in 1974 or even 1979? Our country did not need to land on the moon carrying the symbolic baggage of twenty thousand of Dora's dead.

The perceived need to use the German (and former Nazi) rocket scientists to achieve technical superiority, and their subsequent successes, led NASA's leaders to build our space program on a tainted legacy by placing technical advancements over respect for the humanity of those who were exploited and killed under the Nazi regime. This case shows how administrative evil was well masked and became a hidden yet pervasive part of the organizations built on the foundation of Operation Paperclip. For the most part, its influence remains largely unacknowledged as America continues to celebrate the achievements of the space program and the triumph of technical rationality. Sadly, we see these dynamics at work in the United States much more recently as our nation lost its moral compass—at least for a time—as members of our government engaged in torture and abuse at Abu Ghraib and other locations associated with the "Global War on Terror."

# Administrative Evil in the Twenty-First Century

## Abu Ghraib, Moral Inversion, and Torture Policy

Seven years after Al Qaeda's attacks on America, as the Bush administration slips into history, it is clear that what began on September 11, 2001, as a battle for America's security became, and continues to be, a battle for the country's soul.

—*Jane Mayer,* 2008 (327)

September 11, 2001, was a shocking and traumatizing moment in American history. Terrorists, using passenger jets as missiles, attacked symbolically strategic targets in New York and Washington, killing thousands of innocent civilians. Planning for finding those responsible and bringing them to justice began almost immediately. In November 2001, American forces moved into Afghanistan, toppled the Taliban regime, and launched an intensive search for Al Qaeda and Taliban personnel. As we began to capture and detain elements of both, we were confronted with a consequence of the awkward juxtaposition of "war" and "terrorism." If our action in Afghanistan was indeed a war, we had well-established rules for how to prosecute it; yet, the terrorism we had declared war on was not the product of any one state and in fact was a loosely organized and coordinated worldwide collection of groups operating outside of any government. How then could terrorists be prisoners of war (making them subject to the Geneva Conventions, among other protocols and laws)? If they were not POWs, what exactly were they?

Our answers to these questions, we argue here, combined with events to create a policy that essentially gave permission for the torture and abuse of detainees at Abu Ghraib prison in Iraq, as well as other locations. When the "war on terror" was wrongly diverted and expanded to the invasion and occupation of Iraq, which produced thousands of detainees, the stage was set for an operational fiasco and a moral inversion (Ricks, 2006). The extent of the torture and abuse perpetrated at the Abu Ghraib prison burst upon the American consciousness with the airing of a CBS news magazine *60 Minutes II* episode in April 2004. These abuses, however, were already under investigation and had been previously made public. The Final Report of the Independent Panel to Review Department of Defense Detention Operations, hereafter referred to as the Schlesinger Report, noted that the U.S. Central Command first distributed a press release on the abuses as early as January 2004 (Strasser, 2004, 14). The disturbing photographs of U.S. soldiers, who appeared to be gleefully humiliating, punching, and terrifying naked prisoners with dogs, indicated that things went terribly wrong at Abu Ghraib. The photograph of a hooded prisoner standing on a box connected to wires leading out of view has become an unfortunate and enduring symbol to the world of a superpower that appears to have veered dangerously away from its espoused values. That photograph quickly appeared in downtown Teheran on a billboard with a message that was less than flattering toward the United States.

Even for a nation seared by the attacks of September 11, engaged in continuing military operations in Afghanistan and Iraq, and pursuing a global war on terrorism against a shadowy enemy, these images caused a wave of revulsion. The public recoiled, and the military and intelligence establishments were embarrassed. Protracted warfare has an eroding effect on the moral fabric of any nation, but by any standard the line between military or intelligence necessity and cruelty was crossed at Abu Ghraib. It was as if America walked up to the edge of a moral precipice and, after looking into the abyss, decided that it did not like what it saw. Myriad criminal investigations and administrative inquiries were already under way at the time of the CBS report, and more were to follow.

The torture and abuse of detainees at Abu Ghraib prison and other sites, including Afghanistan and Guantanamo Bay, raises disturbing questions that have few if any easy answers. Were these intentionally evil acts, committed by "a few bad apples" taking advantage of the situation to indulge in the power they wielded over the inmates? Or were they cases of administrative evil, where the obvious evil of torture and abuse was masked from the perpetrators, including those who performed subsidiary and supportive functions? Were those who have been brought to trial the only ones responsible for the abuse, or are they in part scapegoats, deflecting attention from broader, systemic problems (see Zimbardo, 2007)? Even more fundamental is the question of whether torture and abuse are always wrong (see Levinson, 2004 and Rejali, 2007). Can they perhaps be justified, at least in a carefully limited way, in the context of the "Global War on Terrorism" and the need for timely intelligence on potential terrorist attacks (see Mayer, 2005, 2008)? How these questions are answered may well have profound implications for our ability to recognize and avoid acts of administrative evil, and even for the future of democratic governance (see, for example, Terry and Stivers, 2002). Lewis (2002, 61) captures an essential question:

> The world after September 11 presents a particular challenge to all of us. We have to deal with a shadowy enemy that lets nothing, not even human life, get in the way of its terrifying aims. It is a cliché to say that now; we know it too well. But the challenge of dealing with terrorism includes another aspect that we may not understand so well: We have to fight an unprincipled enemy without losing our principles.

These dilemmas have a historical context. Martin Cook observes (2004, 21) that while violent conflict has been a mainstay of the history of mankind, it is also true that the modern world has struggled to, "limit, constrain, and to establish criteria that sanction the use of violence in the name of the state and society." This struggle is apparent in the Judeo-Christian tradition of just war theory where (Glover, 1999, 14), "self-sacrifice for the sake of others is admired, and feelings of guilt are an appropriate reaction to the fact that you have trampled on others in pursuit of your own goals." Codification of the laws of land warfare in conventions and treaties are a means of encouraging, if not enforcing, restraint in what can be a brutal undertaking (Glover, 1999, 48): "Normal moral restraints emphasize the respect for people's dignity, which protects them from barbaric treatment. In war, this inhibition is selectively removed."

In virtually every conflict there are numerous unfortunate examples of violations of the rules and conventions designed to prevent acts of cruelty and inhumanity. Despite the existence of codes and orders designed to limit suffering, the violence that is inherent in war defies constraint even in the most well-trained and disciplined armies (Cook, 2004, 24): "All sides violated these rules in World War II, especially in the use of airpower." In some of the most egregious cases, high-level officials have been held accountable for their actions through tribunals such as those held in Nuremberg and Manila after World War II. For German generals, the defense that they were simply following orders was rejected by the tribunals. Japanese General Tomoyuki

Yamashita was tried and hanged, not for ordering atrocities, but for failing to control the troops that committed them under his command. The lineage of such accountability measures continues today with the International Criminal Tribunals for the former Yugoslavia, Rwanda, and Darfur. In other lesser cases, states have dispensed accountability through internal criminal justice measures as with the prosecution of Lieutenant Calley for the massacre at My Lai during the Vietnam War, and in the courts-martial of soldiers who engaged in prisoner abuse at Abu Ghraib. Indeed, it appears that officials in the Bush administration were concerned about their own future liability for war crimes in the extensive legal memoranda that defined the parameters of the Global War on Terrorism (Mayer, 2008).

If any doubt remains about the capacity of Americans to create and even destroy a surplus population, consider the following two examples. First, as more evidence emerges over time, it has become clear that the United States implemented a policy of extermination in Vietnam (Turse, 2012). General William C. Westmoreland described the North Vietnamese not as an enemy to be defeated, but as "termites" to be exterminated by squashing them one by one, in the context of explaining the proper troop strength for the war effort (Stannard, 1992, 252–253):

> If you crowd in too many termite killers, each using a screwdriver to kill ter-
> mites, you risk collapsing the floors or the foundation. In this war we're using
> screwdrivers to kill termites because it's a guerrilla war and we cannot use
> bigger weapons. We have to get the right balance of termite killers to get rid
> of the termites without wrecking the house.

More than twenty years later, another American general, Norman Schwarz-kopf, lamented the fact that he had been constrained in pursuing a war of annihilation in Iraq, even as American soldiers referred to killed Iraqi women and children as "collateral damage" and to the Iraqi people as "cockroaches" who ran for cover when the bombers appeared overhead (Stannard, 1992, 253). Clearly, despite its democratic traditions and rhetoric, America has the demonstrated capacity to engage in acts of administrative evil and public policies of destruction, as we have seen in both Operations Overcast and Paperclip and the internment of Japanese Americans during World War II. In this chapter we detail the contemporary case of state-sanctioned torture and abuse by the United States in Iraq and elsewhere. While it is clear that the torture and abuse of detainees at Abu Ghraib and other facilities—as bad as it was—pales in comparison to the Holocaust and other genocides, the question we raise here is the degree to which they constitute a case of moral inversion and administrative evil.

## The Road to Abu Ghraib

In January 2002, the U.S. Department of Justice prepared a series of memoranda that argued that both the Taliban and Al Qaeda could be considered as outside the Geneva Conventions, as "unlawful enemy combatants." During this same period, the U.S. Department of State prepared memoranda that argued that whatever advantage might be gained in the war on terrorism by declaring the Geneva Conventions not applicable would be more than outweighed by the disadvantages, including potential loss of the moral high ground accorded to us in the wake of 9/11. Alberto Gonzales, at the time White House counsel and later attorney general, advised the president that he was persuaded by the Justice Department position, and the president issued a memorandum on February 7, 2002, on the "Humane Treatment of al Qaeda and Taliban Detainees." Perhaps the most relevant point from that memo was the following (Strasser, 2004, 145): "As a matter of policy, the United States Armed Forces shall continue to treat detainees humanely and, to the extent appropriate and consistent with military necessity, in a manner consistent with the principles of Geneva." In other words, the Geneva Conventions could apply when convenient. All of these communications are replete with references to a new paradigm of war, a different kind of war, and/or a global war on terrorism. There is inherent ambiguity in a new paradigm, and within that ambiguity is the potential for moral inversion. The memoranda discussed above represent attempts to clarify some of that inherent ambiguity. However, subsequent documents and events suggest that considerable ambiguity about the treatment and interrogation of detainees remained in the system, and had the effect of giving permission for the torture and abuse of detainees.

### Redefining Torture

In a fifty-page memorandum prepared in August 2002 for White House Counsel Alberto Gonzalez, the Justice Department's Jay Bybee (since appointed to a federal judgeship) examined the question of what conduct rises to the level of torture in interrogations. Its summary conclusions bear quoting at length (Bybee, 2002, 1):

> We conclude that for an act to constitute torture as defined in Section 2340, it must inflict pain that is difficult to endure. Physical pain amounting to torture must be equivalent in intensity to the pain accompanying serious physical injury, such as organ failure, impairment of bodily function, or even death. For purely mental pain or suffering to amount to torture under Section 2340, it must result in significant psychological harm of significant duration, e.g.,

lasting for months or even years. We conclude that the mental harm also must result from one of the predicate acts listed in the statute, namely: threats of imminent death; threats of infliction of the kind of pain that would amount to physical torture; use of drugs or other procedures designed to deeply disrupt the senses, or fundamentally alter an individual's personality; or threatening to do any of these things to a third party. The legislative history simply reveals that Congress intended for the statute's definition to track the Convention's definition of torture and the reservations, understandings, and declarations that the United States submitted with its ratification. We conclude that the statute, taken as a whole, makes plain that it prohibits only extreme acts.

The United Nations Convention against Torture and Other Forms of Cruel, Inhuman or Degrading Treatment or Punishment was instituted in 1984, signed by the United States in 1988, and ratified with reservations by the U.S. Senate in 1994. The Convention itself has a rather broad and general definition of torture:

> For the purposes of this Convention, the term "torture" means any act by which severe pain or suffering, whether physical or mental, is intentionally inflicted on a person for such purposes as obtaining from him or a third person information or a confession, punishing him for an act he or a third person has committed or is suspected of having committed, or intimidating or coercing him or a third person, or for any reason based on discrimination of any kind, when such pain or suffering is inflicted by or at the instigation of or with the consent or acquiescence of a public official or other person acting in an official capacity.

The U.S. Senate, which has the constitutional authority to ratify international treaties, insisted on the narrower definition of torture, as outlined in the Bybee memorandum, and specifically developed the language later found in the Bybee memo. That language is included in both the U.S. "Reservations" to the United Nations Convention against Torture, and in Section 18 of the U.S. Code from which Bybee quotes directly. In other words, Bybee did not simply invent a new and narrower definition of torture. However, he did provide arguably the narrowest possible construction of torture.

It is interesting that most of the public debate has focused on torture, and discussed the Convention against Torture as if it were not also about "Other Forms of Cruel, Inhuman or Degrading Treatment or Punishment" as well. In particular, Article 16 of the Convention states:

> Each State Party shall undertake to prevent in any territory under its jurisdiction other acts of cruel, inhuman or degrading treatment or punishment which do not

amount to torture as defined in article I, when such acts are committed by or at the instigation of or with the consent or acquiescence of a public official or other person acting in an official capacity. In particular, the obligations contained in articles 10, 11, 12 and 13 shall apply with the substitution for references to torture of references to other forms of cruel, inhuman or degrading treatment or punishment.

This too is a very broad and general definition, leaving a great deal of room for what might constitute cruel, inhuman, or degrading treatment or punishment. From a legal perspective, one can see why various countries might want to delimit these categories in order to preempt egregious claims in international courts against their own nationals. Further, an activist superpower might be particularly concerned that its officials and military could be especially vulnerable to international courts and claims. However, from a moral perspective, countries that seek leadership in the world might find in that article of the Convention a useful aspirational statement that begins to define the moral high ground that such leadership entails.

### Torture and Abuse in Interrogation Policy and Procedure

All these discussions on torture and abuse were to become a bit less academic in late 2002 (see Bowden, 2003). Conventional interrogation techniques (that is, standard operating procedures as defined in Army Field Manual 34–52) at the Guantanamo Bay facility in Cuba had achieved about as much as they were going to. Some Guantanamo detainees effectively resisted interrogation methods, prompting authorities to request strengthened interrogation techniques in October 2002 (Strasser, 2004, 31). If additional usable intelligence were to come from the detainees, new techniques would have to be introduced, but would need to be duly authorized. Accordingly, the secretary of defense authorized the use of sixteen additional techniques beyond the standard army doctrine in force at the time. By April 2003, these new techniques were mostly rescinded, and additional permissions were put in place in order to use the few of those techniques that remained. Most important, they were limited to use only at Guantanamo.

At Guantanamo, a number of approaches were tried when going by the army book did not yield quick results. Psychologists and psychiatrists were brought in, hoping that their insights could work on the detainees' psyches. Expert and seasoned FBI interrogators were also brought in. The FBI approach to interrogation is a more patient one that is premised on forging a relationship with the subject over time. It works very well, but it typically takes considerable time. According to Daniel Coleman, the senior FBI agent assigned to antiterrorism in the 1990s (Mayer, 2008, 119): "Brutalization doesn't work. We know that. Besides, you lose your soul." Members of the Bush administration, especially Vice President Cheney and Secretary of Defense Rumsfeld, were reacting to what they thought was a high probability of imminent future terrorist attacks, and they created a very high degree of urgency; they wanted results now—the phrase "the gloves are off" was repeated many times (Mayer, 2008). It appears that the impetus for torture, under the assumption that its use would yield actionable intelligence quickly, came either from the vice president (or his chief aide, David Addington) or from the CIA, although this is difficult to know with certainty (Mayer, 2008, 120).

The decision to turn to torture was a curious one (Sands, 2008). Torture was not only a poor choice on moral grounds, but is suspect on pragmatic grounds as well (Intelligence Science Board [ISB], 2006). A pragmatic assessment of torture does not provide a clear example of its effectiveness. As Jane Mayer notes (2008, 134):

> Scientific research on the efficacy of torture is extremely limited because of the moral and legal impediments to experimentation. Before endorsing physical and psychological abuse, the Bush administration did no empirical study. The policy seems to have been based on some combination of political preferences and intuitive belief about human nature.

Indeed, a 2006 report by the Intelligence Science Board, under the auspices of the National Defense Intelligence College, finds very little evidence to support the efficacy of torture and abuse as a means of gathering accurate, much less actionable, intelligence. Quite the contrary, as noted by John Wahlquist in that report (ISB, 2006, xxi): "Why, in the 21st century, with all our accumulated knowledge about how human beings think and interact and function, are we still repeating costly medieval mistakes?"

Everyone's favorite anecdote, which is ubiquitously used to justify torture and abuse, is the ticking bomb scenario (Davis, 2005), in which a detainee knows where the ticking bomb is located (say, a "dirty" atomic bomb planted in a major U.S. city) and when it will be detonated. To save millions of lives, the logic goes, using any and all means—including torture and abuse—is justifiable. As Jamie Mayerfeld notes (2008, 110):

> The ticking bomb argument has exerted enormous influence. Popularized in books, movies, TV dramas, newspaper editorials, TV commentaries, public lectures, journal articles, college courses, and presidential debates, it has persuaded a large portion of the voting public and policy-making elite that torture is warranted on some (larger or smaller) number of occasions. It became an

argument for justifying the massive use of torture by the French army during the Algerian War of Independence. It has been the primary argument for the widespread use of torture by Israeli security forces in the Occupied Territories. It is the main justification for the use of torture by the U.S. government in the "War on Terror."

There are several problems with the ticking bomb scenario—leaving aside the problem of making policy by anecdote. These problems are discussed at great length in Darius Rejali's *Torture and Democracy* (2007). One of the problems with the ticking bomb scenario is limiting torture only to ticking bomb situations; another is the assumption that the ticking bomb situation actually occurs in reality. In March 2008, when the Bush administration threatened to veto new legislation that would restrict the CIA to using only those interrogation techniques available to the military, Senator Jay Rockefeller, the ranking minority member of the Senate Intelligence Committee (in other words, someone privy to any and all ticking bomb scenarios that might have emerged during this entire time frame) said (Mayer, 2008, 330):

> I have heard nothing to suggest that information obtained from enhanced interrogation techniques has prevented an imminent terrorist attack. And I have heard nothing that makes me think the information obtained from these techniques could not have been obtained through traditional interrogation methods used by military and law enforcement interrogators. On the other hand, I do know that coercive interrogations can lead detainees to provide false information in order to make the interrogation stop.

On practical grounds, then, torture is a poor choice. Indeed, the Intelligence Science Board listed seven reasons not to torture (2006, 13–15): Torture undermines international support for the struggle against terrorism; enhances danger to troops and others at risk of capture; entails legal problems for U.S. troops and officials; undercuts U.S. leadership on human rights; creates more enemies (terrorists); corrodes the integrity of the military; and displaces resources that could be better used elsewhere. Against the best available thinking on both moral and practical grounds, the United States chose the path of torture and abuse, first at Guantanamo Bay and in Afghanistan, and then in Iraq.

## Detainee Operations in Untenable Conditions

Operation Iraqi Freedom was a near perfect storm of unexpected and worst-case developments in terms of detainee operations. In the words of the Schlesinger Report (Strasser, 2004, 10), "In Iraq, there was not only a failure to plan for a major insurgency, but also to quickly and adequately adapt to the insurgency that followed after major combat operations." Some of these conditions could have been—and certainly should have been—foreseen better or reacted to better. Early projections estimated the need for twelve facilities to house 30,000 to 100,000 enemy prisoners of war (Strasser, 2004, 11). As the Iraqi Army dissipated in the face of U.S. and allied forces, the estimated number of enemy prisoners of war did not materialize. The planned flow of troops, including military police designated for the detention mission, was adjusted. As the occupation developed and the insurgency grew, the population of the seventeen detention facilities in Iraq began to mushroom with criminals, some enemy prisoners of war and growing numbers of suspected insurgents. In October 2003, Abu Ghraib was manned with a security force of about 90 military police to provide custody and control of 7,000 detainees (Strasser, 2004, 11).

A rather poorly trained and poorly led reserve military police brigade was assigned to Abu Ghraib and fairly quickly partnered with a military intelligence brigade from Germany, some elements of which had already been in theater in Afghanistan. Because the intelligence brigade had been stripped of interrogators (and linguists) during the post–cold war build down, interrogators were gathered and assigned to it from any units where they could be found. Both training and working/command relationships were predictably problematic, and done on the fly. To this already chaotic mix were added OGA (other government agency—a frequent euphemism for the Central Intelligence Agency) personnel, along with large numbers of civilian contractors with variable levels of training and qualifications. There were simply no operational guidelines for how these different elements were supposed to work together (or not), lines of authority were not clear enough, and it was also unclear whose rules applied in what situations. Worse, not only was Abu Ghraib not in a secure area "behind enemy lines" (a fundamental assumption about military detention facilities), it was under more or less constant mortar attack and subject to violent and unpredictable detainee eruptions. Finally, as the insurgency really took hold, the last ingredient to be put in place was urgent prompting for actionable intelligence.

### Detailing the Abuses

Although there is much we do not know—and may never know—about the scope of CIA, special operations, and contract personnel torture and abuse, we now have a clear picture of U.S. military activities. The Schlesinger Report is an authoritative source on detention operations, and the Department of the Army released AR 15–6 reports (Strasser, 2004) conducted by

Lieutenant General Anthony Jones and Major General George R. Fay. The American Civil Liberties Union (2004) also posted numerous redacted Army Criminal Investigation Division reports of investigations obtained through Freedom of Information Act requests at their website and the Center for Public Integrity (2004) has posted an investigation authored by Major General Antonio Taguba. The events at Abu Ghraib brought into question detention operations at other locations such as those in Afghanistan and at Guantanamo Bay.

The evil at Abu Ghraib was revealed when Specialist Joseph Darby first slipped an anonymous note and a CD with pictures under the office door of a special agent with the Criminal Investigation Division (CID) and later provided testimony about the abuses. The U.S. Army CID is a unit designed for one overriding purpose—to investigate felony crimes where the Army is directly involved or has an interest. Agents and officers in CID are not part of the local chain of command as a means to insulate the agents from local interference with their investigations. Their orders come from regional CID headquarters, and their reporting chain extends directly to Command Headquarters in northern Virginia. Once an agent opens an investigation and the reports start to flow into the CID automated reporting system, there is no stopping it unless the agents themselves and their CID supervisors, supported by legal advice from military lawyers, determine that further action is not warranted. This organization emerged from hard lessons learned from the Vietnam experience, and it remains fiercely independent. Although the stovepipe organization may not always be fully appreciated by field commanders, they know that any attempt to influence an ongoing investigation will be immediately reported by the agents to Washington for disciplinary action, so such attempts are infrequent.

In the wake of obvious and incontrovertible evidence of abuse at Abu Ghraib, initial statements by government and military officials described the abuse as anomalous acts of an errant group of poorly led and insufficiently trained reservists. President Bush remarked (White House, 2004), "But I also want to remind people that those few people who did that do not reflect the nature of the men and women we've sent overseas. That's not the way the people are, that's not their character, that are serving our nation in the cause of freedom." Brigadier General Mark Kimmitt, deputy operations director for the Combined Joint Task Force in Iraq pointed out that the 20 soldiers suspected of abuse were among 150,000 who operated properly (Rhem, 2004). Major General Antonio Taguba testified before the U.S. Senate that the cause was the direct result of a (Gilmore, 2004) "failure in leadership . . . from the brigade commander on down," and cited a lack of discipline as well as inadequate training on internment operations and the Geneva Conventions.

In their report, *The Road to Abu Ghraib,* Human Rights Watch (2004) alleges systematic abuse, not just from the acts of a few, but resulting from administration policies that sought to partially circumvent the Geneva Conventions and the UN Convention on Torture. While the Schlesinger Report acknowledged multiple causes for detainee abuse including inadequate or deficient policies at multiple levels extending from the Department of Defense to the various facilities and prisons, it found no evidence that torture and abusive techniques were official policy. The investigation of the Abu Ghraib detention facility and 205th Military Intelligence Brigade conducted by Major General George Fay, hereafter referred to as the Fay Report, found that "abuse was directed on an individual basis and never officially sanctioned or approved" (Strasser, 2004, 109).

As of 2005, there were officially twenty-six detainee deaths that occurred under U.S. custody, and while some of these have been explained, none can be excused (except possibly for the few cases in which detainees had a pre-existing medical condition). While the independent panel rejected the notion that existing policies directed torture and abuse, it did say that "the abuses were not just the failure of some individuals to follow known standards, and they are more than the failure of a few leaders to enforce proper discipline" (Strasser, 2004, 2). A review of the report revealed dozens of contributing factors that combined to result in a moral debacle that centered on Tiers 1A and 1B of the prison at Abu Ghraib. The worst cases of brutality apparently occurred on the night shift.

### A Benighted Prison

The story of Abu Ghraib—a prison built by Saddam Hussein with a well-earned horrific reputation for torture and abuse—is one of chronically under-resourced military police and military intelligence units, and a toxic mix of CIA, special operations, and contractor personnel, located in the middle of a deadly insurgency. These units were faced with an extremely difficult and unfamiliar mission without clear procedural guidelines and under considerable pressure to produce actionable intelligence. Under the best of conditions the running of a maximum security prison is a high-risk operation that requires intensive oversight and professional staff. Firm rules and clear procedures are important control mechanisms, not just for the inmates, but for the staff as well. Military prisons in the United States are staffed and operated by correctional specialists who are trained specifically for that mission. There are just enough of them in the force to secure existing fixed facilities. The number of correctional specialists in the active-duty military-force structure is really not intended to meet the needs of wartime requirements for detention operations. Thus, virtually all of the units designed to deal with detainees existed in the reserve components.

Operations at Abu Ghraib took place in an environment that was inherently complex and dangerous. The fact that the soldiers had to deal with insurgent attacks on the compound in addition to the custody mission made it even more challenging. The 372nd Military Police Company, a reserve unit from Cumberland, Maryland, and its higher headquarters were trained, manned, and equipped for an enemy prisoner of war mission, not for running a prison that housed a volatile mix of hostile insurgents, criminals, and some innocent bystanders simply caught up in extensive sweeps of suspect neighborhoods. Lest it be inferred that the abuses were excusable, there were a number of detention facilities that managed to avoid the extent of problems experienced at Abu Ghraib. Both the Schlesinger and Fay reports cited culpable deficiencies in command and control that extended from the lowest levels to the Commander of the 800th Military Police Brigade, Brigadier General Janice Karpinski, as key contributing factors in the debacle. To help understand in a more direct way what happened on the night shift, it is worth presenting a long summary of the case of Yasser, taken from a June 2008 report by the Physicians for Human Rights (we have highlighted in the text the U.S. personnel who participated in the torture and abuse of this detainee):

Yasser was arrested by the US military on October 13, 2003. He described being *"surprised by two Hummers and one tank"* in the parking lot of the mosque he attended in Baghdad. He was handcuffed behind his back, blindfolded with a hood, placed in one of the trucks, and subsequently transferred into the tank. In the tank the soldiers made him lie down and put their feet on his back. Yasser then was taken to an *"old military area"* in the El Amrea region of Baghdad and was detained in *"a garage for . . . vehicles, surrounded by the fences."* Then he was transferred to Abu Ghraib on October 15, 2003. According to Yasser, he was never informed of the reason for his arrest.

Upon arrival at Abu Ghraib, Yasser recalled that he was not forced to disrobe, although he felt "insulted" by the US personnel as they *"put their hands in my privates."* He said he was forced to sit on the ground with other detainees for four hours and then to crawl on the ground with fellow detainees. Three people conducted the initial interrogation, during which Yasser was commanded to sit on the ground by an area near a putrid, dirty toilet. He reported being handcuffed to a ring in the ground, though he was not physically harmed during this interrogation. Yasser recalled that despite his repeated requests for medical attention for his pre-incarceration injury, he was only given one tablet daily for the pain. When he was transferred to another section of Abu Ghraib he was told to *"take off all [his] clothes."* He followed the order but *"kept the underwear [on]."*

The US soldiers stripped him of his remaining clothing. He subsequently had his face covered and was handcuffed and chained at the feet. Yasser recalled, *"They started hitting and [told] me 'Let's go, let's go'. . . [W]hen they took off the cover . . . I found myself in a very long hall. I used to hear some dogs barking and some people shouting in a loud voice, in Arabic and English. I walked for a few steps and there [were] stairs, and they . . . hit me [and kicked me and told me] to go up . . ."* Yasser tearfully described that when he reached the top of the steps *"the party began . . .* They *started to put the [muzzle] of the rifle [and] the wood from the broom into [my anus]. They entered my privates from behind."* He noted that several other soldiers and civilians were present, including an interpreter with "a Lebanese accent."

Yasser estimated that he was penetrated five or six times during this initial sodomy incident and saw blood *"all over my feet"* through a small hole in the hood covering his eyes. Yasser recalled that this *"party"* of abusive behavior continued for approximately five days. He added that he received no medical care for these injuries, but was occasionally given napkins and coffee grounds to clean the wounds by "the man who takes the garbage—I used to tell him it was for my hand wound because I was shy about the injury."

Many of the abusive incidents described by Yasser occurred in the context of interrogations. On one occasion, Yasser said he passed out on the floor, and a doctor *"opened my mouth with his feet and poured the water in my mouth. Then he said 'continue.'"* Yasser described a number of other abuses, including having his already-injured hand deliberately stepped on and squeezed by American soldiers. Further, soldiers had written degrading phrases in permanent marker on his head, in addition to other writings *"all over my body . . . and they sign[ed] their names on my body."*

Yasser reported that he did not receive any medical care while in the isolation cell. However, he stated, "Doctors . . . *used to be included with the questioning. . . . Sometimes the dog[s] [bit] the prisoner, and [the doctor] gives the needle to the female soldier for stitching—I saw it."* When asked how he knew the individual was a doctor, Yasser replied, *"He had this bag . . . They call him the doctor."* He added that the "two doctor[s]" usually wore *"an Army uniform, but sometimes they wore civilian [clothing]."*

Yasser was released from Abu Ghraib prison in February 2004 without charge.

While Yasser suffered multiple forms of torture and abuse, the Taguba Report (Center for Public Integrity, 2004) detailed a long set of abuses by military police personnel on Tiers 1A and 1B: breaking chemical lights and pouring the phosphoric liquid on detainees; threatening detainees with a 9mm pistol; pouring cold water on detainees; beating detainees with a broom handle and a chair; threatening males detainees with rape; sodomizing a detainee with a chemical light and perhaps a broomstick; using military working dogs to frighten and intimidate detainees; punching, slapping, and kicking detainees; jumping on their naked feet; videotaping and photographing naked male and female detainees; forcibly arranging detainees in various sexually explicit positions for photographing; forcing detainees to remove their clothing and keeping them naked for several days at a time; forcing naked male detainees to wear women's underwear and to masturbate themselves while being photographed and videotaped; arranging naked detainees in a pile and then jumping on them; positioning a naked detainee on an MRE box, with a sandbag on his head, and attaching wires to his fingers, toes, and penis to simulate electric torture; placing a dog chain around a naked detainee's neck and having a female soldier pose for a picture; a male MP guard having sex with a female detainee; and taking photographs of dead Iraqi detainees. How these soldiers came to engage in these reprehensible activities bears further consideration.

### Intelligence Operations in Iraq

The role of intelligence operations warrants special mention. Counterinsurgency operations in Iraq, and indeed in the greater "Global War on Terror," hinge on the collection, analysis, and timely dissemination of intelligence. Intelligence personnel were clearly under pressure to produce information that could be acted on to find weapons of mass destruction, quell the insurgency, and prevent terrorist attacks. Some of the pressure was self-induced, and some was undoubtedly created by a number of visits by senior officers, including one by the commander of the Guantanamo facility, Major General Geoffrey Miller. General Miller, whose military background was in artillery, not in detention or intelligence, was personally selected by Secretary Rumsfeld to command the facility at Guantanamo Bay, after the first months when the detainees failed to provide much usable intelligence. Miller was known as a commander who could make things happen. When the insurgency began to take hold in Iraq, Rumsfeld ordered Miller to take his Tiger team to Iraq because the gloves needed to come off there as well (Mayer, 2008, 241):

> Miller's concept was a change in policy that would place military intelligence officers in charge of prison operations in Iraq, blending the functions of interrogation and detention. Miller also recommended that interrogations be centralized at Abu Ghraib so that intelligence could be processed more efficiently. And in a break with traditional military doctrine, Miller advocated using ordinary military police officers who worked as guards in the prison to participate in

the interrogation process, even though they had not been trained for this. The guards, he wrote, "must be actively engaged in setting the conditions for successful exploitation of the internees." Miller also recommended using military dogs for interrogation.

Due to decisions made during the drawdown of the army after the end of the cold war, there were too few linguists and human intelligence operatives to meet the demand. There was a critical shortage not only of experienced and well-trained interrogators, but of interpreters as well. Civilian contractors, some with dubious expertise, provided almost half of the interrogators at Abu Ghraib and were involved in more than a third of the abuses (Schooner, 2005; see also O'Toole and Meier, 2004; and Singer, 2003). The Schlesinger Report indicated that the Joint Interrogation and Debriefing Center was cobbled together from six different units (Strasser, 2004, 71). Intelligence personnel involved in interrogations were implicated in a number of excesses. Specialist Charles Graner Jr., a military policeman and central figure in the abuses, steadfastly maintained at his court-martial that he was just following orders; that he was encouraged to soften up inmates for interrogation.

### Blurring the Boundaries

Obviously, the military police mission of providing custody and control became enmeshed with the mission of producing actionable intelligence. This was deliberately done at Guantanamo Bay and migrated to Iraq under the auspices of General Miller. Techniques that may have been authorized at one time or another at Guantanamo and those used in Afghanistan (apparently by CIA personnel and perhaps by special operations personnel), including the use of stress positions, removal of clothing, isolation, and sleep deprivation, found their way to Iraq (Strasser, 2004, 72). The commanding general in Iraq at that time, Ricardo Sanchez, authorized Miller's program in a memo on September 14, 2003 (Zimbardo, 2007, 412).

The line between the permissible and the prohibited was blurred by varying legal opinions, the lack of clearly established written procedures, and a perceived need to adapt to a new paradigm of warfare in which the enemy did not adhere to the established rules of land warfare (Mayer, 2008). Rule and procedure ambiguity may provide beneficial space for flexibility and creativity when individuals have a clear sense of professional ethics and a well-grounded moral compass. Without ethical and moral anchors and lacking clear procedural guidelines or solid supervision, some military police soldiers at Abu Ghraib increasingly moved from passive observers and reporters of prisoner conduct to active participants in the process of breaking inmates down for interrogation purposes. It was an inappropriate function for which they were ill-suited on multiple levels. The prison was under the tactical control of a military intelligence brigade, and intelligence production clearly trumped what would be recognized as good practices of custody and control in the field of corrections.

The Fay Report observed that the Central Intelligence Agency conducted unilateral detention and interrogation operations at Abu Ghraib that contributed to abuse and a lack of accountability (Strasser, 2004, 111). The Schlesinger Report also noted that the CIA was allowed to conduct its interrogations separately and "under different rules" (Strasser, 2004, 75). Both reports noted the existence of unregistered "ghost" detainees that complicated prisoner reporting processes, quite apart from violating inspection and reporting protocols with the International Red Cross. Neither report addressed the specific interrogation tactics used by the CIA (OGA), and instead focused on the absence of a memorandum of agreement between the military command and the CIA. Civilian contractors may well have been in an even more ambiguous situation. The extent to which CIA tactics influenced the conduct of interrogations by military intelligence personnel is not clear, but remains an obvious possibility. Accounts of the death of an Iraqi general in November 2003 during interrogation by CIA personnel, their hired Iraqi mercenaries, and an army interrogator in Qain, suggest that this was indeed a toxic mix (White, 2005).

The torture and abuse perpetrated on Iraqi prisoners in Tier 1 at Abu Ghraib fit the clear definition of evil as acts of knowing and deliberate infliction of pain and suffering on other human beings. The moral inversion of reducing all detainees at Abu Ghraib and elsewhere to "terrorists" gave sufficient permission for many personnel to rationalize their actions as acceptable and justified. For examples of administrative evil whereby people can "engage in acts of evil without being aware that they are in fact doing anything wrong," and by "acting appropriately in their organizational role," we must look both to those guards and interrogators—and their officers—who did not participate directly in the abuse, but ignored what they saw or failed to act on it, and to the myriad other personnel who intersected with the detention and intelligence systems (Zimbardo, 2007, 395–396). Dr. William Winkenwerder addressed the role of military health workers in the Abu Ghraib scandal at a media roundtable in 2004 (Funk, 2005; see also, Lifton, 2004). While denying any evidence that health workers took part in abuse, there were clearly a number of doctors and other health workers who observed suspicious injuries or evidence of abuse (see, however, the report of the Physicians for Human Rights, 2008) but did not report it to authorities. They may have remained within the boundaries of professional practice by recording the injuries in medical records, but did not raise an alarm to stop the abuse. Thus we see an important aspect of administrative evil: actions that were viewed as appropriate in the professional role are viewed as morally questionable in retrospect. We are left to wonder how much sooner the evil might have been unmasked had the medical workers not only recorded the injuries but reported them through their chain of command. And there were a number of other groups that chose not to "see" the torture and abuse they were in fact witnessing (Zimbardo, 2007).

## Making Sense of the Senseless

The choice in the wake of 9/11 to redefine the rules of war to fit a new paradigm—the "Global War on Terrorism"—set off a stream of memos on torture. We believe this series of discussions and events became a "defining moment" for our country in which we crossed over the threshold of overtly sanctioning torture and other abusive practices, and walked down the pathway toward a moral inversion (Mayer, 2008; Pfiffner, 2009). This moral inversion created the permission that enabled the migration of practices and attitudes from Afghanistan to Guantanamo to Iraq. Much as in other historical examples of moral inversions and administrative evil, there was no overt paper trail, no explicit orders were given to torture anyone, but permission was given that said in essence: Because these terrorists are so thoroughly bad, we are justi-fied in approaching this war differently from all other wars, and redefining the rules accordingly. While detainee abuse within the military system has been drastically reduced, it remains unclear whether we are still on that path of moral inversion or not, given what we now know about CIA renditions and "black site" prisons (Mayer, 2008, 145), and given that much remains unknown about special operations and contract personnel, along with the sustained stonewalling of the Bush administration.

With all of these elements combined in an unholy mix, one almost had a field replication of the Stanford Prison Experiment (Zimbardo, 2007), and, indeed, a number of individuals answered the invitation to sadism that is ir-resistible to the handful of thugs who seem always available and waiting in the wings. There were also presumably well-intentioned people who found them-selves drawn in both passively and actively based on the social-psychological cues that were loaded into the situation.

Contributing to the permission that enabled the abuses was the perception that we were now engaged in a new form of warfare. Some argued that new warfare calls for new rules. A number of attorneys from the Department of State as well as military attorneys felt that traditional interpretations of the Geneva Conventions provided a sufficient framework for the "Global War on Terror" (Strasser, 2004, 4). The navy's general counsel, Alberto Mora, wrote (Zimbardo, 2007, 423):

> If cruelty is no longer declared unlawful, but instead is applied as a matter of policy, it alters the fundamental relationship of man to government. It destroys the whole notion of individual rights. The Constitution recognizes that man has an inherent right, not bestowed by the state or laws, to personal dignity, including the right to be free of cruelty. It applies to all human beings, not just in America—even those designated as "unlawful enemy combatants." If you make this exception, the whole Constitution crumbles. It is a transformative issue.

Others, including the Department of Justice Office of Legal Counsel, proffered differing opinions leading to a number of policy changes about how to deal with "unlawful combatants" between December 2002 and April 2003 (Strasser, 2004, 6). The result was permission-giving ambiguity and uncertainty about rules that our military had come to rely on after hard-won experience. Still, there are several possible explanations for why the prisoner abuses occurred.

### The Individual Perpetrator

One possible explanation centers on those who were directly involved. The simplest of these is that the perpetrators were a "few bad apples," who committed crimes on their own with no one else responsible for their heinous acts. In effect, this is the explanation, or theory-in-use, behind the trials and convictions of Specialist Charles Graner and others. The trials do not seek to assign responsibility or accountability beyond the scope of the accusations of prisoner abuse by an individual (nor is it typically their role to do so).

Whether Graner and others followed orders is a separate issue. All that the trials focus on is whether the abuses (and conspiracy to abuse) occurred and whether they were illegal acts. Whatever the outcome of an individual trial, questions remain about what other factors may have been involved. As all the investigations note, commanding officers claimed that no orders were given to torture prisoners. On May 11, 2004, Major General Antonio Taguba told the Senate Arms Services Committee (Gilmore, 2004) that he "did not find any evidence of a policy or direct order given to these soldiers to conduct what they did. I believe that they did it on their own volition and I believe that they collaborated with several MI (military intelligence) interrogators at the lower level." On the other hand, the low-ranking personnel accused of abuse in the prisons claim that they "were just following orders," and cannot be expected to disobey directives from their superiors in a wartime situation. While some have stated that they felt uncomfortable about some of the acts they were involved in, they also felt that they were doing what was expected of them. In the end, this explanation falls far short of providing a satisfactory account.

**Administrative Evil and Dehumanization**

The Stanford Prison Experiment (Zimbardo, 2007) suggests that the social and psychological dynamics at Abu Ghraib carried with them the potential for abuse. But it also does not fully fit the specifics of the situation. Unlike the Stanford experiments, the guards did not act in an isolated and controlled environment, but were part of a larger organizational structure and political environment. They interacted regularly with all sorts of personnel, both directly and indirectly involved with the prisoners. They were in a remarkably chaotic environment, were by and large poorly prepared and trained for their roles, and were faced with both enormous danger and ambiguity. But most important, as in the Stanford Prison Experiment, permission to torture and abuse was available to those who chose to accept it.

In his groundbreaking book, *The Destruction of the European Jews,* Raul Hilberg (2003, 55) observed that a consensus for and the practice of mass murder coalesced among German bureaucrats in a manner that "was not so much a product of laws and commands as it was a matter of spirit, of shared comprehension, of consonance and synchronization." In another study of mid-level bureaucrats and the Holocaust, Christopher Browning (1992, 141–142) describes this process in some detail as he also found that direct orders were not needed for key functionaries to understand the direction that policy was to take:

> Instead, new signals and directions were given at the center, and with a ripple effect, these new signals set in motions waves that radiated outward . . . with the situations they found themselves in and the contacts they made, these three bureaucrats could not help but feel the ripples and be affected by the changing atmosphere and course of events. These were not stupid or inept people; they could read the signals, perceive what was expected of them, and adjust their behavior accordingly. . . . It was their receptivity to such signals, and the speed with which they aligned themselves to the new policy, that allowed the Final Solution to emerge with so little internal friction and so little formal coordination.

If something as horrific and systematic as the Holocaust could be perpetrated based as much on a common understanding and permission to test moral boundaries as upon direct orders, it should not be difficult to imagine how the torture and abuse of detainees in Iraq and elsewhere occurred, with otherwise unacceptable behaviors substituting for ambiguous, standard operating procedures. While the Nazi Holocaust was far, far worse than anything that has happened during the American occupation of Iraq, it has been amply demonstrated that Americans were not immune to the types of social and organizational conditions that made it possible and even permissible to violate the boundaries of morality and human decency, in at least some cases, without believing that they were doing anything wrong.

It would be naive to assume that the "few bad apples" acted alone, and that others in the system did not share and support the torture and abuse as they went about their routines and did their jobs. Before and surrounding overt acts of evil, there are many more and much less obviously evil organizational activities that lead to and support the worst forms of human behavior. Moreover, without these instances of masked evil, the more overt and unmasked acts are less likely to occur (Staub, 1992, 20–21). The apparent willingness and comfort level with taking photos and being photographed while abusing prisoners seems to reflect the "normalcy" of the acts within the context of at least the night shift on Tiers 1A and 1B at Abu Ghraib (and is hauntingly similar to photos of atrocities sent home by SS personnel in World War II) (Klee, Dressen, and Hess, 1988). In the camps and prisons run by the U.S. military in Iraq and Afghanistan, orders and professional standards forbidding the abuse of prisoners and defining the boundaries of acceptable behavior for prison guards could be found in at least some locations posted on some walls, but were widely ignored by the perpetrators. Instead, we find a high stress situation, in which the expectation was to extract usable intelligence from detainees in order to help their comrades suppress a growing insurgency, find weapons of mass destruction, and prevent acts of terrorism. In this context, the power of group dynamics, social structures, and organizational ambiguities can be readily seen.

The normal inhibitions that might have prevented those who perpetrated the abuses from doing these evil deeds may have been further weakened by the shared belief that the prisoners were somehow less than human, and that getting information out of them was more important than protecting their rights and dignity as human beings. For example, in an interview with the BBC on June 15, 2004, Brigadier General Janis Karpinski stated that she was told by General Geoffrey Miller—later placed in charge of Iraqi prisons—that the Iraqi prisoners, "are like dogs and if you allow them to believe at any point that they are more than a dog then you've lost control of them." Just as anti-Semitism was central to the attitudes of those who implemented the policy of mass murder in the Holocaust, the policy of torture and abuse at Abu Ghraib and elsewhere was facilitated by an atmosphere of dehumanization. The detainees, with their ambiguous legal status, were in effect treated as a "surplus population," terrorists living outside the protections of society and state (Rubenstein, 1983). And when organizational dynamics combine with a tendency to dehumanize and/or demonize a vulnerable group, the stage is set for and by the mask of administrative evil.

Given the complexity of this case, with its individual, group, organizational, and institutional dimensions, it would be presumptuous to claim that all abuse could or should have been prevented. As we have said, protracted warfare is corrosive to the moral fabric of any nation, and actionable intelligence (i.e., information that could save the lives of fellow soldiers) is nearly always motivation enough for at least some abuses. At the same time, Abu Ghraib serves well as an example of what the road to administrative evil looks like. While we can take some comfort in the fact that the abuses were uncovered at a fairly early stage and that reforms were instituted, the full extent of the harm done to the reputation and credibility of the United States in the world and what it may mean when American soldiers are taken prisoner by hostile forces remains to be seen. Clearly, it would have been better had the torture and abuse never taken place. This whole sad episode raises the specter of possible war crimes trials for senior U.S. officials such as former Secretary of Defense Rumsfeld, former Vice President Cheney, and former CIA director George Tenet.

Our human capacity for cruelty has been unmasked, along with our willingness to lower our constitutional and moral standards in the name of the "Global War on Terrorism," in this case in our own time and our own culture within the world's "most advanced democracy." And there seems to be little or no concern about cruelties that are outsourced to others even as we condemn them as enemies of freedom (Schooner, 2005). The program of "extraordinary rendition" in which certain detainees are transferred (without due process) to other countries, some among them well known for their torture and abuse of detainees, continued well into the first decade of the twenty-first century (Mayer, 2008). And there is no foreseeable accountability for the actions of the CIA, special operations units, and civilian contractor personnel, who operate largely in secret but with the written permission of the U.S. president (Warrick, 2008, A01). In the meantime, Canada placed the United States on its list of nations that practice torture (Mayer, 2008, 332).

Major General Antonio Taguba, now retired, wrote the preface for the report of the Physicians for Human Rights, and it is worth quoting at some length (2008, viii):

> This report tells the largely untold human story of what happened to detainees in our custody when the Commander-in-Chief and those under him authorized a systematic regime of torture. This story is not only written in words: It is scrawled for the rest of these individuals' lives on their bodies and minds. . . . The profiles of these eleven former detainees, none of whom were ever charged with a crime or told why they were detained, are tragic and brutal rebuttals to those who claim that torture is ever justified. . . . In order for these individuals to suffer the wanton cruelty to which they were subjected, a government policy was promulgated to the field whereby the Geneva Conventions and the Uniform Code of Military Justice were disregarded. The UN Convention Against

Torture was indiscriminately ignored. And the healing professions, including physicians and psychologists, became complicit in the willful infliction of harm against those the Hippocratic Oath demands they protect. . . . There is no longer any doubt as to whether the current administration has committed war crimes. . . . The former detainees in this report, each of whom is fighting a lonely and difficult battle to rebuild his life, require reparations for what they endured, comprehensive psycho-social and medical assistance, and even an official apology from our government. But most of all, these men deserve justice as required under the tenets of international law and the United States Constitution. And so do the American people.

General Taguba, we suggest, is an American profile in courage, during a time when our country had too few such exemplars. Perhaps he might also serve as a model for a public service that is less apt to be complicit in future events that could lead to evil and administrative evil.

Clearly, the cruelties that we did not wish to see or did not commit ourselves were at least temporarily considered acceptable tactics in the war on terror (Shklar, 1984, 43):

We have learned to shrug at massacres, especially among peoples whom we cruelly disdain as our racial or cultural inferiors, but we still react to those that occur in our own cultural orbit . . . they reveal not only our capacity for cruelty, but also an infinity of illusion and hypocrisy. And it is the latter, rather than the cruelty they seek to mask, that appear to arouse the greatest public censure.

The torture and abuse at Abu Ghraib should prompt us not only to punish the perpetrators and better train their replacements (technical rational "solutions") but also to think more deeply about the contradictions and challenges of how to govern a democracy in the context of the "Global War on Terror" (see Adams and Balfour, 2009; Kettl, 2004). Our capacity for cruelty and administrative evil has been briefly unmasked, and so has our hypocrisy and reluctance to confront the full implications of these sorry events. Abu Ghraib prison was finally closed on August 15, 2006. Only time will tell if Abu Ghraib may serve as a lesson for achieving a more humane and democratic governance, or if it will fade into obscurity behind the masks of moral certainty and technical solutions.

Torture is the extreme of cruelty. One person subjects another, held captive and help-less, to possible pain. Cruelty is combined with cowardice, because the captive not only cannot escape, but cannot fight back or retaliate. . . . We do not need a lengthy discourse on the immorality of torture. If torture is not wrong, nothing is wrong.

—*Jamie Mayerfeld,* 2008 (109)

# Administrative Evil and Public Ethics in Praetorian Times

> If history is a nightmare, it is because there is so much cruelty in it. In peace as in war members of our species are cruel to one another, and human progress seems to consist not so much in diminishing that cruelty as in finding more impersonal and efficient ways of crushing and grinding one another.
> —*Philip Hallie,* 1969 (xv)

Administrative evil fundamentally challenges the ethical foundations of public and organizational life. Our reluctance to recognize the importance of administrative evil as part of the identity and practice of public policy and administration reinforces its continuing influence and increases the possibility of future acts of dehumanization and destruction, even in the name of the public interest. During the twentieth century, the Holocaust and other eruptions of evil and administrative evil showed that the assumptions and standards for ethical behavior in modern, technical-rational systems are ultimately incapable of preventing or mitigating evil in either its subtle or its more obvious forms. New patterns of institutional and public corruption in the twenty-first century—what we call Praetorian times—create conditions that seem likely to increase instances of administrative evil. This final chapter considers the nature of and prospects for ethics in public and organizational life, living as we do in Praetorian times and the shadow of administrative evil.

## Ethics and Administrative Evil

Despite the extensive literature on public service ethics, there is little recognition of the most fundamental ethical challenge to the professional within a technical-rational culture: that is, one can be a "good" or responsible administrator or professional and at the same time commit or contribute to acts of administrative evil (Adams and Balfour, 2010). As Harmon (1995) has argued, technical-rational ethics has difficulty dealing with how the professional or administrator can meet the ethical expectations of the hierarchy of authority, public policy, and the performance requirements of the job or profession, while abdicating any personal, much less social, responsibility for the content or effects of decisions or actions. There is little in the way of coherent justification for the notion of a stable and predictable distinction between the individual's personal conscience guided by higher values that might resist moral inversion, and the socialized professional or administrator who internalizes organizational values and obedience to legitimate authority. In the technical-rational conception of ethics, the personal conscience is always subordinate to the structures of authority. The former is "subjective" and "personal," while the latter is characterized as "objective" and "public."

The specter of moral inversion and the tightly controlled, dedicated, but soulless functionary, and the need for administrative discretion, helps explain why much of the recent literature in public service ethics has leaned toward internal control and personal conscience as the center of ethical behavior and standards. But some see this trend as leading to the usurping of democratic controls over public policy and a slippery slope toward government by bureaucracy (see Lowi, 1993).

This conundrum is starkly illustrated in the Third Reich and the Holocaust. Many of the administrators directly responsible for the Holocaust were, from the technical-rational perspective, effective and responsible administrators who used administrative discretion to both influence and carry out the will of their superiors. Professionals and administrators such as Eichmann, Speer, and Arthur Rudolph diligently obeyed orders, followed proper protocol and procedures, and were often innovative and creative while carrying out their assigned tasks in an efficient and effective manner (Cesarani, 2006; Harmon, 1995; Hilberg, 1989; Keeley, 1983; Lozowick, 2000). Ironically, the SS was very concerned about corruption in its ranks and with strict conformance to the professional norms of its order (Sofsky, 1997).

Rubenstein (1975) points out that the Holocaust was perpetrated without breaking any laws against genocide or dehumanization. Everything was legally sanctioned and administratively approved by a legitimated authority, while at the same time a number of key programs and innovations were initiated from within the bureaucracy (Browning, 1989; Sofsky, 1997). Even within the morally inverted universe created by the Nazis, professionals and administrators carried out their duties within a framework of ethics and responsibility that was consistent with the norms of technical rationality (Lifton, 1986). Hilberg

(1989) points out that the professions were "everywhere" in the Holocaust. Lawyers, physicians, engineers, planners, military professionals, accountants, and more contributed to the destruction of the Jews and other "undesirables." Scientific methods were used in ways that dehumanized and murdered innocent human beings, showing clearly how the model of professionalism consistent with modernity empties out moral reasoning. The moral vacuity of professional ethics is clearly revealed by the fact that the vast majority of those who participated in the Holocaust were never punished, and many were placed in responsible positions in post-war West German government or industry, as well as our own NASA and other public and private organizations in the United States. The need for "good" managers to rebuild the German economy and to develop our own rocket program outweighed any consideration of the reprehensible activities in which they were complicit.

The historical record is such that we must conclude that the power of the individual's conscience is very weak relative to that of legitimated authority in modern organizations and social structures more generally, and that current ethical standards do too little to limit the potential for evil in modern organizations. Even if the individual finds the moral and cognitive resources to resist administrative evil, the technical-rational perspective provides little in the way of guidance for how to act effectively against evil. A public servant can voice disagreement with a public policy privately, but if this does not result in a change of policy, the only acceptable courses of action that remain are exit or loyalty (Harmon, 1995; Hirschman, 1970). One can resign and seek to change policy from the outside (leaving only silent loyalists in the organization), or remain and carry out the current policy. This was the choice faced by German civil servants in the early 1930s, as observed by Brecht (1944). If legitimate authority leads in the direction of administrative evil, it will certainly not provide legitimate outlets for resistance. In a situation of moral inversion, when duly constituted authority leads in the direction of evil, public and organizational ethics provide very little help, as we saw in Chapter 7.

Why, one might ask, do professional ethics focus so much on the decision processes of individual administrators at the expense of collective outcomes? Why is the individual conscience primarily responsible for ethical behavior, when political and managerial authority determine public policy and organizational standards? Because, operationally (theory-in-use), the guiding value in most organizations is compliance with legitimated authority. Or, put another way, doing the right thing is almost always what is deemed good for the organization. This is buttressed by the focus on the utility-maximizing individual as the locus of ethical decision making. In short, the ethical problem is construed as one of individual conformance to legitimate authority as a function of self-interest. The fact–value distinction (Simon, 1976) further separates the individual administrator from making substantive judgments by limiting the field of ethical behavior to questions of efficiency and proper or innovative implementation of policy as determined by those who deal in the realm of values (policy makers). In effect, the ethical purview validated by technical rationality relieves, and even prohibits, individual administrators from making substantive value judgments.

Within the technical-rational tradition, there seems to be little or no room for allowing or encouraging public servants to publicly disagree with policies that threaten the well-being of members of the polity, particularly policies that may produce or exploit surplus populations. Rather than expecting the individual public servant to exit voluntarily when in serious disagreement with such public policies, public disagreement might press those in authority either to dismiss the offending administrator or to engage in a public debate over the policy. Or, public servants may pursue the tactics of "guerilla government" (O'Leary, 2013), engaging in a kind of civil disobedience and pursuing a vision of social responsibility even in the face of breaking the law or subverting public policy (and suffering the consequences).

If the Holocaust teaches us anything, it is that individual administrators and professionals, far from resisting administrative evil, are most likely to be either helpless victims or willing accomplices. The ethical framework within a technical-rational system posits the primacy of an abstract, utility-maximizing individual while binding professionals to organizations in ways that make them into reliable conduits for the dictates of legitimate authority, which is no less legitimate when it happens to be pursuing an evil policy. An ethical system that allows an individual to be a good administrator or professional, while committing acts of evil, is necessarily devoid of moral content, or perhaps better, morally perverse. When administrative evil can be unmasked, no public servant should be able to rest easy with the notion that ethical behavior is defined by doing things the right or acceptable way. Norms of legality, efficiency, and effectiveness—however "professional" they may be—do not necessarily promote or protect the well-being of individuals, especially that of society's most vulnerable members, whose numbers are growing in the turbulent years of the early twenty-first century.

## Public and Organizational Ethics in the Nation-State

Administrative evil flourished in the twentieth century when the public service and its ethical regime were wedded with the values of the nation-state, a mode of governance that derived its legitimacy and dominance from the expectation that both government and the private sector would promote and provide for the welfare of the nation (Bobbitt, 2002; Reich, 2007). In the United States, government did its part to advance the interests of its people by providing a social and economic safety net and through the application of technical rationality and public policies to social, economic, and political problems, while major corporations and other businesses provided jobs, health care benefits, and retirement pensions.

Public service in the United States in the last century conceived of the public bureaucracy largely as an instrument of democratic rule. The goals of the nation were formulated within the democratic process, but the efficient and effective achievement of those goals depended upon a bureaucratic command structure rooted in technical rationality and professionalism (Waldo, 1948). This approach to governance produced unprecedented innovations, organizations, and programs: reformed city governments, the New Deal, a reorganized and expanded federal government, a "military-industrial complex," the Great Society, the war on poverty, the social and economic "safety net"—the very infrastructure of twentieth century industrial society. Large and powerful bureaucracies, both public and private, provided a critical part of the structure of the nation-state and the means for achieving its goals (Judt, 2008). However over time, the intrinsic limitations of basing public and organizational ethics on technical rationality and professionalism emerged.

Both public service and business ethics—as well as professional ethics more generally—in the technical-rational tradition draw upon both teleological and deontological ethics, and focus on the individual's decision-making process in the modern, bureaucratic organization and as a member of a profession. In the public sphere, deontological ethics are meant to safeguard the integrity of the organization by helping individuals conform to professional norms, avoid mistakes and misdeeds that violate the public trust (corruption, nepotism, etc.), and assure that public officials in a constitutional republic are accountable through their elected representatives to the people. At the same time, public servants are encouraged to pursue the greater good by using discretion in the application of rules and regulations and creativity in the face of changing conditions (teleological ethics). The "good" public servant should avoid both the extremes of rule-bound behavior and the undermining of the rule of law with individual judgments and interests. Like most people, public servants operate within a partly tacit mix of different ethical orientations, with the mix often shifting from one situation to the next. Virtue ethics, with its focus on moral character and citizenship, does not align well with either the organizational or cultural context of technical rationality, especially if virtue ethics is understood to be a social, and not just an individual, construct. It is fairly self-evident that public (and private) organizations depend on at least this level of ethical judgment in order to function efficiently and effectively, and to maintain public confidence in government (and business). At the same time, it has to be recognized that these ethical standards of an organization or profession are only safeguards, not fail-safes, against unethical behavior and administrative evil. Nor do they necessarily help individuals to resolve tough moral dilemmas that are often characterized by ambiguity and paradox in rapidly changing times.

## The Emergence of the Market State

By the closing decade of the twentieth century a new world order emerged (for discussions, see Bauman, 1999; Bobbitt, 2002; Farazmand, 1999; Friedman, 1999; Fukuyama, 1992; Huntington, 1996; Reich, 2007; Sassen, 1998) that transformed states and institutions based upon the dynamics of a global political economy and ushered in new ethical regimes (Adams and Balfour, 2010; 2014). Where once a few great nation-states defined the parameters of the world's political and economic systems, we found instead a constantly shifting balance of powers in the relationships between states, between these states and super-markets (such as NAFTA and the European Union), and between states, super-markets, and super-empowered corporations and individuals (Friedman, 1999). Old boundaries—organizational, regional, and national—mattered less as the world moved toward greater integration of markets, labor, states, and technology. These developments have created phenomenal opportunities to create wealth and prosperity, but have also opened the doors to new conflicts and to deepening poverty and deprivation among the multitudes who lacked access to these new opportunities, or whose fortunes were tied to the "old" economy. And there has been considerable worldwide backlash to the spread of economic rationalism; much of this backlash is fueled by various versions of tribal or religious fundamentalism.

The waves of change and reform in the public service—new governance, for one example (Kettl, 1993)—during this same time frame were a direct response to the undermined credibility of the state as a means for assuring continuous improvement in the welfare of its people. The end of the Cold War and of the era of nation-states was hastened by innovations in rapid computation, international travel and communication, and their integration and application to markets and organizations (Friedman, 2007). The expansion of markets across national boundaries in a global system increasingly limited governments' ability to effectively promote the welfare of citizens or to limit the purview of international corporations. At the organizational level, these developments have made it very difficult for even the most capable managers to create the "lean" and "nimble" organizations demanded by the global marketplace and also promote the welfare of their communities (Bobbitt, 2002). Cutbacks in the labor force and in the benefits offered by employers have been accepted as normal—and necessary—operating procedures in the global economy of the twenty-first century.

Translated to the individual level, the short-term orientation of the new market state has tended to undermine character, especially those qualities that bind people to each other and furnish the individual with a stable sense of self. Callahan notes three recent shifts in the United States that, taken together, undermine the possibilities for ethical action (2004, 107): individualism has shifted to a hard-edged selfishness, money has become more important (well-being is understood as financial), and harsher norms of competition have emerged. All three are consistent with globalization and the rise of the market state.

### A More Challenging Context for Public and Organizational Ethics

Given the changes associated with market-based government, along with globalization and economic rationalism, the changed requirements for success in organizations have made the prospects for ethical behavior and unmasking administrative evil even more uncertain (Barley, 2007). While bureaucracy and stable lines of authority and routine were valued in a nation-state environment, market state organizations emphasize flexibility and autonomous action. Corporations and governments prefer employees who can think on their feet and adjust to rapid change, but also insist on the right (in the name of adaptability to market imperatives) to let these employees go at any time for the good of the organization. While the welfare of the people remains a concern for government and the stated aim of public policies, it takes a less prominent role in the emerging system of market states to efforts to maximize economic opportunities for citizens and business. Whereas nation-states primarily used rules and regulations to achieve desired behaviors and results, market states in a new governance context rely upon incentives and penalties, not to achieve specific results, but to create a stable market place and favorable economic conditions conducive to maximizing opportunities. As Don Kettl put it (1993, 22): "Instead of a chain of authority from policy to product, there is a negotiated document that separates policy makers from policy output. Top officials cannot give orders to contractors. They can only shape the incentives to which the contractors respond." Market states thus de-emphasize the programmatic and legal/Constitutional aspects of governance in favor of mechanisms for enhancing opportunities (Bobbitt, 2002; Rosenbloom and Piotrowski, 2005).

Under such conditions, governments have been under pressure to devolve much of their service delivery to private organizations via contracts, networks, and privatization (Cooper, 2003). Most agree on what happened: in the United States and, to an increasing extent in other countries, government became less and less responsible (and trusted to provide) for the delivery of what had been thought of as public services, including social services, health care, corrections, and basic municipal services. A new mode of governance emerged that relies upon networks of public, nonprofit, and for-profit organizations and market-based management, with less commitment to public values and far lower expectations for providing for the welfare of the nation, and a greater emphasis on expanding opportunities in a global political economy (see Van der Wal, de Graaf, and Lasthuizen, 2008). At the same time, cutbacks in government budgets and personnel have made it more difficult for regulatory and other agencies to monitor the ethical practices of contracting organizations and protect the public interest (Adams and Balfour, 2010; Frederickson, 2005; Frederickson and Frederickson, 2006).

Government contracting is not a new phenomenon. The Defense Department has long relied on contracting as a means for procuring all kinds of material, from high-tech bombers to toilet seats (Feeney, 2008). The "military-industrial complex" was born in the era of the nation-state and is still largely defined by the huge defense contracts with major corporations such as Lockheed-Martin, Northrop, Boeing, General Dynamics, and more recently, Halliburton. After a series of scandals and public outcry in the 1980s over reports that the Pentagon paid highly inflated prices for commercially available products, Congress overhauled government procurement processes. The result was the Federal Acquisition Streamlining Act of 1994, which, in line with the "reinventing government" movement (Gore, 1995), simplified procurement regulations to make it easier for federal agencies to buy products at competitive prices from the private sector and to encourage "entrepreneurial government" (Peterson, 2003).

These and other reforms, the emergence of the market state, and the policies of the second Bush administration, opened the door for the private sector to take advantage of hitherto unimagined opportunities for contracts and other market-based mechanisms with governments at all levels. From FY 2000 to FY 2006, federal spending on contracts more than doubled from $208.8 billion per year (11 percent of all spending) to $415 billion (14.4 percent), with a total of $2.28 trillion spent over the six-year period (OMB Watch, 2008). This growth in federal contracting was more than five times faster than the inflation rate and almost twice as great as the growth in other discretionary federal spending over this period, with nearly 40 cents of every discretionary federal dollar now flowing to private contractors (Committee on Government Reform—Minority Staff, 2006). The increased reliance on contracting has been driven not only by structural changes in an increasingly competitive global economy, but also by an ideological preference for smaller (if not less costly) government and the presumed efficiencies to be derived from the discipline of the marketplace over rule-bound bureaucracies (Frederickson, 2005).

Government spending via contracts has not only grown, it has also expanded into new areas. Whereas government contracting was once primarily about procuring goods, the majority of contracts and dollars spent are now for a wide range of services (Center for Public Integrity, 2003). For FY 2006 (and since 2000), the second largest category of federal contracts (after R&D, $52.5 billion) was professional, administrative, and management support services at $50.7 billion ($20.1 billion in FY 2000) or 12.2 percent of all contract dollars (OMB Watch, 2008). Many of these dollars were once spent for a federal workforce of civil servants which has been cut significantly over the past two decades while spending on private sector contractors increased almost exponentially, creating what some critics (Klein, 2007; Reich, 2007) have called a "shadow government," a phenomenon that accelerated dramatically under the second Bush administration.

This combination of increased spending on service contracts and cutbacks in the federal workforce has severely strained the government's ability to properly award and manage contracts, making it difficult to assure that contractors are accountable for their performance (Frederickson and Frederickson, 2006). And, because service contracts are more difficult to write than an order for a commercial item or construction job, the result is more ambiguity and less oversight (Center for Public Integrity, 2003). The combined effect of these forces has produced a vast new system that is running ahead of efforts to insure accountability and uphold ethics and public values (if indeed such ethics and values are even considered). Rosenbloom and Piotrowski (2005) argued persuasively that legal/Constitutional norms and values—which overlap considerably with the larger body of ethics and public values—have been essentially left behind as contracts are written and managed. Moreover, congressional critics of the growth in contracting argue that not only have the presumed efficiencies of the marketplace not been achieved by the increased reliance on contracts but that it has resulted in greater costs for taxpayers and higher levels of waste, fraud, and abuse (Committee on Government Reform—Minority Staff, 2006). Indeed, there has been some compensatory reaction in the form of "contracting back in" (Chen, 2009).

There is considerable evidence to suggest that almost taken-for-granted public values and ethics—such as stewardship of public funds, accountability, and effectiveness—have taken a back seat to expediency and favoritism in the drive to privatize government services. The Committee on Government Reform reported that contract mismanagement has grown in tandem with the increase in contracting and occurs at virtually every stage of the process, from pre-contract planning through contract award and oversight to recovery of overcharges. Many of the recently documented cases of noncompetitive bids, poor contract management, and waste, fraud, and abuse occurred in contracts granted in response to the 9/11 attacks (homeland security), the Katrina disaster, and for the war in Iraq, for example (Committee on Government Reform, 2006, 9):

> Hurricane Katrina provides a case study in how the exemptions to full and open competition have been stretched to justify the award of noncompetitive contracts. The urgent needs in the immediate aftermath of Hurricane Katrina provided a compelling justification for the award of noncompetitive contracts. Yet as the immediate emergency receded, the percentage of contract dollars awarded without full and open competition actually increased. In September 2005, the month after Hurricane Katrina, 51% of the contract dollars awarded by the Federal Emergency Management Agency were awarded without full and open competition. Rather than declining after September, the percentage of contract dollars awarded noncompetitively increased to 93% in October 2005. As late as December 2006, FEMA was still awarding 57% of the total dollar value of its contracts without full and open competition. In total, 66% of the contract dollars awarded by FEMA for the period ending May 29, 2006, were issued noncompetitively.

It seems that when it comes to the ethics of contracting, the federal government itself often promotes neither basic compliance nor social responsibility.

One of the most disturbing practices pointing toward the abandonment of ethics and public values is the contracting out of contract management and oversight, a kind of second level of privatization that contributes to and masks unethical behaviors, and insulates contractors from accountability to the public (Klein, 2007, 417):

> The actual state, meanwhile, has lost the ability to perform its core functions without the help of contractors. Its own equipment is out of date, and the best experts have fled to the private sector. When Katrina hit, FEMA had to hire a contractor to award contracts to contractors. Similarly, when it came time to update the Army Manual on the rules for dealing with contractors, the army contracted out the job to one of its major contractors, MPRI—it no longer had the know-how in-house.

Klein (2007) argues further that the behaviors of the government and its contractors in at least some of these cases take advantage of a crisis situation or disaster to advance an aggressive economic program to remake communities and organizations and extend new business opportunities to corporations and cronies. At the very least, the shift of funding from government organizations to contractors has created a level of dependence on the private sector to carry out public functions that goes well beyond the benefits of using market forces to improve the efficiency and effectiveness of government agencies.

As the transition from the nation-state to the market state unfolded in an era of new governance, it is important to note that the core assumptions of liberal democracy still dominate the American context. Liberalism and democracy of course came together in the American founding period (Macpherson, 1977). The core values of classical liberalism are individualism, the notion of rights (particularly to property), the sanctity of contracts, and the rule of law. Classical liberalism set the ideational foundation for American society, which allows for and encourages differential achievement by individuals. Democracy's chief value—equality—has often been outweighed within this framework. The transition to the market state dramatically accentuated the core assumptions of classical liberalism even as it diminished the capacity of governments to achieve advances in democratic practices: Indeed in public discourse today, a "free market" is thought by many to constitute democracy (Sandel, 2012), creating the conditions under which unethical behavior becomes normal and acceptable. With regard to ethics and public values, it is perhaps not an exaggeration to suggest that the U.S. public and private sectors have slipped into a condition that we describe as "Praetorian," and a new mask of administrative evil.

## Praetorian Times

The Praetorian Guard was an elite military force that was originally created to protect the Roman emperors (perhaps analogous in some respects to the Waffen SS in Nazi Germany and more recently, Iraq's Republican Guard). Over several hundred years of Roman history, the Guard gradually became a symbol of pervasive corruption and venality, and this is the sense in which the term is evoked here. There is a rich scholarly tradition on Praetorianism, much of it associated with its obvious military connection (see, e.g., Huntington, 1965, or Rapoport, 1960). Much of the literature, however, uses the term more generally, to refer to social, political, and economic (cultural) corruption and decay—again, the sense in which it is used here.

Some of the literature analyzes Praetorianism as it manifested in nation-states undergoing modernization—specifically, the transition from traditional to modern social, political, and economic institutions. As Perlmutter stated (1969, 385): "praetorianism is generally associated with the disintegration of an old order and the rise of a decapitated new one." Instead of "decapitation," implying a headless new order, the emerging new order might better be thought of as "heartless." It appears possible that a transition of similar magnitude is now underway, perhaps captured by "globalization" (also called by some a transition to post-modernism). While the parameters and destination of this transition remain opaque, one can at least identify some of the characteristics of Praetorianism as it manifested in the earlier transition from the traditional to modernity, and ask how these characteristics are emerging in the current situation—even if the result is only in the form of tentative suggestions.

Perlmutter identifies four social conditions that can give rise to Praetorianism in traditional societies undergoing modernization (1969, 385–388): a low degree of social cohesion; the existence of fratricidal classes; social polarity and nonconsolidated middle class; and weak mobilization of resources (for the state). One indication that these phenomena may indeed be relevant in the current transition is the point made by some economists (e.g., Johnson, 2009; Stiglitz, 2010), who suggest the applicability of developing country models (bubble economies; debt crises; risk of deflation) to "fully developed" states such as the United States. Seen from a cultural perspective, the current Praetorian times suggest a quite limited capacity to develop and sustain strong public cultures. The example offered by the financial meltdown of 2007–8 and its evolution is a case in point of the new Praetorian times.

### Market Triumphalism: Enron as Harbinger of Praetorianism

If the film *The Graduate* had been made in the 1990s or 2000s instead of the 1960s, the conversation between the newly minted college graduate Benjamin Braddock and businessman Mr. McGuire might have gone like this:

> Mr. McGuire: I just want to say one word to you—just one word.
> Ben: Yes sir.
> Mr. McGuire: Are you listening?
> Ben: Yes I am.
> Mr. McGuire: *Derivatives.*
> Ben: Exactly how do you mean?
> Mr. McGuire: There's a great future in derivatives. Think about it. Will you think about it?
> Ben: Yes I will.
> Mr. McGuire: Shh! Enough said. That's a deal.

Like plastics as a metaphor for avarice in the 1960s, derivatives became the new opportunity for making money in the maturing market state of the

1990s. Although derivatives had been present as a risk management tool for over a century, they were a very small part of the financial markets until they came to be seen, in an unprecedented way, as an opportunity to make vast fortunes with the creative use of mathematical modeling (quantitative finance) and new securitized financial instruments—in some respects, a new level of global economic technical rationality (Stiglitz, 2010) and mask of administrative evil.

At the forefront of innovation in derivatives was the corporate superstar of the 1990s, Enron Corporation, and its CEO, Jeffrey Skilling. Enron played a key role in the creation of a global market for energy-based derivatives. The company generated an apparent financial bonanza by trading contracts for electricity and natural gas, and later, other more creative products such as rights to high-speed telecommunications networks and even financial hedges against changes in the weather. As late as April 2000, when Enron was careening toward financial collapse, Skilling was the featured speaker at the annual meeting of the International Swaps and Derivatives Association. In a foreshadowing of what was yet to come in the markets, those in attendance were very eager to learn Skilling's tricks of the trade.

In hindsight, Enron can clearly be seen as one of the most notorious and spectacular corporate failures in U.S. history, and even as a criminal organization (Adams and Balfour, 2012). As David Callahan notes: "Enron's corporate culture in particular will endure as an archetype of bad values in high places. The company is a vivid example of what can happen when you stir together the leading moral toxins of the 90s—extreme individualism, money obsession, and social Darwinism" (2004, 126–127). Enron went bankrupt at the end of 2001, owing billions of dollars to creditors and harming its employees, consumers, and investors across the country. Much of the company's debt had been creatively hidden from view by disguising loans as derivative swaps with major financial institutions and invested in fictitious partnerships. Nevertheless, Enron's business model, based on mathematical modeling (quantitative finance) and creative packaging of financial instruments, remained an irresistible temptation and continued to proliferate throughout the economy (Stiglitz, 2010).

During the 1990s, concerns emerged that derivatives had become so vast, intertwined, and inscrutable that additional regulation was needed to protect the financial system (McLean and Nocera, 2010). The burgeoning financial industry, however, lobbied successfully against such measures with the support of free market ideologues, including Alan Greenspan, chair of the Federal Reserve Bank from 1987 to early 2006. These efforts culminated in the Commodity Futures Act of 2000, a law authored primarily by Senator Phil Gramm of Texas (a doctor of economics) that actually prohibited the regulation of the trading of credit default swaps, a new level of derivatives trading partly responsible for the economic meltdown of 2007–8. Not only was federal regulation prohibited, but the law also prohibited any regulation by the fifty states (Stiglitz, 2010).

### Praetorian Capitalism

The financial crisis of 2008 was the culmination of nearly thirty years of deregulation and public policies designed to unleash the creative powers of the free market (Baily, Litan, and Johnson, 2008, 40). As it turned out the collapse of the dot-com bubble and the wave of corporate scandals at the turn of the century, symbolized by the Enron case discussed here, were just a warm up for what was to come. The American economy had been shifting from a manufacturing base to a financial services base for many years. By the first decade of the twenty-first century, the financial sector achieved an unprecedented place in the economy at 41 percent of corporate profits (Johnson, 2009, 4). Thirty years of deregulation and neglect had the cumulative effect of creating what might best be called "Praetorian capitalism," a corrupt and venal set of institutional relations; in this instance, political economic institutions. In the United States, public policies fostering Praetorian capitalism have led to an economy built largely on successive bubbles, the most recent of which was the housing bubble (Baker, 2009). It is important to note here that Praetorian capitalism has enormous creative and constructive capacity—it can foster whole new areas of economic activity and generate opportunities for some to accumulate stunning amounts of wealth almost overnight. The other side of Praetorian capitalism—widespread individual and social chaos and destruction—is not one of its selling points. If the chaotic and destructive downside risks can be avoided for some by displacing all or a large part of the risk on others, one practically has a license to print money. And this is precisely what the financial sector was able to do.

On Wall Street, any bank or investment company that failed to take maximum advantage of these opportunities was in effect unilaterally disarming, and would have been considered to have failed management and would have had its stock severely pummeled in the market. In a corporate world driven by a short-term orientation (the next quarter's earnings—the next year being considered the long term), one kept up with the competition by escalating the securitization bubble. Like most situations that produce corrupt or unethical actions, and administrative evil, those involved felt they had "no other choice" with the destructive consequences conveniently masked:

> In today's financial markets, almost everyone claims innocence. They were all just doing their jobs. And so they were. But their jobs often entailed exploiting others or living off the results of such exploitation. There was individualism but no individual responsibility. In the long run, society cannot function well if people do not take responsibility for the consequences of their actions. "I was just doing my job" cannot be a defense. (Stiglitz, 2010, 282)

In fact, the main beneficiaries of these three decades of market triumphalism have done their job very well by achieving a consistent trend toward concentrating wealth in the top 1 percent or less of the U.S. population, a trend that accelerated dramatically in the first decade of the twenty-first century (Hacker and Pierson, 2010). It has continued regardless of the political party in power and can be traced to political decisions to either deregulate or to allow policies and regulation to "drift" and be outstripped by innovative financial instruments and rapid computation. Hacker and Pierson (2011, 80) provide ample evidence that the rise of the market state (and Praetorian times) was not due only to impersonal, global, economic forces, but also to political action (and inaction) in response to powerful, organized economic interests, that seem to wear the mask of administrative evil:

> (The) preoccupation with specific personalities and insistence on attributing everything that happens to the qualities of individuals is a form of blindness. We see individuals, but not the organizations that help to pool their resources and can vastly extend their range of social action . . . To understand our politics, and the remarkable transformation it has undergone, we need to cultivate a different sixth sense: a deeper awareness of the powerful role of organization.

These organizations, from the Chamber of Commerce to the many organizations lobbying for individual industries, have not only weakened government regulation and oversight, but also the very nature of democracy and our ethical sensibilities.

### The New Praetorianism: Corrupt Risk Assessment and Regulation

Among the outcomes of the last wave of corporate and financial meltdowns that included Enron is the passage of the Sarbanes-Oxley Act and the Financial Reform Act of 2010. These measures intended to create enough of a regulatory regime that would prevent similar failings in the future, but even they have been under very heavy fire as overregulation from free market ideologues and industry advocates. Sarbanes-Oxley was directed in considerable part toward the failures of accountancy firms, whose conflict of interest between their auditing and consulting arms was a major factor in the lack of warning about various imminent corporate collapses. However, the new legislation did not foresee a similar conflict of interest of a key player in the meltdown of the financial sector—namely the ratings agencies, such as Moody's or Standard and Poor's. The ratings agencies (which bestow AAA, AA, A, and other such ratings) received very large payments for their ratings of collateralized debt obligations (CDOs), and the quite favorable ratings given by them were instrumental in convincing investors, brokers, and banks of the safety of what turned out to be far more risky investments. As Baily, Litan, and Johnson point out (2008, 35): "Moody's profits tripled between 2002 and 2006 to $750 million, mostly because of fees from structured finance products (CDOs) . . . fees from structured finance products made up 44 percent of Moody's revenue in 2006." When organizations whose role includes protecting the public interest are corrupted, it seems reasonable to characterize the times as Praetorian.

Praetorianism has become a self-sealing appreciative system. The more pervasively corrupt and venal institutions and organizations become, the more people mistrust them. Institutions become the last place that individuals look to for the nurturing of affirmative public values; individuals instead see institutions as settings in which only the foolish or stubborn act with high ethical standards (Callahan, 2004). Consider the list—only partial—of individual corporate scandals provided by Heclo (2008, 15): Adelphia, AIG, Cendant, Global Crossings, Tyco, Phar-More, HealthSouth, Waste Management, WorldCom, and leading the way, Enron. He goes on to list categories of corporate misconduct (2008, 15): Savings and Loan; Junk Bond; BCCI Money Laundering; Mutual Funds; Public Accounting Firms; Investment Banks. For the public sector, Heclo (2008, 17–21) presents a long table of 39 scandals in the United States stretching from 1958 (Sherman Adams— President Eisenhower's chief of staff—acceptance of bribes in the form of gifts) to 1999 (President Clinton's impeachment after lying to cover up an affair with a White House intern). A list nearly as lengthy could be constructed just for the decade since. Contemporary Praetorianism has sent an unfortunate signal around the globe: that corruption runs rampant even in the most advanced democracy in the world.

> In the developing world people look at Washington and see a system of government that allowed Wall Street to write self-serving rules, which put at risk the entire global economy, and then when the day of reckoning came, Washington turned to those from Wall Street and their cronies to manage the recovery—in ways that gave Wall Street amounts of money that are beyond the wildest dreams of the most corrupt in the developing world. They see

corruption American-style as perhaps more sophisticated—bags of money don't change hands in dark corners—but just as nefarious . . . They see, in short, a fundamental problem of political accountability in the American system of democracy. (Stiglitz, 2010, 225–226)

While one might prefer a cultural milieu that would foster and sustain public virtues that would pervade social, political, and economic institutions, organizations, and even individuals, instead cultural conditions are such that progress might be best served by initiating a sustained discussion of public vices and processes for expiating the inevitable evils that humans commit (see the Afterword). These seem more relevant in Praetorian times.

## Toward a New Context for Public Ethics

As the twenty-first century unfolds, we find a context that appears perhaps more friendly than ever to eruptions of evil and administrative evil. And that context is as problematic as it has ever been for developing the kind of political arrangements that would be least conducive to them. We find more surplus populations appearing, and being created, at the fringes of American society and around the world. Unfortunately, the possibilities for coercive power and even public policies of elimination, the most perversely tempting technical-rational solution to social and political disorder (Rubenstein, 1975, 1983), are no longer scenarios confined to science fiction. As we have seen in the response to 9/11, the framing of the "Global War on Terror," and the torture and abuse of detainees at Abu Ghraib, an authoritarian and unilateral America has been partially realized, one in which the barriers to "final solutions" can all too easily fail. Many political, economic, and social responses to these conditions have been suggested from a wide variety of perspectives. However, any viable response must be plausible within the American political system of liberal democracy.

### Putting Cruelty First

"Putting cruelty first," our first scenario, is more apparent in American public life at the national level; it gives precedence to liberty within the pantheon of American political values and offers a public ethics which at best provides a scant defense against administrative evil. This version of liberalism is perhaps best articulated by Judith Shklar in *Ordinary Vices* (1984), in which she advances a "liberalism of fear" predicated on the rather dismal track record of human beings, particularly in the twentieth century. Among the pantheon of human vices, including treachery, disloyalty, tyranny, dishonesty, and cruelty,

Shklar argues for "putting cruelty first" (1984, 7–44). If our first consideration in public life is the cruelty that human beings all too often inflict on one another, our normal response is a healthy fear of cruelty, leading us to a liberalism of fear; one whose first and foremost mission is to avoid the worst excesses of state power run amok (Shklar, 1984, 5):

> Tolerance consistently applied is more difficult and morally more demanding than repression. Moreover, the liberalism of fear, which makes cruelty the first vice, quite rightly recognizes that fear reduces us to mere reactive units of sensation. . . . The alternative . . . is . . . between cruel military and moral repression and violence, and a self-restraining tolerance that fences in the powerful to protect the freedom and safety of every citizen, old or young, male or female, black or white.

A polity based on the liberalism of fear is focused on avoiding its worst proclivities. It is, essentially, a negative approach to ethics where the bottom line is to do no harm, and to especially avoid doing great, catastrophic harm. At the same time, it paradoxically makes strenuous ethical demands on citizens: "liberalism imposes extraordinary ethical difficulties on us: to live with contradictions, unresolvable conflicts, and balancing between public and private imperatives which are neither opposed to nor at one with each other" (Shklar, 1984, 249). In a liberalism of fear, into which we are prompted by our "ordinary vices" and by the forces of globalization, we are left utterly dependent on the development of the character of our citizens—too many bad characters and we lapse into the excesses of evil. Too much of an organized, systematic program by government or by religious or social institutions to reform character on a large, social scale, and we risk falling into evil through arrogance, "Nothing but cruelty comes from those who seek perfection and forget the little good that lies directly within their powers" (Shklar, 1984, 39). It is just as easy to overreach as to underreach for character development within a liberalism of fear, leading to cruel consequences that surely warrant a deep concern for the future of democracy.

In this first scenario, one is left with minimalist public ethics. Transparency becomes the chief principle, under the assumption that when people can see the worst excesses they will respond to correct them. A system of laws and regulations that make public deliberations and decisions *visible* to the public becomes the pillar of public ethics. Along with a system of transparency, public ethics under a liberalism of fear would include a program of laws and regulations that set minimum floors below which we would not want to allow people's behavior to sink (in full knowledge and expectation that at least from time to time it will). This is not a version of public ethics that inspires much optimism about future instances of administrative evil. The assumptions about human nature under a liberalism of fear are essentially misanthropic, anticipating the worst from human beings, having been given so little encouragement from the events of the twentieth and early twenty-first centuries. Indeed, the difficulties of getting liberalism right, in combination with the fear engendered by 9/11, has led to examples of administrative evil in our time and culture.

### *Deliberative Democracy*

The second scenario for public ethics focuses on the democratic aspect of our political heritage—in particular, deliberative democracy—and has been more visible at the local level of our polity (Chaskin et al., 2001; Nabatchi, 2010; Rosenberg, 2007). In its most basic sense, deliberation is careful thought and discussion about issues and decisions. Deliberative processes comprise discussion and consideration by a group of persons of the reasons for and against a measure, or, put another way, consulting with others in a process of reaching a decision (Fishkin, 1991). According to Dryzek (2012), deliberation is a process of social inquiry in which participants seek to gain understanding of themselves and others, to learn and to persuade. Thus, one of the cornerstones of deliberative processes is the nature of the communication involved: participants strive to rise above win–lose exchange; over time, they may aspire to dialogue, and even to become a learning community (Yankelovich, 1999).

Participants in deliberative processes are expected to be open to change in their attitudes, ideas, and/or positions, although such change is not a required outcome of deliberation. It is a process that can, over time, grow citizens, fostering growth both in the capacity for practical judgment and in the art of living together in a context of disagreement—hence, a public ethics. As in a liberalism of fear, tolerance is elevated to a central virtue in public life.

Deliberative democracy insists on a meaningful role for citizens in public decisions, although sorting out which citizens and what decisions are appropriate for deliberation represent ongoing problems (Dryzek, 2012). There is a considerable theoretical literature on both deliberative democracy (Dryzek, 1990; Gastil and Levine, 2005; Gutmann and Thompson, 1996; Leighninger, 2006; Nabatchi, 2010) and deliberative governance (deLeon, 1997; Fischer, 2000; Forester, 1999; Hajer and Wagenaar, 2003). Deliberative processes have seen use at all levels of government (although perhaps most effectively at the local level) and share in common involving citizens in public discussion and decision making (Dryzek and Torgerson, 1993; Parkinson, 2006). Insistence on "full" deliberation sets a very high standard that has been met only rarely, and then only after multiple iterations. Publicness is a key aspect in this develop-ment as Ventriss (1993, 201) notes: "A public, therefore, is a community of citizens who attempt to understand the substantive interdependency of social and political issues on the community, and who maintain a critical perspective on the ethical implications of governmental policy making." In this view, it would be unethical for public servants *not* to speak publicly to policy issues. As citizen professionals and administrators in a democratic community, they would have a special responsibility to guard against policies and practices that might engender eruptions of administrative evil.

This critical and active citizenship is a key aspect of building a viable deliberative democracy, and clearly makes demands on individuals, and on individuals acting together in the public interest. It views exclusion and non-participation in public life as major problems in and of themselves. Public policies based on exclusion and exploitation are entirely inimical to a delib-erative democracy because they "weaken the community by undermining the civic bonds that unify it, while eroding the political process by converting what should be a dialogue between fellow citizens into a repressive hierar-chy" (Farber, 1994, 929). This of course is precisely what occurred in Nazi Germany. Under the rhetoric of a unified community, the Nazis' racist and exclusionary policies created a polity held together not by civic bonds but by the terror of the concentration camps (Gellately, 2001; Sofsky, 1997).

### Cruelty, Deliberation, and Administrative Evil

Within our liberal democratic polity, at least these two versions of public eth-ics can be imagined. The first, based on a liberalism of fear, stems from an essentially misanthropic view of human nature: We have repeatedly seen the worst from human beings, and we should expect no better. In this scenario, we should understand that only a minimalist public ethics can be expected to be workable, but even more important, we must beware the arrogance of a public ethics based on grand designs about human perfectability—for such designs are the well-traveled avenues to those horrific eruptions of evil that we have seen throughout human history, and especially in the last century.

The second version, based on deliberative democracy, while not blind to human vices, including cruelty, does assume that humans can—with hard work and great vigilance—do better. In this scenario, we can strengthen our public life and our public ethics through the rigor and tribulations of delibera-tive processes. This is not an easy road; not only does it risk arrogance and a concomitant descent into evil, but it assumes more—perhaps far more—than we have yet achieved. Yet it does have the considerable attraction of imagining a future that can hope for fewer lapses into administrative evil.

Regardless of which assumptions about human nature one holds—and which version of public ethics one thus finds persuasive—no human communities, even deliberative and democratic ones, offer any guarantees against administrative evil. And they certainly offer no escape from evil itself, which remains a part of the human condition. Still, one might hope—perhaps without lapsing into fantasy—that administrative evil may not be so easily masked in deliberative democratic communities. And public servants might not so easily wear the mask of administrative evil when their role entails a critically reflexive sense of the context of public affairs, and a duty to educate and build an inclusive and active citizenry. Our argument in this book thus offers no easy or sentimental solutions. It offers no promise of making anything better, but only offers an inevitably small and fragile bulwark against things going really wrong—those genuinely horrific eruptions of evil that modernity has exacerbated very nearly beyond our willingness to comprehend.

> Do not despair. You need not worry so much about the future of civilization, for mankind has not yet risen so far, that he has so very far to fall.
>
> —*Sigmund Freud, Vienna, the 1920s*
> *(personal recollection of Raul Hilberg)*

# Afterword

## Expiating Evil and Administrative Evil

What of evil's aftermath? While some aspects of evil's aftermath are clear enough through the trail of mass graves, broken bodies and lives, and transgenerational reverberations, the possibilities of expiating evil, including administrative evil, through processes of forgiveness, reconciliation, and reparation, especially on the part of organizations and cultures, remain underexplored. Victims, perpetrators, and bystanders are all marked by evil activities, whether that evil takes the form of genocide, other forms of mass violence, organizational malevolence, or the torture, abuse, or killing of even a single individual. Both the doers of evil and those to whom it was done can never be the same in the aftermath of evil. But to what extent can they, over time, through processes of reparation, be made whole enough again to move on with productive and meaningful lives? We have a reasonably good understanding of the intrapsychic process of reparation, and a great many cases in which successful therapy has moved that process along. How reparation works—and how well it can work—at the interpersonal, group, intergroup, organizational, cultural, and national levels are less clear. And given that these levels are all in some degree interactive with each other, the possibilities for expiating evil become quite murky.

There are significant barriers—at the individual, organizational, and cultural levels—to the expiation of evil acts, although some processes of reparation offer hope for reconciliation and the rebuilding of shattered lives. The *Oxford English Dictionary* defines reparation as: (1) a. the action of restoring to a proper state, restoration or renewal; b. spiritual restoration, salvation; (2) the action of repairing or mending; (3) repairs; (4) the action of making amends for a wrong done, amends, compensation. We have a fairly well-developed framework for reparation in a clear-cut instance of an evil act involving a perpetrator and a victim. Although the process is subject to many kinds of disruptions and goes astray more often than not, victims can move through several stages (closely akin to the process of grieving) (Marris, 1974), to forgiveness, and onto reparation. Similarly, with just as many caveats, perpetrators can move through a process of repentance, and onto reparation (and perhaps even redemption). While these processes can move on parallel tracks, most often they do not move at the same pace. Moreover, there are many situations in which either the victim or perpetrator are not available (perhaps dead, perhaps missing), not interested, or not willing or able to forgive or to repent. The framework for reparation may be understood, but realizing it is a rare and fragile process.

As complex and complicated as these processes have the potential to be, they seem almost straightforward compared with the analogous processes at the group and intergroup levels, at the organizational level, and at the cultural and national levels (Bersani, 1990; Bloomfield, Barnes, and Huyse, 2003; Cose, 2004; Derrida, 2001; Douglas, 2003; Gibson, 2004; Stover and Weinstein, 2004). Not only is there not as clear a set of frameworks, but these processes are not understood as well, and are subject to even more complexity and convolutions. How exactly does a group forgive a group? Large group processes of expiation do not straightforwardly mimic the process between two individuals. Given that government and public institutions can be complicit in evil actions, how these processes might work organizationally is also of considerable relevance. The concept of large group identity is helpful in understanding these dynamics at the organizational and social levels.

## Large Group Identity

Identity is an important concept for understanding the dynamics of evil and its expiation at the organizational and cultural levels. Vamik Volkan gives us insight into large-group identities (1997, 22): "Large group identities are the end result of a historical continuity, geographical reality, a myth of a common beginning, and other shared events; they evolve naturally." Humans have always lived in emotionally bonded large groups, such as tribes and clans, and the large group identities that are bound up in such groups continue underneath the patina of modernity within organizations and cultures.

Much like individuals, large groups can and often do regress under stress. Volkan uses the concept of the "ethnic tent" to describe one way that large groups come together and stay together. While each of us has a personal identity, our large group identity is often focused around this ethnic tent. The center pole is symbolically represented in the leader (usually the political leader), whose most primal task is to hold the group together, by keeping the tent secure and in good repair, as Volkan notes (1997, 28):

When there is shared anxiety and regression, besides rallying around the pole, the members become preoccupied with repairing and mending the tears in the canvas of the large-group tent. In fact, the main reason for rallying around the pole is to protect the large-group identity. Under certain conditions, efforts to stabilize the tent and repair the canvas after it shakes may include violent mass behavior.

Volkan uses the concept of "shared trauma" to describe a past wrong that was done to the large group. Both Pearl Harbor and 9/11 are American examples. For Serbs, Kosovo (as symbolized by the fourteenth-century Battle of Kosovo) is another, and in this case, an excellent example of transgenerational transmission—that is, the trauma is passed emotionally from one generation to the next. In the case of Kosovo, the trauma occurred in the loss of a battle in 1389. Consider also the various "shared traumas" of many North American Native American tribes (the "Trail of Tears" being just one example; see Ehle, 1988). Volkan suggests that the dynamics of such intergenerational transmission go beyond telling stories and the like, and calls it almost psychological DNA. When these "shared traumas" are not dealt with through a social process akin to mourning, which includes acknowledging and naming them, they remain traumatic for the group (Marris, 1974). Under stress, time, in effect, collapses and the trauma becomes a part of present dynamics, skewing interpretations and actions in unpredictable and often violent, even evil, ways. There is little indication, for example, that the trial of Slobodan Miloŝević at the International Criminal Court at the Hague contributed to better relations between Serbs and Albanians in Kosovo, even though bringing perpetrators to justice can be—and is often thought to be—part of a reparative process (Robertson and Roth, 2006). An organization or culture with a deeply held shared trauma has great difficulty either acknowledging evil or foreswearing revenge.

## The Myth of Pure Evil

The "myth of pure evil," as discussed in Chapter 1, is relevant for large group identity, and for organizational and cultural evil. From the victim group's perspective, an act of cruelty or violence (or the perpetrator group of that act—or both), is typically described as evil—most typically, as wholly evil. Baumeister refers to this as the *myth of pure evil* (1997, 17). In the minds/bodies of the victim group, what was done was "pure evil." The "reality" is always more complex. Mitigating circumstances and competing interests can dilute justice; perpetrator groups may be benevolent in other spheres of life, and none of us (including victim groups) is without "sin."

The myth of pure evil is compounded by the psychological concept of splitting (also discussed in Chapter 1), which projects those aspects of the psyche seen as "all bad" outward onto some object (typically a person or persons). The myth of pure evil thus represents a dangerous propensity to cast moral questions in absolute terms, which in turn makes them easier to reverse, facilitating moral inversion (in which evil activity is convincingly repackaged as good; see Staub [1992, 83] for a closely similar argument).

The perpetrator group's description of the same act differs from that of the victim group, often dramatically. We have already referenced what Baumeister called the *magnitude gap* (1997, 18), in which the significance of the evil or destructive act is always far greater for the victim than for the perpetrator. As we have seen, the activity may be seen by the perpetrator as routine, or under conditions of moral inversion, even a good thing to have done. The magnitude gap can become a veritable chasm when approaching processes of expiation.

As we have seen, administrative evil most often occurs when people in organizations engage in or contribute to acts of evil without recognizing that they are doing anything wrong. Recent events, such as the moral debacles of the U.S. occupation and reconstruction in Iraq and the failed response to Hurricane Katrina in the United States, suggest that acts of omission and incompetence may also be unethical and fit within the definition of administrative evil, a kind of "structural violence" (see, for example, Adams and Balfour, 2009, and Christie, Wagner, and Winter, 2000) wherein administrators act appropriately in roles as others would expect them to from an organizational or policy perspective, and yet do harm to vulnerable populations. Administrative evil thus further complicates processes for expiating evil, because its mask makes it more difficult to identify and name, especially in one's own time and culture.

## Financial Reparations

Forgiveness may or may not be within the purview of groups and organizations, but the historical record suggests at least the possibility of reparation and some degree of reconciliation—usually only after time has passed allowing for the mask of administrative evil to be pulled back (which can result in a potential mismatch between individual healing and group/national healing). Institutional or state-level reparation may move too fast and/or too slow for individuals. And financial reparation, even though it at least acknowledges that evil happened, may fall too short for many people to move beyond wounded and broken lives. Consider the example of the internment of Japanese-American citizens in the United States during World War II, which we discussed in Chapter 6. Only decades later did the U.S. government acknowledge its past and offer small reparations, which allowed the nation to reach some sense of closure, while leaving most of the victims with little enough sense of reparation or reconciliation. One has to turn to literature like David Guterson's *Snow Falling on Cedars* (1995) to capture some sense of the emotional and psychological toll on members of victim groups.

Much the same has happened to child survivors of the Holocaust. Surveys of child survivors (Danieli, 2006; Moskovitz and Krell, 2001) have found the experience of applying for financial reparations to be negative and even a source of trauma rather than relief. Nations and organizations only undertook to provide financial reparations long after the event, and then imposed myriad requirements and limitations that served to add insult to injury for those seeking, and deserving, at least a degree of compensation for their irrecoverable losses. In a tragic and ironic way, formal reparations processes can replicate a kind of administrative evil, where administrators in the course of doing their jobs, and conforming to legal and procedural requirements, inflict more suffering on those they are supposedly helping. For example, (Moskovitz and Krell, 2001, 935):

> We learn about being re-traumatized by government bureaucrats who want you to prove your suffering with documents, tell you you're too late, that you don't qualify; or do not respond. We learn about French officials who tell child survivors that since they were young children and too young to work, there is nothing to compensate them for, since they lost no work. We learn about Jewish agencies who treat you like a beggar and stall and delay for years "just like the Germans." And we learn about lawyers, some of whom have pocketed most of the survivors' claims.

These cases lead us to ask whether or how forgiveness can be attained, and whether such efforts can even at times paradoxically contribute to the masking of evil. Forgiveness without truth telling, acknowledgment, and accountability is likely to be an empty, and even harmful, exercise in futility. Just as important, exclusive reliance on the state and public bureaucracies to facilitate reparation seems to limit the extent to which such criteria can be realized. To be expiated, evil needs to be made public and recognized for what it is and has done—with processes that are not constrained by the demands and shortcomings of technical rationality.

## Forgiveness and Repentance

Both forgiveness and repentance (or redemption) are rooted in religion. Finding our way to processes that can work in a secular world is perhaps complicated by that history (Schwann, 1998). One is reminded of Jesus's dying words: "Father, forgive them, for they know not what they do." While Christianity typically interprets the ignorance of the perpetrators in terms of not knowing Jesus's true identity, a secular understanding of the nature of evil suggests another interpretation: that evil is often masked from those who do it. Jesus's executioners were just doing their job. In order to function well, executioners must learn to have little or no empathy for their victims; evil, especially when given state (or even, organizational) sanction, is made into a routine, a method, without feeling.

Forgiveness and repentance can be understood as the opposite of evil: they stem from empathy and a deep understanding by both victim and perpetrator of what has occurred. Some have suggested that empathy-based forgiveness may be more lasting and more effective than self-enhancement–based forgiveness (Enright and North, 1998). Forgiveness on the basis of self-enhancement seems a clear second choice in those instances where it is possible to have a process in which both victim and perpetrator move more or less at the same time through forgiveness and repentance, respectively. Because evil is relational, relational expiation seems clearly preferable, even if the "other" is not always available, and a surrogate "other" must be constructed or found. Both forgiveness and repentance are processes, as well as capacities or potentials (Davis et al., 1992; Karen, 2001; Wiesenthal, 1998). Forgiveness involves four steps: naming of the wrong (or evil); stepping back from revenge; developing empathy for the perpetrator; and being open to reconciliation (a future if not together in friendship, at least of mutual toleration). Steps in repentance for the perpetrator mirror those for forgiveness.

Translating forgiveness to large group levels (institutions or states) is problematic (Hamber and Wilson, 2002; Holtzman, 2003; Neal, 1998; Stover and Weinstein, 2004). Legal and administrative systems normally include processes for enforcing rules and laws, and remedies or punishments for those who violate them. But, such systems, rooted as they are in technical rationality, are not well equipped to help us to expiate evil through forgiveness or repentance (redemption). In spite of what may appear to be real and significant benefits arising from the Truth and Reconciliation Commission process in South Africa, it is clear that reparation has not occurred for many individuals, and the jury is still out on both organizational and cultural reparation (Gibson, 2004).

Thus, current institutional processes rarely produce outcomes that can be deemed satisfactory for the victims of evil and can even at times be complicit in acts that they are charged with punishing or reconciling. Paul Digeser's (2001) attempt to develop a concept of political forgiveness illustrates this difficulty in part. Digeser turns forgiveness into a transaction between a debtor (perpetrator) and creditor (victim). Basically, the creditor releases what is due, and thus "forgives" the debtor. It is hard to imagine either victim or perpetrator groups really becoming able to move on so easily. The question of whether some evil-doing organizations can even merit forgiveness bears consideration; Claudia Card (2002, 177) argues that, "some organizations, like the National Socialist Party or the KKK, are unforgivable. Unlike people who create and belong to them, organizations need have no dignity or inherent worth. The worth of an organization is a function of the principles and procedures that define it."

Managing the transitional time that inevitably follows mass violence, especially when it is within a nation-state (or even a culture), is very difficult. It is easy to have either too much or too little acknowledgment (truth telling), judgment (justice/punishment), and/or reconciliation/reparation. These difficult processes are still of course attractive compared with doing nothing. Trials, truth commissions, and financial reparations are all processes that engage the process of reinterpretation (Haynor, 2001). This works best when participants are far enough along a process akin to mourning. They must be ready to integrate current life with enough strands from the past (irretrievably lost, as it once was) to produce a reinterpretation that enables moving on.

For victim groups and for perpetrator groups, forgiveness and repentance take active psychological work, in order to reach a place where either can be genuine. Evil acts cause real pain—personal, unfair, and deep. What is even more problematic at the level of the individual is that evil actions diminish the moral capacity of *both* perpetrators and victims, even to the extent that the pursuit of reconciliation may itself stem from a denial or masking of evil and the nature of evil acts. Regarding attempts to bring some sort of heroic or comforting closure to Holocaust narratives, Langer (1991, 167) writes:

> But such tact provides insulation, not insight . . . it seems a frail conclusion to the chronicle of atrocities . . . as if the destruction of European Jewry signified little more than a temporary foray against these bulwarks of civilization. One is reminded of attempts to read into the ending of King Lear the triumph of the family reunited under the sanction of Christian love. Understanding here is somehow bound up with the idea of reconciliation, though if the testimony of former victims teaches us anything, it is the permanent *impossibility* of that expectation. The integrity of the (victims') testimonies . . . depends on our willingness to accept that harsh principle. Such an acceptance depends in turn on the idea that an un-reconciled understanding has a meaning and value of its own, one of the most disruptive being that violence, passivity, and indifference are natural and unsurprising expressions of the human will under certain circumstances.

Forgiveness is equally difficult in its own way, and both forgiveness and repentance can be paradoxical processes, in some instances, making things worse.

## On the Potential for Expiation

The challenges and issues explored earlier provide some guidance as to what is necessary to expiate evil acts by one group or nation against another. Complementary efforts need to be undertaken at the individual, societal, national, and international levels. These measures include reestablishing the victim's equality of value, power, and esteem through compensation, restitution, and commemoration; relieving the victim's stigmatization and separation from society through commemoration and education; restoring the nation's ability to provide and maintain the rule of law and justice through prosecution, apology, public records, education, and conflict resolution; and engaging the international community in attaining justice and redress, monitoring conflict resolution, and preventive interventions (Danieli, 2006, 343).

The emerging practice of *restorative justice* (see, for example, Bazemore and Schiff, 2001; Perry, 2002; Strang and Brathwaite, 2001; Sullivan and Tifft, 2006) takes additional complementary steps toward offering some measure of hope that communities torn by evil or violence can reconstitute themselves and even prevent future evil acts. Restorative justice draws upon premodern and nonbureaucratic models and processes that are less reliant upon technical rationality for reconciliation and healing, and that emphasize the primacy of the needs and interests of the victim and the entire community (Sullivan and Tifft, 2006, 17): "A restorative justice response creates a process within which all those affected by a harm come together to collaboratively decide how to respond to its aftermath and its implications for the future."

Dinnen, Jowett, and Cain, in their examination of restorative justice in the Pacific Islands, maintain that achieving some degree of reparation after many years of violence and injustice requires an inclusive and participatory process (2003, 4), "in contrast to the exclusionary character of formal court proceedings under state justice." In the wake of a long and bloody conflict not unlike what is now under way in Darfur and throughout the Middle East, the Pacific Islanders—particularly in Bougainville—have managed to achieve a degree of expiation of evil by engaging in multiple processes in diverse organizational settings—public, private, and third sector—over an extended period of time in ways that are resonant with their culture. In other cases of massive trauma, with varying levels of success, including that in South Africa and Serbia (Sullivan and Tifft, 2006), emphasis is placed on the needs of the victims, on process, not outcomes, and the building of relationships and a civil society with the potential to confront and resist the impulse to do evil. Restorative justice processes seem most likely to succeed using a contemporary new governance approach, in which public institutions partner with other sectors and with the various associations and institutions of civil society to create a protective state. To be able to contribute to such processes, those in the public service need to develop the skills and abilities associated with restorative justice, or risk repeating the failures of the past (Adams and Balfour, 2008).

A core principle of restorative justice is that it does not seek to move on from the tragedy with a quick fix or verdict that purports to put an end to the problem. Rather, communities are encouraged to engage in a form of deliberative democracy (Dryzek, 2000) with multiple and ongoing mediations, conflict resolution, and conferences, aimed at healing the wounds inflicted by those who perpetrate evil without regard for others. Healing for victims and their communities requires including all parties in the process—victims, perpetrators, and bystanders—and dedication to sustaining the effort over a significant period of time. Technical-rational solutions and final verdicts are subordinated to building the community's capacity to heal itself and live with the scars inflicted by evil acts. Consistent with Judith Shklar's (1984) notion of "putting cruelty first," which we discuss in Chapter 8, restorative justice provides some cautious optimism about the possibility to expiate even the most heinous of evil acts. Even then, we must remain vigilant for further eruptions of evil in our midst, knowing that forgiveness in itself does not magically make us less susceptible to or more aware of the masks of evil. Consider the words of Emmanuel Levinas (1998, 37): "Such a rectification (of human violence) does not put an end to violence: evil engenders evil and infinite forgiveness encourages it. Such is the march of history." It is perhaps easiest simply to despair in the face of history's worst atrocities. With all of the difficulties we have seen in expiating evil and administrative evil, especially at the organizational and social levels, the options seem quite limited. Yet as Martha Minow suggests (1998, 147):

> Responses to collective violence lurch among rhetorics of history (truth), theology (forgiveness), justice (punishment, compensation, and deterrence), therapy (healing), art (commemoration and disturbance), and education (learning lessons). None is adequate. Yet, invoking any of these rhetorics, through collective steps such as prosecutions, truth commissions, memorials, and education, people wager that social responses can alter the emotional experiences of individuals and societies living after mass violence. . . . The wager is that social and political frameworks can make a difference to how individuals emerge from devastating atrocities.

Whenever evil and administrative evil are unmasked, institutions and administrators have the responsibility to respond, seeking ways to move forward that promote justice, accountability, and healing.

# Appendix A

# Foreword to the Third Edition

Sometimes evil enters on soft cat paws, and sometimes on hard cloven hoofs, but it always leaves an indelible imprint on human affairs. Lucifer (see my book, *The Lucifer Effect*, 2007) is satisfied to be a bit player in evil's scenario, never taking on leading roles, willing to speak his lines in the subtext, slipping his actions into the small details of the situation, and restricting his direction to the marginal stage settings. Lucifer conceals his charismatic power behind a variety of masks. Curiously, his most preferred disguises are masks of patience, of seeming indifference, and of good-naturedness. He views our world through the loopholes of legality, where good men can convince themselves that a wrong can be righted simply by a turn of phrase.

Most of all, Lucifer delights in the challenge of seducing really good people, disdaining as unworthy of his efforts those who have already had a "push from nature" toward the dark side. At the top of his list of take-down candidates are those who possess the arrogance of invulnerability. They are the easiest marks because they never see his power skirting around or under their illusory veil of personal fortitude. When we steady ourselves for encounters with evil, we are apt to imagine that it will appear amid bright lights in a slam-bam head-on blast. When evil really confronts us, we may notice no more than a blur in the side-view mirror, a gentle nudge, or a momentary reflection in our celebratory glass held high. Evil undoes us because its presence is subtle and disguised. It is a pervasive perturbation of the human condition.

"Mind your own business; don't get involved!" That is the mantra of most mothers to their children. While it might help ensure a longer life for the children who obey this mantra, it will be no advantage to people who need their help. The first step on the path to evil is flowered with buds that never blossom. Evil gets its initial operating permit from those who do nothing when something is demanded, refrain from action when intervention is required, and look away when watchful observation is urgent. Perpetrators of evil rely on the passivity of those observing them, making the observers accomplices who enable them to continue their evil actions without challenge. Inaction can be construed as tacit approval. Very subtly a nonverbal conspiracy is forged between an actor and his passive supporting actor(s), which puts into play the drama of the evil of inaction.

What could make that mother, father, teacher, or preacher happier than a good little kid, who respects authority and does what he or she is told to do without question or hassle? Such obedience to authority is an essential ingredient in those who would respect their elders, follow the leader, and be useful, cooperative citizens. Authorities are often those who make the rules, or at least present them as the "shoulds" and "oughts" of moral behavior, and enforce the rules with appropriate rewards or punishments. Rules are impersonal ways to control interpersonal behavior. Authority proclaims semi-legal status and defines the necessary limits on individual freedom. Curiously, the ones who make the rules often claim not to fall under the control of those rules, instead using the rules, especially vague and changing ones, to control the behavior of people who might question the legitimacy of their authority. Nevertheless, no one teaches us to distinguish just from unjust authority. No one highlights the difference between benevolent and corrupt authority, until it is too late. In fact, rules that are designed to serve the social good should be more recognizable and more highly valued than those designed merely to bend the will of the people to the dictates of authorities. Authority gains more power as greater numbers of citizens obey its arbitrary rulings. Blind obedience to unjust authority and mindless adherence to coercive rules can transform freedom-loving democracies into fascist dictatorships. Another big win for that wily old Lucifer.

All for one, one for all; the team comes first; sacrifice personal ambition for the success of the group. When such reasonable sport slogans are mindlessly translated into the realms of business or politics, they become simply, "Be a team player!" Individual ethical values are forced aside when an unethical system intrudes upon personal decision making. Lying, cheating, cooking the accounting books, and tolerating corruption become the individual player's way of being a valued team player. Lucifer loves teams like those.

We spend much of our lives seeking the goodwill of people we care about and people who are like us. They form the inner circle of family and friends who can do no wrong in our eyes. We trust them without question, give them the benefit of the doubt when their actions seem to violate social norms, hire them over others more competent or more honest than they. The way we honor commitment to them is by contrasting "us" with all those "others." "They" are the out-group. Once we so categorize the "other," we discover differences that lead us to set them apart from ourselves, and we deem them unacceptable, inferior, untrustworthy, and dangerous. It becomes vital to keep them in their place because their very existence threatens our way of life. Stereotypes help us to do that for they allow us visibly and verbally to mark those "others" as less than human. Lucifer is a master of dehumanization. Dehumanization is like a cortical cataract; it impairs the mind's perception of other people as people like us, rendering them instead as blurry, threatening objects. Those objects then must be contained, restrained, and even destroyed. Dehumanization is at the core of prejudice, discrimination, mass murders, torture, and rape. It operates at both individual psychological levels and system/formal levels of propaganda, as we witnessed in Nazi Germany's depiction of Jews as "vermin," and recently Rwanda's Hutu leaders' characterization of Tutsi neighbors as "cockroaches" that must be destroyed. (Indeed, civilians and military butchered 800,000 of them in eight months with machetes and clubs.)

But what about men and women of conscience who might resist taking actions that appear immoral, unethical, or illegal? It is easier to commit questionable acts if those in authority over us are ready to accept the burden of responsibility for us and defuse the consequences of going down a dark, unmarked path. Shedding or shredding the mantle of responsibility reduces our personal accountability for behavior unbecoming to a citizen of conscience. In addition, we can persuade others to evade taking responsibility for their actions when we assure them that we will share some of the blame. In short, we can help them slip across the illusory boundary separating good from evil.

We all want to believe in a just world where those in power have our best interests at heart and will use their resources to make our lives better. Often they pretend to do that by proclaiming adherence to some high-minded principle outlining an abstract goal that is readily accepted as desirable. Ideologies are only systems of ideas, but it is all too easy for us to become "true believers" in them. In the hands of ideologues, ideologies can be used to justify any and all means to such worthy ends. Ideology can become the system's most dangerous weapon of mass deception and mass destruction.

My personal interest in evil began as a child growing up in New York City's South Bronx ghetto, where violence flourished around me and good kids were seduced into doing bad things, such as running drugs, and reputations were made by time in the juvenile authority facility or jail. Robert Louis Stevenson's fable of the good Dr. Jekyll's transformation into the evil Mr. Hyde by ingesting some strange elixir made me realize that the comforting line supposedly separating good from bad people was not fixed and impermeable, but flexibly permeable. It initiated my interest in investigating the social-situational conditions that might induce those who are clearly "good" at one point in time to inch across that boundary and become "bad" at another time. My research on the effects of anonymity, or deindividuation, as a cause of vandalism and violence set the stage for my Stanford Prison Experiment. In 1971, my assistants and I put college student volunteers who were preassessed as normal, healthy, and even wholesome into a mock prison, as randomly assigned prisoners or guards. To my surprise, I had to terminate the designated two-week study after only six days because it had spun out of control. It had become not a mock prison experiment, but a tough maximum-security prison run by psychologists and not by the state. Our analytic observations and evidence led to the conclusion that the cruelty and inhuman behavior of those in the guard role and the pathological reactions of those in the prisoner role were the direct result of a host of situational variables and processes.

That experience led me to conjecture that the abuses of Iraqi detainees by military police (MPs) in Abu Ghraib prison were not—as the Bush administration and military command had declared—the work of a "few bad apples." Rather, perhaps similar to the findings of my Stanford Prison Experiment, it was the "bad barrel" that corrupted previously good apples. I was able to test that hypothesis by becoming an expert witness for one of the MP guards charged with some of those crimes. In that capacity, I had access to all of the investigative reports as well as thousands of horrendous images the soldiers had taken of their abuse and torture of those they were supposed to protect. I also had access to the guard (interviews, psychological assessments, prior military and civilian job checks, and more). My conclusion presented to the judge at the guard's court martial was that although he was guilty of the crimes as charged, his behavior was under profound situational control and thus his sentence should be mitigated. The prosecutor's summation hinted that his behavior and that of the other MPs threatened the well-being of all captured U.S. soldiers because they could not count on humane treatment as prisoners of war, and therefore, he should be severely punished.

That prosecutor was invoking the Geneva Convention rationale, without naming it as such because it had been revoked in the case of all those captured as "enemy combatants," and not as "real soldiers." U.S. Justice Department lawyers and officials developed that new definition, disregarded the Uniform Code of Military Justice, and created a new legal rationale for suspending habeas corpus, arresting anyone anywhere in the world on suspicion of terrorism, holding them indefinitely without formal charge or legal defense. That view was embodied in the Military Commissions Act, and filled Guantanamo Bay prison with hundreds of those arrested around the world in the most totalitarian actions that the United States has ever taken. The soldier I defended was dishonorably discharged, received an eight-year prison sentence, was stripped of his nine medals and awards, and had his twenty-two-year retirement fund rescinded. So much for the system recognizing situational influences over individual behavior.

However, as I became immersed in trying to understand how these young army reservists had come to behave so badly when they were playing the roles of MPs on the night shift of Tier 1 A (the interrogation center), it became clear that I was missing the big picture by focusing on person versus situation (see *The Lucifer Effect*). Like most social scientists, I had ignored the system that creates such evil-breeding situations. Those systems contain the "bad barrel makers" who use their power to redefine reality and legality; they can even justify genocide. The system in the case of the Abu Ghraib abuses includes those in charge of creating and maintaining those situations by means of resource allocation, legal rules, and top-down pressures for "actionable intelligence," by all means necessary. Like Mafia dons, these officials—elected, appointed, or born to the realm—always have consiglieri who find a legal loophole to circumvent the law, or provide plausible deniability when challenged publicly. They use and abuse the law as a tool to conveniently skirt morality and ethics as long as their lawyers can persuade some judge that it is all OK because it is legal.

Adams and Balfour's *Unmasking Administrative Evil* confirms my original convictions about evil. Its many fascinating case studies reveal evil done by ordinary people working in corporations and institutions. My view has been that most evil is indeed done by ordinary people, certainly by those underlings who do the dirty work of the boss man. Adolph Eichmann was merely a functionary doing his job as a planner of mass executions of Jews and other undesirables at Auschwitz, following the rules and laws created by the Nazi party. Hannah Arendt described such criminals as "terrifyingly normal," given that they look like our next-door neighbors, not comic-book monsters. Accountants in the Arthur Andersen firm were also doing their job in helping to "cook the books" for Enron officials engaged in massive fraudulent activities. And what about lawyers for cigarette companies challenging opposition to their death-dealing product? The same is true of lawyers defending various destructive cult groups, or oil and gas companies that contaminate the lands of indigenous people around the world, or vehicles proven dangerous to drive.

Big evil is always systemic evil, writ large by powerful institutions: social, political, and economic. Because they control enormous resources, they can redefine reality in the best Orwellian tradition, especially if they can manipulate the media and influence education and political choice. Such systems almost always function from behind a veil of secrecy—like the Wizard of Oz behind green curtains—that obscures their comings and goings. Thus, for example, correctional institutions that cost taxpayers billions of dollars annually are shrouded in secrecy to conceal their ineptitude, high recidivism rates, and failure to influence crime or promote positive reentry of paroled inmates.

In a similar show of power, the military system that sent the soldier I defended to a long prison term along with other MPs on his shift did not try a single officer who should have had command responsibility for knowing what evil their subordinates were doing at Abu Ghraib month after month. On the other hand, they did punish General Anthony Taguba for filing a critical investigative report that singled out officers who were derelict in their duty, and made it clear that those abuses would not have occurred were it not for a failure or absence of leadership. He was forced to retire when notified he would never get his next star. Even more egregious use of military power to punish "whistle-blowers" and "dissidents" is revealed in the sad case of former army sergeant Sam Provance. Sam was one of the heroes of the Abu Ghraib scandal, the only uniformed military intelligence officer at the Iraq prison to testify about the abuses during the internal army investigation. The military had arranged a cover-up to pin the abuses solely on the lowly MPs and not on any higher-ups who had brought the lessons of "alternative interrogation techniques" from the Guantanamo Bay prison to Abu Ghraib. Because Sam refused to go along with that ruse, he was threatened with punitive action, had a gag order issued against him, and was pushed out of the military after eight years of decorated service.

Corporate evil should be everyone's concern because corporations are the dominant institution on our planet. The job of corporations is to amass wealth as a legal entity structured to maximize profit for shareholders and owners via prudent policies while minimizing accountability for any negative collateral damage of such wealth seeking. Of the top 100 world economies, at least fifty are corporations with a greater net income than that of the other nations. With such considerable wealth comes political lobbying and support for corporations' wealth-generating practices. Corporations were originally formed to serve the public trust licensed by local communities to perform specific functions for limited time periods. Over time, that conception changed to corporations as serving primarily the demands for profit of shareholders and not the needs of stakeholders. Paradoxically corporations are legally "persons" under the Fourteenth Amendment to the U.S. Constitution. Corporations are persons who conduct business. What kinds of persons are corporations? Noam Chomsky cynically asserts that they are persons without moral conscience; corporations are persons with "no soul to save, no body to incarcerate."

If stockholder interest is placed above the public good, then the negative consequences to society of business practices are "externalized." Corporations have become "externalizing machines," letting the third party consequences of their business dealings become simply part of the cost of doing business, and not their primary concern. No malevolence, no personal harm intended, it is only business when it all hits the corporate fan. In the 2003 documentary *The Corporation*, such externality is described as: "harm to others," people and animals, workers and citizens affected by their products; and "harm to the biosphere" through polluting environments with their chemical by-products. When accused of engaging in dangerous illness-generating activities, big corporations settle out of court and move on with their reputations intact. The Monsanto Corporation was the distributor of the chemical known as Agent Orange used in Vietnam to defoliate the jungle, but it also devastated the health of many Vietnamese civilians and American soldiers. The corporation paid $800 million in an out-of-court settlement—and it never admitted any guilt. Similarly, the Catholic Church in the United States has paid out hundreds of millions of dollars across many parishes to settle suits against priests who had raped children over decades—without a single priest being tried for sexual molestation.

So evil is really about the exercise of power to inflict harm, hurt, and destruction on others individually or collectively, and when it occurs on an institutional scale, to commit crimes against humanity. The importance of international tribunals is to recognize a higher level of morality and justice that transcends national boundaries or the might and self-arrogated rights of powerful dictators at a given time in a given place. Polish lawyer Raphael Lemkin, who successfully argued, in 1944, that genocide be recognized by the United Nations as a crime against humanity and its perpetrators tried in international tribunals, is our counter-model to all lawyers who sell their souls out daily to defend their corporations' wrongdoing through their administratively shrewd, legal wheeling and dealing.

I would like readers of *Unmasking Administrative Evil* to go beyond being intellectually engaged with the vital messages contained in its every chapter, and not to remain socially passive. It is time to put on your mental and spiritual armor, and to realign your moral compass using common but effective mental strategies that we all have available, but too often allow to rust by disuse. Assume your adversary is really shrewd and has eons of experience to rely upon in his or her bag of tricks. You have the most powerful, dynamic organ in the universe on your side, the human mind. Use it or lose the battle. The key to resisting evil then starts and ends with the exquisite development of three skill sets—self-awareness, situational sensitivity, and street smarts. You must be more mindful of the influences affecting your personal decisions. You must begin to recognize the power of social situations to shape your attitudes and actions. You must be wary of accepting "facts" at face value, of consuming "free lunches," of buying into something "too good to be true," or trusting without question false political prophets or Wall Street wizards (e.g., Bernie Madoff and his multibillion dollar Ponzi scheme). Street-smart people have suspicion alerts primed to detect and set off alarms when they perceive discontinuities between words and deeds, promises and evidence, claims and consequences.

What is at stake is not just your individual soul, but our collective civic virtue. In my most recent research, I am working with a team to explore how ordinary people can use new media to join forces and take action against corruption (see www.IntegrityCapitalism.com). When enough of us live as citizens rather than just consumers and form an alliance against all forms of institutional corruption—through community awareness, participation, and taking an active stand—we can perhaps begin to unmask administrative evil.

Philip G. Zimbardo
Stanford University

# Appendix B

# Foreword to the Second Edition

This is a disturbing book. It makes one realize how much organizational theory (and worse yet, public administration theory) has largely ignored, or sanitized, the notion of evil.

We have reasonable taxonomies of organizational forms, organizational environments, success and failure, even types of leadership. But we have no taxonomies of organizational evils. The notion of organizational evils merely conjures up images of pollution, mismanagement, corruption, or law breaking. But, the authors of this disturbing book argue, there is something beyond this: organizations inflicting pain and suffering unto death *willingly*. Not inadvertently, or accidentally. They have many examples, from the clear one of the Holocaust to the murky one of the *Challenger* disaster. And this administrative evil is organizational, formal, rational, efficient evil—not the work of a crazy leader, personal failings, lax controls, or racist ideologies. Though these may be involved, they would be less consequential without modern organizations and their efficiency and professionalism. It is unsettling to have a review of these evils, but it is just as disturbing to realize how little attention my field of organizational analysis has given to the subject. Organizational analysis has moved beyond "operator error" as an explanation for failures to notions of high- and low-reliability organizational types, and on to notions that I have been advancing of error-avoiding and error-inducing systems (see the Afterword in the 1999 edition of *Normal Accidents*). But Adams and Balfour are after something more basic: an inherent characteristic of modern organizations that allows evil to be administratively "sanitized," accepted as rational and proper in terms of efficiency, and the masking may be inadvertent.

In the most striking illustration of this phenomenon, the authors describe the efficient, bureaucratic, rationalized system of exterminating Jews in Nazi

Germany. The retelling of parts of this horrific story is needed. I knew many of the details but still was brought up sharply with the retelling because it has an added dimension of horror for those of us seeking to understand and improve organizations—the application of rational-legal principles and bureaucratic efficiency to the task of extermination: "The destruction of the Jews became procedurally indistinguishable from any other modern organizational process. Great attention was given to precise definition, to detailed regulation, to compliance with the law, and to record keeping. In other words, the modern, technical-rational approach to public service was adhered to in every aspect." Among the many examples, the German Rail Authority billed the Gestapo at the third-class rate, one way, with discounts for children and group rates for 400 or more passengers on their journey to the death camps: "With this routine, matter-of-fact calculation, whole communities were transported to their deaths."

The second major case is more equivocal. Wernher von Braun was technical director of the project to build the V-2 rocket, and he explicitly adopted the policy of using SS-provided slave labor at the various production sites. Mittelbau-Dora, built to supply slave labor for the Mittelwerk factory, was the last and among the worst of the SS concentration camps, which von Braun often visited and from which he selected prisoners for special technical tasks. The factory produced 6,000 rockets and 20,000 deaths in two years. More humans were killed in making the rockets than in the explosions in Britain. Other Nazi officials associated with the camp were tried at Nuremberg after the war, but the United States whisked von Braun and 117 members of his team, half of them Nazi party members and virtually all familiar with the slave labor camps, to the United States. (They might otherwise have escaped to South America or been taken by the Russians.) The Americans needed them. They were sanitized and their records hidden, given charge of our missile program, well paid, and lionized for their role in arming us against the USSR.

The example is equivocal because, in the case of the slave labor camps, von Braun could have said, "Just following orders, where the failure to do so might have meant punishment." But like the Eichmann defense, it does not wash. As with the huge bureaucracy that supported the extermination camps, von Braun and Eichmann worked hard, ingeniously, and innovatively to execute their orders with all possible efficiency, perhaps even enthusiasm. It was not about keeping one's job.

More equivocal is the case of the U.S. government protecting and using von Braun. There was a "higher good" of getting better missiles than our enemy the USSR could get, or we all might be dead. The goals of the system, rather than its administrative evil, would seem to be the problem. This ambiguity deserves further exploration—there can be evil goals, and if so, is "administrative" evil all that important? We can say that the goals of the

Nazis were evil, and administrative evil allowed them to be carried out. But if the U.S. officials feared that Russian nuclear superiority could lead to our enslavement or worse, and thus believed we must retain nuclear superiority even if we whisked away a few Nazis and hid their crimes, perhaps it was justified—a "necessary evil for the greater good." (The Nazis could hardly make a comparable case that the Jews threatened their nation, though they tried.) What, then, is the role for administrative evil?

Administrative practices made it possible to whisk the crew away, keep those who knew of their crimes from identifying them, hide them for a time, give them new records, and celebrate their accomplishments when it was time to reward them. (Here is how it might work: "I am repelled by what these Nazis did, but my bosses embrace them, and the personnel department treats them well, and they work hard and rationally at the tasks they are given, so I have no *organizational* grounds for criticizing or sounding any alarms. It is probably okay, or my organization would not be supporting them.") The more efficient the bureaucracy, the more likely there would be no leaks or protest. In the same way, back in the concentration camp, handling schedules, production targets, raw materials, and supplies probably served to avert to some extent (never completely) von Braun's gaze when visiting the camp and seeing the conditions. (Those who resisted were routinely left hanging at the entranceway of the camp, then buried in a mountain; hard to miss even from a staff car.) The truly remarkable U.S. administrative accomplishment was to identify this monster in public ceremonies as the basis of our security from the threat of Russian domination. Public awards and ceremonies are administrative tools, and can be evil as well as good.

A further case is made about the subsequent trajectory of the missile program and then the space program, under von Braun. A defensive organizational culture was created by the von Braun team, and it turned "destructive" under the leadership of Dr. William Lucas, leading to the *Challenger* tragedy. The history here is quite interesting and offers a quite different view of the events leading to the *Challenger* accident than that of Diane Vaughan's "normalization of deviancy" account. Here we have much more "agency," in the form of political actors with political goals exercising bureaucratic power over dissenting engineers. The authors admit that the "identification of administrative evil is problematic" in the *Challenger* account.

I can think of other examples where the designation of "necessary evil" may be more appropriate than administrative evil. Workers in U.S. atomic weapons plants were knowingly exposed to unnecessary radiation, but safer procedures would slow up the war effort, it was said at the time. (The evil, for me, is the lack of informed consent, though this might have precluded the workers' cooperation, and worse yet, the lack of medical follow-up—both administrative evils.) President Eisenhower was informed that soldiers placed a few thousand feet from an atomic test blast would be seriously irradiated, but he approved of the experiment because fighting communism demanded sacrifice. (Test animals would tell us just as much, and in any event it appears that there was little follow-up of the exposed troops, so this compounded the evil with bungling.) The authors mention the Tuskegee experiments on African-American prisoners, internment of Japanese Americans in World War II, and other cases to remind us that "American public administration also possesses a well-developed capacity for administrative evil." But most of these are easily rationalized in terms of some "higher good." (The Tuskegee case could have been so rationalized initially, but not later on; the cruel experiments continued even after a cure for syphilis had been found.) Another case comes to mind that is not suitable for such rationalization and thus is a pristine example of administrative evil: that of the U.S. tobacco industry. In this case, scientists and upper management knew full well the suffering they were inflicting on others as they sought to increase nicotine addiction rates. The penalties for refusing to cooperate were minor—job loss by people with marketable skills. But most important, they could not rationalize this in terms of any higher national or scientific good. It took a rare individual, a whistle-blower, to break out of the administrative routine that for decades produced and rewarded this evil. As I will note later, this range of examples implies that a scale of administrative evil might be uncovered.

For this writer, there are several issues and questions that need to be cleared up as this very important perspective is refined and expanded. We need to be more precise about when the virtues of modern administrative practices will be realized without encouraging administrative evil. It is claimed that these practices make possible dehumanization and destruction of human values and dignity, and thus that administrative rationality creates the possibility for administrative evil (rather than causing it directly). And, of course, no one would suggest that we try the alternatives—nonrationality in administration, inefficiency, or nontechnical rationality, if there be such a thing. But, focusing on the dark side, the administrative urge toward human rights that has begun to assert itself in the world is not addressed. The human rights record of the United States, where technical rationality reigns, compares rather favorable with that of Russia, China, and many Middle Eastern states, where it is absent. The countries with the best human rights records—thus, presumably the lowest level of administrative evil—are the most technically rational, the Scandinavian countries. Some reflection on the circumstances for administrative good, as well as evil, would sharpen their case.

There is a danger that the message could be read as follows: given the advance of science and rationality and bureaucracy, things can only get worse.

(I think things are getting worse, but the cause is political and religious, not administrative.) They say the "scientific-analytic mindset and technical-rational approach to social and political problems enables a new and frightening form of evil—administrative evil." Since our very public service ethics and professional ethics are anchored in this mindset, this implies these ethics are useless in the face of administrative evil. They say, "modern management is founded on and sustained by systematic dehumanization, exploitation, and even extermination." That is far too strong. The Scandinavian countries are exemplars of modern public administration and the least likely to dehumanize, exploit, and exterminate. Somehow or other, we have to identify the conditions under which modern public administration can lead to one or the other.

But I think they are on the right track to do that, and the answer could be enticed from their work, though it is a tough problem. The Holocaust case is crystal clear. So, I think, is the tobacco case, the Tuskegee case, and plenty of cases of victims in the pharmaceutical area, where the companies have knowingly suppressed knowledge of disastrous side-effects that they surprisingly do not examine. All need more systematic analysis, using some of the variables they sprinkle throughout the book, and some new ones, such as regulatory failures and the complicity of elected officials outside the organization.

Then, let us dig into the more murky and difficult cases. The space shuttle offers two good examples whose differences offer more variables. In the case of the *Challenger*, we have top management pressing for a launch, middle managers obeying, and the engineers pounding the table and shouting about the dangers of a launch in unprecedentedly low temperatures, where cold is a risk factor. A risk would be taken because powerful people wanted it taken and the careers of the middle managers would suffer. It would create a lot of problems to delay the launch, and the launch was almost successful (an unprecedented windshear probably tipped the scale). NASA clearly would not have launched had they read the data on previous launches correctly. But they did not want to see the data that way. The administrative evil here is that the procedures and the authority structure suppressed unwanted analysis. The lesson: do not undertake risky ventures if you might be subject to production pressures that will distort the administrative process.

The *Columbia* accident is probably even more problematic, but examining it allows us to suggest the range of the concept's applicability. In this case—and I am writing before the report of the official investigating committee has even come out—it looks as if Diane Vaughan's concept of "normalization of deviancy" is very applicable, along with a cultural drift toward sloppy work, especially the poor supervision of extensive subcontracting. Still, I find the concept of administrative evil attractive here. Linda Ham was the official responsible for handling the investigation of the foam that hit the wing of the shuttle. A rationalized administrative system meant that you relied upon specialists' conclusions (no problem with the foam; it has happened before, said the Boeing specialist), without carefully examining the data presented. A Yale professor, Edward R. Tufte, examined the crucial slide Ms. Ham was given and told reporters it was "a PowerPoint festival of bureaucratic hyper-rationalism" (Adams and Balfour should love that quote) because it concealed more than it revealed. The real fault of upper management, he said, was that "they did not look beneath the optimistic surface of the reports of their subordinates." Administrative evil resides here because presenting only the optimistic surface did not get the Boeing engineers in trouble (and it is not clear that they even had the experience to do the analysis—an administrative failure). Moreover, Ms. Ham's readiness to accept the optimism (she cut off the engineer who attempted to express some of the reservations that did not make it to the slide), and subsequent dissembling, according to press reports, about not knowing that three groups had pressed for photographs of the foam impact area, and finally, her refusal to order the photos— all suggest that the organization had promoted someone who was not going to say, "Hey, this is a serious matter, it could result in human deaths, we had better go into this in more detail and get some more opinions. I want someone to play the devil's advocate here." (Nor did NASA demote her after these revelations.) Several knowledgeable observers within and outside of NASA characterized the shuttle project as "complacent." Given its mission, and previous charges of complacency in the *Challenger* case, it should have been well above the average organization in utilizing devil's advocates, or "red teams," in military parlance, to challenge Ham's conclusion that the foam strike was a "nonissue."

We should not be surprised at this; such personnel failures occur all the time in organizations. But the point of Adams and Balfour is just that. Administrative rationality is procedural, rather than substantive; if the procedures are correct, the substance will take care of itself. The rationality they propose, concerned with the quality of the output, the substance, rather than the steps to get to it, requires a quite different kind of organization. The last chapter provides some help on this type of organization but tends toward enumerating virtues rather than describing structures that might generate the virtues, but we are all guilty of that. It will take much more work, and more evidence from both successful and unsuccessful cases of avoiding administrative evil, to make more progress. But they have made a beginning. No other book that I am aware of in mainstream organizational theory has even noticed the problem of administrative evil. They have to draw upon works outside of my discipline, and for me, that is quite disturbing. I admire their courage as much as their analysis.

Charles B. Perrow
Yale University

# Appendix C

# Foreword to the First Edition

In 1961, for a series of articles Hannah Arendt was going to write for *The New Yorker*, she traveled to Jerusalem to attend the trial proceedings of the notorious war criminal Adolf Eichmann. As she sat in the back of the courtroom taking copious notes, she heard Eichmann, among other things, repeatedly claim that he was in many ways actually sickened by some of the mass murdering he witnessed in the concentration camps. He went on to reiterate, with almost an eerie calmness to his voice as he stood within his bulletproof glass cage, that he had nothing personal against the Jews (or anybody else for that matter), even as, in his next breath, he admitted that with meticulous care he organized the deportation of hundreds of thousands of people to their deaths. Moreover, Eichmann claimed that as much as some of the camps he visited were (at times) repugnant to him, he never let those feelings—at any time—interfere with his more important role in performing the administrative duties consistent with the goals and purposes of the Third Reich.

Ironically, Eichmann tried to invoke nothing other than Immanuel Kant's categorical imperative to justify his behavior: if he had disobeyed these administrative orders, then every soldier (from any army) would have the right, if not the obligation, to disobey any order found to be personally objectionable. It was an argument, as Arendt has pointed out, deeply ingrained in the subversion of language and the atrophy of thought itself—an instrumental perspective that found its most frightening expression in administrative language that attempted to mask the conduct of Nazi administrative operations: mass killings replaced by the new word "evacuation" or deportation by the new phrases of "resettlement" and "labor in the East." The argument also reflected Eichmann's mechanical thoughtlessness as well as his inability to exhibit any independent critical thinking. Eichmann's "banality of evil" (as Arendt called it) even today is an unsettling dimension of public affairs. Even as he was going to be hanged for his crimes against humanity, he remained captive to this thoughtlessness, thanking his beloved homeland, Austria; praising Germany as a country he tried to serve so well; and finally thanking Argentina for giving him a place to hide until he was captured by Israeli agents. He voiced how he would never forget them. No thought—even in his last words—was ever expressed to those he had played such a major role in systematically murdering.

Many aspects of Arendt's controversial argument concerning Eichmann need not concern us here. What is salient about Arendt's basic argument, particularly in the light of Guy Adams and Danny Balfour's important new book about administrative evil, is that Eichmann represented a new kind of evildoer whose evil was accomplished within and conforming to acceptable organizational roles and policies. According to their analysis, the Holocaust was (obviously) a clear instance of administrative evil, an evil unmasked. At times, administrative *evil* (a word rarely referred to in the fields of public administration and public policy) can be more subtle and opaque. At this point, they explain, administrative evil becomes masked. Herein lies, I think, Adams and Balfour's important contribution to public ethics. They anchor their argument within the broader milieu of technical rationality—a rationality that essentially has stripped reason of any normative role in shaping human affairs. Specifically, in regard to public administration and public policy, they trace how technical rationality has, to a large degree, determined the boundaries of these respective fields, starting in the Progressive Era of a century ago.

As they argue, this analytical-technical mindset does not offer enough of a bulwark against what they refer to as "moral inversion"—that is, an invitation to administrative evil that can come in the form of an expert or technical role working on what supposedly is a good and worthy project. What is particularly troubling to Adams and Balfour is that public service ethics and professional ethics are, by and large, both embedded in a technical-rational approach to public affairs. As they assert in Chapter 1, "since administrative evil wears many masks, it is entirely possible to adhere to the tenets of public service and professional ethics and participate in even a great evil and not be aware of it until it is too late (or perhaps not at all)."

Within this context, they discuss the Marshall Space Flight Center and how the von Braun team of scientists came to the United States, even though close to 20,000 individuals died at Mittelbau-Dora in less than two years. Concomitantly, they posit the serious normative implications of a defensive organizational culture that developed at the Marshall Space Flight Center and explain how, almost inevitably, it set in motion a destructive culture that, to some degree, contributed to the space shuttle *Challenger* disaster. As polemic as this argument may seem, they proceed to address some major policy programs and how they represent disturbing reminders concerning the role of public service in possessing a capacity for administrative evil. If nothing else, this part of their argument will provoke a debate, long overdue, concerning the nature and scope of administrative evil as part of public administration and public policy.

The challenge confronting us, Adams and Balfour maintain, is how we can unmask administrative evil, which will imply a fundamental rethinking of our field's fixation on technical rationality. It will mean, at a minimum, fostering a critical view of public (and private) organizations and the instrumental-technical culture in which they are embedded. Although, it is true, they offer no definitive way of overcoming administrative evil, they do indicate that by developing a historical consciousness and a "public ethics" we can at least resist the more tempting moral inversions that are often clothed in managerial and analytical approaches.

I know—given the controversial nature of this book—that many will disagree with certain aspects of the arguments posed by the authors. I suspect many will also find themselves getting somewhat defensive about the broader implications of the book's lucid analysis. Whatever the reaction, we have here a book that will compel us to look at administrative evil in a way that we can no longer ignore. Perhaps, as we try to comprehend how administrative evil can take place and construe the different and subtle forms in which it can manifest itself, we might in fact be taking the first step in increasing our ability to resist it in whatever forms, or behind whatever masks, it tries to hide itself. In the end, Adams and Balfour echo a point made by Arendt (1958, viii) that is worth pondering: "Comprehension does not mean denying the outrageous, deducing the unprecedented from precedents, or explaining phenomena by such analogies and generalities that the impact of reality and the shock of experience are no longer felt. It means, rather, examining and bearing consciously the burden which our century has placed on us—neither denying its existence nor submitting meekly to its weight. Comprehension, in short, means the unpremeditated, attentive facing up to, and resisting of, reality—whatever it may be."

Curtis Ventriss
University of Vermont

# References

Adam, U.D. (1989). "The gas chambers." In F. Furet (Ed.), *Unanswered questions: Nazi Germany and the genocide of the Jews* (134–154). New York: Schocken Books.

Adams, G.B. (1992). "Enthralled with modernity: The historical context of knowledge and theory development in public administration." *Public Administration Review,* 52: 363–373.

———. (1993). "Organizational metapatterns: Tacit relationships in organizational culture." *Administration and Society,* 25: 139–159.

Adams, G.B., and Balfour, D.L. (2008). "Expiating evil: Reflections on the difficulties of cultural, organizational and individual reparation." *Public Administration,* 86 (4): 881–893.

———. (2009). "Ethical failings, incompetence and administrative evil: Lessons from Katrina and Iraq." In R. Cox (Ed.), *Ethics and integrity in public administration* (40–64). Armonk, NY: M.E. Sharpe.

———. (2010). "Market-based government and the decline of organizational ethics." *Administration and Society,* 42 (6): 615–637.

———. (2012). "Toward restoring integrity in 'Praetorian Times': The value of 'putting cruelty first.'" *Public Integrity,* 14 (4): 325–339.

———. (2014). "Towards a political economy of regime values, ethics, and institutions in a context of globalization and hypermodernity." *Administration and Society,* 46 (2): 131–140.

Adams, G.B., Balfour, D.L., and Reed, G.E. (2006). "Abu Ghraib, administrative evil, and moral inversion: The value of 'putting cruelty first'." *Public Administration Review,* 66 (5): 680–693.

Adams, G.B., Bowerman, P.V., Dolbeare, K.M., and Stivers, C. (1990). "Joining purpose to practice: A democratic identity for the public service." In H.D. Kass and B.L. Catron (Eds.), *Images and identities in public administration* (219–240). Newbury Park, CA: Sage.

Adams, G.B., and Ingersoll, V.H. (1990). "Culture, technical rationality and organizational culture." *American Review of Public Administration,* 20: 285–302.

Adams, M.M., and Merrihew, R. (Eds.) (1990). *The problem of evil.* New York: Oxford University Press.

Alford, F.C. (1990). "The organization of evil." *Political Psychology,* 11: 5–27.
———. (2001). *Whistleblowers: Broken lives and organizational power.* Ithaca, NY: Cornell University Press.
Allcorn, S., and Diamond, M.A. (1997). *Managing people during stressful times: The psychologically defensive workplace.* Westport, CT: Quorum Books.
Allen, M.T. (2002). *The business of genocide: The SS, slave labor, and the concentration camps.* Chapel Hill: University of North Carolina Press.
Allison, G.T. (1971). *The essence of decision: Explaining the Cuban Missile Crisis.* Glenview, IL: Scott Foresman.
Aly, G. (1999). *"Final Solution": Nazi population policy and the murder of the European Jews.* New York: Arnold.
American Civil Liberties Union (ACLU). 2004. CIA Copy of CNN Article: Details of Army's Abuse Investigation Surface. Available at https://www.thetorturedatabase.org/document/cia-copy-cnn-article-details-armys-abuse investigation-surface? (accessed April 6, 2014).
Anna, H.J. (1976). *Task groups and linkages in complex organizations: A case study of NASA.* Beverly Hills, CA: Sage.
Archibold, R.C. (2007). "At the U.S. border, the desert takes a rising toll." *New York Times,* September 15. Available at www.nytimes.com/2007/09/15/us/15border. html.
Archibold, R.C., and Becker, A. (2008). "Border agents lured by the other side." *New York Times,* May 27. Available at www.nytimes.com/2008/05/27/us/27border. html?_r=1&oref=slogin.
Arendt, H. (1954). *Between past and future.* Cleveland: World Publishing.
———. (1958). *The human condition.* Chicago: University of Chicago Press.
———. (1963). *Eichmann in Jerusalem: A report on the banality of evil.* New York: Viking Press.
Baily, M., Litan, R. and Johnson, M.S. (2008). *The origins of the financial crisis.* Washington, DC: Brookings Institution Press.
Baker, D. (2009). *Plunder and blunder: The rise and fall of the bubble economy.* Washington, DC: Polipoint Press.
Balfour, D.L. (1996). "Historiography of the Holocaust: A cautionary tale for public administration." *American Review of Public Administration,* 27 (2): 133–144.
Bandura, A., Underwood, B., and Fromsen, M.E. (1975). "Disinhibition of aggression through diffusion of responsibility and dehumanization of victims." *Journal of Research in Personality,* 9: 253–269.
Barley, S.R. (2007). "Corporations, democracy, and the public good." *Journal of Management Inquiry,* 16: 201–215.
Barrett, W. (1979). *The illusion of technique.* Garden City, NY: Anchor Doubleday.
Bauman, Z. (1989). *Modernity and the Holocaust.* Ithaca, NY: Cornell University Press.
Baumeister, R.F. (1997). *Evil: Inside human cruelty and violence.* New York: W.H. Freeman.
Bazemore, G., and Schiff, M. (2001). *Restorative community justice: Repairing harm and transforming communities.* Cincinnati, OH: Anderson.
Bellah, R.N. (1971). "Evil and the American ethos." In S. Nevitt and C. Comstock (Eds.), *Sanctions for evil* (177–191). San Francisco: Jossey-Bass.
Bellush, J., and Hausknecht, M. (Eds.) (1967). *Urban renewal: People, politics and planning.* Garden City, NY: Doubleday Anchor.

Bendix, R. (1956). *Work and authority in industry*. New York: Harper and Row.

Bentham, J. (1989, orig. 1789). *Vice and virtue in everyday life*. New York: Harcourt Brace Jovanovich.

Beon, Y. (1997). *Planet Dora: A memoir of the holocaust and the birth of the space age*. Boulder, CO: Westview Press.

Berenbaum, M. (1993). *The world must know*. Boston: Little, Brown.

Berger, P.L., and Luckmann, T. (1967). *The social construction of reality*. Garden City, NY: Doubleday.

Berlin, I. (1991). *The crooked timber of humanity*. New York: Alfred A. Knopf.

Bernstein, R.J. (Ed.). (1985). *Habermas and modernity*. Cambridge, MA: MIT Press.

———. (2002). *Radical evil: A philosophical investigation*. Cambridge, England: Polity Press.

———. (2005). *The abuse of evil: The corruption of politics and religion since 9/11*. Cambridge, England: Polity Press.

Bersani, I. (1990). *The culture of redemption*. Cambridge, MA: Harvard University Press.

Bilstein, R.E. (1980). *Stages to Saturn: A technological history of the Apollo/Saturn launch vehicles*. Washington, DC: National Aeronautics and Space Administration.

Blanco, H. (1994). *How to think about social problems*. Westport, CT: Greenwood Press.

Blank, R.M., and Kovak, B. (2008). *Helping disconnected single mothers*. Washington, DC: Brookings Institution Press.

Bloomfield, D., Barnes, T., and Huyse, L. (Eds.). (2003). *Reconciliation after violent conflict: A handbook*. Stockholm: International IDEA.

Bloxham, D. (2009). *The final solution: A genocide*. New York: Oxford University Press.

Bobbitt, P. (2002). *The shield of Achilles: War, peace, and the course of history*. New York: Knopf.

Boisjoly, R. (1997). Personal telephone conversation with author. July 17.

Bok, S. (1978). *Lying: Moral choice in public and private life*. New York: Vintage Books.

Borenstein, S. (2008). "Analysis: Is the right stuff now lost in space?" *Washington Post,* September 29: B-1.

Borjas, G.J. (1996). "The new economics of immigration." *Atlantic Monthly,* 278 (5): 72–80.

Bowden, M. (2003). "The dark art of interrogation." *Atlantic Monthly,* October: 1–22.

Bower, T. (1987). *The Paperclip conspiracy*. London: Michael Joseph.

Brecht, A. (1944). *Prelude to silence*. New York: Oxford University Press.

Broszat, M. (1981). *The Hitler state: The foundation and development of the internal structure of the Third Reich*. London: Longman.

Browne, M.N., Kubasek, N.K., and Giampetro-Meyer, A. (1995). "The seductive danger of craft ethics for business organizations." *Review of Business,* 17 (Winter): 23–29.

Browning, C. (1983). "The German bureaucracy and the Holocaust." In A. Grobman and D. Landes (Eds.), *Genocide: Critical issues of the Holocaust*. Los Angeles: Simon Wiesenthal Center.

———. (1989). "The decision concerning the final solution." In F. Furet (Ed.), *Unanswered questions: Nazi Germany and the genocide of the Jews* (96–118). New York: Schocken Books.

————. (1992). *The path to genocide.* Cambridge: Cambridge University Press.

Burleigh, M. (2000). *The Third Reich: A new history.* New York: Hill and Wang.

Bybee, J.S. (2002). *Memorandum for Alberto R. Gonzales, Counsel to the President. Re: Standards of conduct for interrogation under 18USC2340–2340A.* Washington, DC: Department of Justice, Office of Legal Counsel.

Callahan, D. (2004). *The cheating culture: Why more Americans are doing wrong to get ahead.* Orlando, FL: Harvest Books.

Card, C. (1998). "Stoicism, evil and the possibility of morality." *Metaphilosophy,* 29 (October): 245–253.

————. (2002). *The atrocity paradigm: A theory of evil.* New York: Oxford University Press.

Center for Public Integrity. (2004). *The Taguba report.* Available at www.publicintegrity.org/report.aspz?aid=396&syd=100/.

Cesarani, D. (2006). *Becoming Eichmann: Rethinking the life, times, and trial of a "desk murderer."* Cambridge, MA: Da Capo Press.

Chapman, R.L. (1973). *Project management at NASA: The system and the men.* Washington, DC: National Aeronautics and Space Administration.

Chaskin, R.J., Brown, P., Venkatesh, S., and Vidal, A. (2001). *Building community capacity.* New York: Aldine.

Chen, C.A. (2009). "Antecedents of contracting-back-in: A view beyond the economic paradigm." *Administration and Society,* 41: 101–126.

Christensen, K.S. (1985). "Coping with uncertainty in planning." *Journal of the American Planning Association,* 51: 63–73.

Christie, D.J., Wagner, R.V., and Winter, D. (2000). *Peace, conflict and violence.* New York: Pearson Education.

Clarke, S., and Simpson, E. (1989). *Anti-theory in ethics and moral conservatism.* Albany: State University of New York Press.

Cole, P. (2006). *The myth of evil.* Edinburgh: University of Edinburgh Press.

Columbia Accident Investigation Board. (2003). Report. Washington, DC: US Government Printing Office.

Committee on Government Reform, Minority Staff. (2006). *Dollars, not sense: Government contracting under the Bush Administration.* Available at http://oversight-archive.waxman.house.gov/story.asp?ID=1071.

Committee on Science and Technology. (1986). *Investigation of the Challenger accident: Hearings before the Committee on Science and Technology.* Washington, DC: U.S. House of Representatives. 2 vols.

Cook, M.L. (2004). *The moral warrior: Ethics and service in the U.S. military.* Albany: State University of New York Press.

Cook, R. (1986). "The Rogers Commission failed: Questions it never asked, answers it didn't listen to." *Washington Monthly* (November): 13–21.

Cooper, P.J. (2003). *Governing by contract: Challenges and opportunities for public managers.* Washington, DC: CQ Press.

Cose, E. (2004). *Bone to pick: Of forgiveness, reconciliation, reparation and revenge.* New York: Atria Books.

Countryman, E. (1985). *The American revolution.* New York: Hill and Wang.

Covault, C. (2003). "Foam jars t-seal: Initial impact test that a foam strike can dislodge the critical seal between RCC panels." *Aviation Week and Space Technology,* June 2: 3–5.

Danieli, Y. (2006). "Essential elements of healing after massive trauma: Complex needs voiced by victims/survivors." In D. Sullivan and L. Tifft (Eds.), *Handbook of restorative justice* (343–354). London: Routledge.

Daniels, R., Taylor, S.C., and Kitano, H.H.L. (1986). *Japanese Americans: From relocation to redress*. Salt Lake City: University of Utah Press.

Darley, J.M. (1992). "Social organization for the production of evil." *Psychological Inquiry*, 3: 199–218.

———. (1995). "Constructive and destructive obedience: A taxonomy of principal-agent relationships." *Journal of Social Issues*, 51 (3): 125–154.

———. (1996). "How organizations socialize individuals into evildoing." In D.M. Messick and A.E. Tenbrunsel (Eds.), *Codes of conduct: Behavioral research into business ethics*. New York: Russell Sage Foundation.

Davis, G., Messner, H., Umbreid, M., and Coates, R. (1992). *Making amends: Mediation and reparation in criminal justice*. New York: Taylor and Francis.

Davis, M. (2005). "The moral justifiability of torture and other cruel, inhuman or degrading treatment." *International Journal of Applied Philosophy*, 19: 161–178.

Dawidowicz, L. (1975). *The war against the Jews, 1933–1945*. New York: Holt, Rinehart and Winston.

Delbanco, A. (1995). *The death of Satan: How Americans have lost the sense of evil*. New York: Farrar, Strauss and Giroux.

Delbecq, A.L. (2001). "'Evil' manifested in destructive individual behavior: A senior leadership challenge." *Journal of Management Inquiry*, 10 (September): 221–226.

Delbecq, A.L., and Filley, A. (1974). *Program and project management in a matrix organization: A case study*. Madison: Bureau of Business Research and Service, University of Wisconsin–Madison.

deLeon, P. (1997). *Democracy and the policy sciences*. Albany: State University of New York Press.

Denhardt, R.B. (1981). *In the shadow of organization*. Lawrence: Regents Press of Kansas.

Derrida, J. (2001). *On cosmopolitanism and forgiveness*. London: Routledge.

Dews, P. (2008). *The idea of evil*. Oxford, England: Blackwell.

Diamond, M.A. (1988). "Organizational identity: A psychoanalytic exploration of organizational meaning." *Administration and Society*, 20: 166–190.

———. (1993). *The unconscious life of organizations: Interpreting organizational identity*. Westport, CT: Quorum Books.

Digeser, P.E. (2001). *Political forgiveness*. Ithaca, NY: Cornell University Press.

Dinnen, S., Jowett, A., and Cain, T.N. (2003). *A kind of mending: Restorative justice in the Pacific Islands*. Canberra: Pandanus Books.

Douglas, H. (2003). "Redeeming the wages of sin: The workings of reparation." *Perspectives on Evil and Human Wickedness*, 1 (3) (July): 47–58: www.wickedness.net.

Dryzek, J. (1990). *Discursive democracy: Politics, policy and political science*. Cambridge: Cambridge University Press.

———. (2000). *Deliberative democracy and beyond*. Oxford, England: Oxford University Press.

———. (2012). Foundations and frontiers of deliberative governance. New York: Oxford University Press.

Dryzek, J., and Torgerson, D. (1993). "Democracy and the policy sciences: A progress report." *Policy Sciences*, 26: 127–137.

Dwork, D., and Van Pelt, J.R. (1996). *Auschwitz: 1270 to the present*. New York: W.W. Norton.

*Economist.* (2008). "Good neighbors make fences." October 4, 25–27.

Edelman, M.J. (1977). *Political language: Words that succeed and policies that fail.* New York: Academic Press.

Ehle, J. (1988). *The trail of tears*. New York: Anchor Books.

Eisenhower, M. (1974). *The president is calling*. Garden City, NY: Doubleday.

Eliot, G. (1972). *The twentieth century book of the dead*. New York: Scribner.

Ellul, J. (1954). *The technological society*. New York: Vintage Books.

Enright, R.D., and North, J. (Eds.). (1998). *Exploring forgiveness*. Madison: University of Wisconsin Press.

Farazamand, A. (1999). "Globalization and public administration." *Public Administration Review,* 59: 509–522.

Farber, D.A. (1994). "The outmoded debate over affirmative action." *California Law Review,* 82: 893–934.

Feeney, M. (2008). "Public wars and private armies: Militaries, mercenaries, and public values." Unpublished paper presented at the Copenhagen International Public Values Workshop.

Fischer, F. (2000). *Citizens, experts and the environment: The politics of local knowledge.* Durham, NC: Duke University Press.

Fishkin, J.S. (1991). *Democracy and deliberation*. New Haven, CT: Yale University Press.

FitzGibbon, C. (1969). *Denazification*. London: Michael Joseph.

Forester, J. (1999). *The deliberative practitioner: Encouraging participatory planning processes.* Cambridge, MA: MIT Press.

Formosa, P. (2006). "Moral responsibility for banal evil." *Journal of Social Philosophy,* 37: 501–520.

———. (2008). "A conception of evil." *Journal of Value Inquiry,* 42: 217–239.

Frankena, W. (1973). *Ethics* (2d ed.). Englewood Cliffs, NJ: Prentice Hall.

Friedlander, S.J. (1997). *Nazi Germany and the Jews*, vol. I: *The years of persecution.* New York: HarperCollins.

———. (2007). *Nazi Germany and the Jews*, vol. II: *The years of extermination.* New York: HarperCollins.

Friedman, T. (1999). *The Lexus and the olive tree*. New York: Farrar, Straus and Giroux.

Fukuyama, F. (1992). *The end of history and the last man*. New York: Free Press.

Fritz, M. (1999). *Lost on earth: Nomads of the new world*. Boston: Little, Brown.

Funk, D. (2005). "No proof found that medics took part in abuse, torture." *Army Times,* February 10.

Furner, M.O. (1975). *Advocacy and objectivity: A crisis in the professionalization of social science.* Lexington: University of Kentucky Press.

Garlinski, J. (1978). *Hitler's last weapons: The underground war against the V1 and V2.* New York: Times Books.

Garrard, E. (1998). "The nature of evil." *Philosophical Investigations,* 1 (January): 43–60.

———. (2002). "Evil as an explanatory concept." *Monist,* 85 (April): 320–337.

Gastil, J., and Levine, P. (Eds.). (2005). *The deliberative democracy handbook: Strategies for effective civic engagement.* San Francisco: Jossey-Bass.

Geddes, J.L. (2003). "Banal evil and useless knowledge: Hannah Arendt and Charlotte Delbo on evil after the Holocaust." *Hypatia*, 18: 104–115.

Gellately, R. (2001). *Backing Hitler: Consent and coercion in Nazi Germany*. New York: Oxford University Press.

Gibson, J.L. (2004). *Overcoming apartheid: Can truth reconcile a divided nation?* New York: Russell Sage Foundation.

Gilmore, G.J. (2004). "Abuse resulted from leadership failure, Taguba tells Senators." *American Forces Press Service*, May 11.

Gimbel, J. (1986). "U.S. policy and German scientists: The early Cold War." *Political Science Quarterly*, 101: 433–451.

———. (1990). "German scientists, United States denazification policy and the 'Paperclip Conspiracy.'" *International History Review*, 12: 441–485.

Glass, J.M. (1997). *Life unworthy of life: Racial phobia and mass murder in Hitler's Germany*. New York: Basic Books.

Glover, J. (1999). *Humanity: A moral history of the twentieth century*. New Haven, CT: Yale University Press.

Goldhagen, D.J. (1996). *Hitler's willing executioners: Ordinary Germans and the Holocaust*. New York: Alfred A. Knopf.

Graebner, W. (1987). *The engineering of consent: Democracy and authority in twentieth century America*. Madison: University of Wisconsin Press.

Graham, J.F. (1995). *History of Apollo and Saturn*. Washington, DC: National Aeronautics and Space Administration.

Greenberg, J., and Mitchell, S. (1983). *Object relations in psychoanalytic theory*. Cambridge, MA: Harvard Uitversity Press.

Grodzins, M. (1949). *Americans betrayed: Politics and the Japanese evacuation*. Chicago: University of Chicago Press.

Guerreiro-Ramos, A. (1981). *The new science of organization*. Toronto: University of Toronto Press.

Guterson, D. (1995). *Snow falling on cedars*. New York: Vintage Books.

Gutmann, A., and Thompson, D.F. (1996). *Democracy and disagreement*. Cambridge, MA: Harvard University Press.

Haber, S. (1964). *Efficiency and uplift: Scientific management in the Progressive Era, 1890–1920*. Chicago: University of Chicago Press.

Hacker, S.J., and Pierson, P. (2011). *Winner take all politics: How Washington made the richer richer—and turned its back on the middle class*. New York: Simon and Schuster.

Hajer, M., and Wagenaar, H. (2003). *Deliberative policy analysis: Understanding governance in the network society*. Cambridge: Cambridge University Press.

Hallie, P. (1969). *Cruelty*. Middletown, CT: Wesleyan University Press.

———. (1997). *Tales of good and evil, help and harm*. New York: HarperCollins.

Hamber, B., and Wilson, R. (2002). "Symbolic closure through memory, reparation, and revenge in post-conflict societies." *Journal of Human Rights*, 1 (1) (March): 42–66.

Hammer, E. (2000). "Adorno and extreme evil." *Philosophy and Social Criticism*, 26 (4): 75–93.

Haney, C., Banks, C., and Zimbardo, P. (1974). "Interpersonal dynamics in a simulated prison." *International Journal of Criminology and Penology*, 1: 69–97.

Harmon, M.M. (1995). *Responsibility as paradox: A critique of rational discourse on government*. Thousand Oaks, CA: Sage.

Haskell, T.L. (1977). *The emergence of professional social science.* Urbana: University of Illinois Press.

Haybron, D. (2002). *Earth's abominations: Philosophical studies of evil.* New York: Rodopi.

Hayes, P. (1989). *IG Farben in the Nazi era.* New York: Cambridge University Press.

————. (2004). *From cooperation to complicity: Degussa in the Third Reich.* New York: Cambridge University Press.

Haynor, P.B. (2001). *Unspeakable truths: Facing the challenges of truth commissions.* London: Routledge.

Heclo, H. (2008). *On thinking institutionally.* Boulder, CO: Paradigm Press.

Hegel, G.W.F. (1965, original 1807). "Preface to the phenomenology of mind." In W. Kaufman (Ed.), *Hegel: Texts and commentary.* Notre Dame, IN: Notre Dame University Press.

Heidegger, M. (1977, original 1926). *Basic writings.* New York: Harper and Row.

Herrnstein, R., and Murray, C. (1994). *The bell curve.* New York: Free Press.

Hilberg, R. (1989). "The bureaucracy of annihilation." In F. Furet (Ed.), *Unanswered questions: Nazi Germany and the genocide of the Jews* (119–133). New York: Schocken Books.

————. (2003). *The destruction of the European Jews* (3d ed.). New York: Holmes and Meier.

Hills, S.L. (1987). *Corporate violence.* Totowa, NJ: Rowman and Littlefield.

Hirsch, H. (1995). *Genocide and the politics of memory.* Chapel Hill: University of North Carolina Press.

Hirschman, A. (1970). *Exit, voice and loyalty.* Cambridge, MA: Harvard University Press.

Holtzman, K. (2003). "Renewing our minds: Political forgiveness and leadership in the former Yugoslavia." Unpublished paper.

Horkheimer, M. (1947). *The eclipse of reason.* New York: Oxford University Press.

Houston, J.W., and Houston, J. (1966). *Farewell to Manzanar.* New York: Bantam.

Human Rights Watch. (2004). *The road to Abu Ghraib.* Available at http://hrw.org/reports/2004/usa0604/.

Hunt, L. (1991). *Secret agenda: The United States government, Nazi scientists, and project Paperclip.* New York: St. Martin's Press.

Hunter, D.H. (1991). *Culture wars: The struggle to define America.* New York: Basic Books.

Huntington, S.P. (1996). *The clash of civilizations and the remaking of the world order.* New York: Simon and Schuster.

Hurt, R.D., and Robertson, C.R. (1998). "Prying open the door to the tobacco industry's secrets about nicotine." *Journal of the American Medical Association,* 280 (October): 1173–1205.

Huxley, A. (1952). *The devils of Loudon.* New York: Harper and Row.

Ingersoll, V.H., and Adams, G.B. (1992). *The tacit organization.* Greenwich, CT: JAI Press.

Intelligence Science Board (ISB). (2006). *Educing information: Interrogation science and art.* Washington, DC: National Defense Intelligence College.

Ishiguro, K. (1988). *The remains of the day.* New York: Alfred A. Knopf.

Janis, I. (1982). *Groupthink.* Boston, MA: Houghton Mifflin.

Jencks, C. (1992). *Rethinking social policy: Race, poverty and the underclass.* Cambridge, MA: Harvard University Press.

Johnson, E.A. (1999). *Nazi terror: The Gestapo, Jews, and ordinary Germans*. New York: Basic Books.

Johnson, S. (2009). "The quiet coup." *Atlantic Online*, April 3, 2009.

Juergensmeyer, M. (2000). *Terror in the mind of God: The global rise of religious violence*. Berkeley: University of California Press.

Kahn, P.W. (2007). *Out of Eden: Adam and Eve and the problem of evil*. Princeton, NJ: Princeton University Press.

Kant, I. (1959, original 1786). *Metaphysical foundations of morals*. Indianapolis: Bobbs-Merrill.

Kaplan, M. (1998). *Between dignity and despair: Jewish life in Nazi Germany*. Oxford, England: Oxford University Press.

Karen, R. (2001). *The forgiving self*. New York: Doubleday.

Kateb, G. (1983). *Hannah Arendt, politics, conscience, evil*. Totowa, NJ: Rowman and Allanheld.

Katz, F.E. (1993). *Ordinary people and extraordinary evil: A report on the beguilings of evil*. Albany: State University of New York Press.

Katz, J. (1988). *Seductions of crime: Moral and sensual attractions in doing evil*. New York: Basic Books.

Katz, M.B. (1989). *The undeserving poor: From the war on poverty to the war on welfare*. New York: Pantheon Books.

Kearney, R.C., and Sinha, C. (1988). "Professionalism and bureaucratic responsiveness: Conflict or compatibility." *Public Administration Review*, 48: 571–579.

Keeley, M. (1983). "Values in organizational theory and management education." *Academy of Management Review*, 8 (3): 376–386.

Kekes, J. (1990). *Facing evil*. Princeton, NJ: Princeton University Press.

———. (2005). *The roots of evil*. Ithaca, NY: Cornell University Press.

Keller, D.F. (1985). *Reflections on gender and science*. New Haven, CT: Yale University Press.

Kennedy, D.M. (1996). "Can we still afford to be a nation of immigrants?" *Atlantic Monthly*, 278 (5): 52–68.

Kennedy, G.P. (1983). *Vengeance weapon 2*. Washington DC: Smithsonian Institution Press.

Kettl, D.F. (2004). *System under stress: Homeland security and American politics*. Washington, DC: CQ Press.

Kitigawa, D. (1967). *Issei and Nisei: The internment years*. New York: Simon and Schuster.

Klee, E., and Merk, O. (1965). *The birth of the missile: The secrets of Peenemünde*. New York: Dutton.

Klee, E., Dressen, W., and Hess, V. (1988). *The good old days: The Holocaust as seen by its perpetrators and bystanders*. New York: Free Press.

Klein, M. (1964). *Love, hate and reparation*. New York: Free Press.

Klein, N. (2007). *The shock doctrine: The rise of disaster capitalism*. New York: Henry Holt.

Kneebone, E., and Berube, A. (2008). *Reversal of fortune: A new look at concentrated poverty in the 2000s*. Washington, DC: Brookings Institution. http://www.brookings.edu/papers/2008/08_concentrated_poverty_kneebone.aspx.

Kohn, R.D. (1922). "The significance of the professional ideal: Professional ethics and the public interest." *Annals of the American Academy of Political and Social Science*, 101: 1–4.

Kultgen, J. (1988). *Ethics and professionalism.* Philadelphia: University of Pennsylvania Press.

Lang, B. (1991). "The history of evil and the future of the Holocaust." In Hayes, P. (Ed.), *Lessons and legacies: The meaning of the Holocaust in a changing world* (90–105). Evanston, IL: Northwestern University Press.

Langer, L. (1991). *Holocaust testimonies: The ruins of memory.* New Haven, CT: Yale University Press.

Larson, M.L. (1977). *The rise of professionalism.* Berkeley: University of California Press.

Lasby, C.G. (1971). *Project Paperclip: German scientists and the Cold War.* New York: Atheneum.

Lawler, J. (2012). "The new welfare: Fast, cheap, out of control." *Atlantic Online,* May 25, 2012.

Leighninger, M. (2006). *The next form of democracy: How expert rule is giving way to shared governance—and why politics will never be the same.* Nashville, TN: Vanderbilt University Press.

Leighton, A. (1945). *The governing of men: General principles and recommendations based on experience at a Japanese relocation camp.* Princeton, NJ: Princeton University Press.

Levinas, E. (1998). *Otherwise than being, or, beyond essence.* Pittsburgh: Duquesne University Press.

Levine, A.S. (1982). *Managing NASA in the Apollo era.* Washington, DC: National Aeronautics and Space Administration.

Levinson, S. (Ed.). (2004). *Torture: A collection.* New York: Oxford University Press.

Levy, M.B. (1982). *Political thought in America: An anthology.* Homewood, IL: Dorsey Press.

Lewis, A. (2002). "Fear, terrorism and the Constitution." *Public Administration Review,* 62 (September special issue): 61–67.

Lifton, R.J. (1986). *The Nazi doctors: Medical killing and the psychology of genocide.* New York: Basic Books.

———. (1999). *Destroying the world to save it: Aum Shinrikyo, apocalyptic violence and the new global terrorism.* New York: Henry Holt.

———. (2004). "Doctors and torture." *New England Journal of Medicine,* 351: 415–416.

Lindbergh, C.A. (1978). *Autobiography of values.* New York: Harcourt Brace Jovanovich.

Lippman, M. (1995). "War crimes: American prosecution of Nazi military officers." *Touro International Law Review,* 6: 243–276.

Lower, W. (2013). *Hitler's furies: German women in the Nazi killing fields.* New York: Houghton Mifflin Harcourt.

Lowi, T.J. (1993). "Legitimizing public administration: A disturbed dissent." *Public Administration Review,* 53: 261–264.

———. (1995). *The end of the republican era.* Norman: University of Oklahoma Press.

Lozowick, Y. (2000). *Hitler's bureaucrats: The Nazi security police and the banality of evil.* New York: Continuum.

Lynn, L.E., Jr. (1996). *Public management as art, science, and profession.* Chatham, NJ: Chatham House.

Machiavelli, N. (1961, orig. c.1520). *The prince*. London: Penguin.

Macidull, J.G., and Blattner, L.E. (2002). *Challenger's shadow: Did government and industry management kill seven astronauts?* Coral Springs, FL: Lumina Press.

MacIntyre, A. (1984). *After virtue* (2d ed.). Notre Dame, IN: Notre Dame University Press.

Macpherson, C.B. (1977). *The life and times of liberal democracy*. New York: Oxford University Press.

Mann, M. (2000). "Were the perpetrators of genocide 'ordinary men' or 'real Nazis'? Results from fifteen hundred biographies." *Holocaust and Genocide Studies*, 14: 331–366.

Mannheim, K. (1940). *Man and society in an age of reconstruction*. New York: Harcourt Brace and World.

Marie, L. (2012). *Social death: Racialized rightlessness and the criminalization of the unprotected*. New York: New York University Press.

Marris, P. (1974). *Loss and change*. London: Routledge.

Mason, T. (1981). "Intention and explanation: A current controversy about the interpretation of National Socialism." In A. Hirschfeld and L. Kettenacker (Eds.), *Der Fuhrerstaat: Mythos und realitat* (21–40). Stuttgart: Klett-Cotta.

Mathewes, C.T. (2000). "A tale of two judgments: Bonhoeffer and Arendt on evil, understanding, and the limits of understanding evil." *Journal of Religion*, 80 (3): 375–423.

Matthaus, J. (2004). "Historiography and the perpetrators of the Holocaust." In D. Stone (Ed.), *Historiography of the Holocaust*, 197–215. New York: Palgrave.

Mayer, J. (2005). "Outsourcing terror." *New Yorker,* February 14: 1–14.

———. (2008). *The dark side: The inside story of how the war on terror turned into a war on American ideals*. New York: Doubleday.

Mayerfeld, J. (2008). "In defense of the absolute prohibition of torture." *Public Affairs Quarterly,* 22: 109–128.

McConnell, M. (1987). *Challenger: A major malfunction*. New York: Doubleday.

McCurdy, H.E. (1993). *Inside NASA: High technology and organizational change in the U.S. space program*. Baltimore: Johns Hopkins University Press.

McElheran, B. (1995). *V-bombs and weathermaps: Reminiscences of World War II*. Montreal and Buffalo: McGill-Queen's University Press.

McGinn, Colin. (1997). *Ethics, evil and fiction*. Oxford, England: Clarendon Press.

McGovern, J. (1964). *Crossbow and overcast*. New York: Morrow.

McLean, B., and Nocera, J. (2010). *All the devils are here: The hidden story of the financial crisis*. New York: Penguin.

Meier, M. (1992). *A major malfunction: The story behind the space shuttle Challenger disaster*. Binghamton, NY: SUNY Research Foundation.

Merkle, J.A. (1980). *Management and ideology*. Berkeley: University of California Press.

Michel, J. (1979). *Dora*. London: Weidonheld and Nicolson.

Milgram, S. (1974). *Obedience to authority*. New York: Harper and Row.

Miller, A.G., Gordon, A.K., and Buddie, A.M. (1999). "Accounting for evil and cruelty: Is to explain to condone?" *Personality and Social Psychology Review,* 3: 923–937.

Minow, M. (1998). *Between vengeance and forgiveness: Facing history after genocide and mass violence*. Boston, MA: Beacon Press.

Mintz, M. (1985). *At any cost: Corporate greed, women and the Dalkon Shield.* New York: Pantheon.

Morton, A. (2004). *On evil.* New York: Routledge.

Moskovitz, S., and Krell, R. (2001). "The struggle for justice: Survey of child survivors' experiences with restitution." In J.K. Roth and E. Maxwell (Eds.), *Remembering for the future: The Holocaust in an age of genocide,* vol. 2 (923–937). New York: Palgrave.

Murray, C. (1984). *Losing ground.* New York: Basic Books.

Myer, D.S. (1971). *Uprooted Americans.* Tucson: University of Arizona Press.

Mynatt, C., and Sherman, S.J. (1975). "Responsibility attribution in groups and individuals: A direct test of the diffusion of responsibility hypothesis." *Journal of Personality and Social Psychology,* 32: 1111–1118.

Nabatchi, T. (2010). "Addressing the citizenship and democratic deficits: The potential of deliberative democracy for public administration." *American Review of Public Administration,* 40 (4): 376–399.

Neal, A.G. (1998). *National trauma and collective memory: Major events in the American century.* Armonk, NY: M.E. Sharpe.

Neiman, S. (2002). *Evil in modern thought: An alternative history of philosophy.* Princeton, NJ: Princeton University Press.

Neufeld, M.J. (1996). *The rocket and the Reich.* Cambridge, MA: Harvard University Press.

Neumann, F. (1944). *Behemoth.* New York: Oxford University Press.

Nevitt, S., and Comstock, C. (Eds.). (1971). *Sanctions for evil.* San Francisco: Jossey Bass.

Nicholson, I. (2011). "Torture at Yale: Experimental subjects, laboratory torment and the rehabilitation of Milgram's "Obedience to Authority." *Theory & Psychology,* 21: 737–761.

Niebuhr, R. (1986). *The essential Reinhold Niebuhr: Selected essays and addresses.* Robert McAfee Brown, ed. New Haven, CT: Yale University Press.

Nietzsche, F. (1956, orig. 1872). *The birth of tragedy and genealogy of morals.* F. Golffing, trans. Garden City, NY: Anchor Doubleday.

Noakes, J. and Pridham, G. (1984). *Nazism: A history in documents and eyewitness accounts, 1919–1945.* New York: Schocken Books.

Norden, M.F. (2006). "Introduction: The changing face of evil in film and television." *Journal of Popular Film and Television,* 28 (Summer): 50–60.

O'Leary, R. (2014). *The ethics of dissent: Managing guerilla government* (2d ed.). Washington, DC: CQ Press.

OMB Watch. (2008). "Top 100 Recipients of Federal Contract Awards for FY 2008." Available at http://www.fedspending.org/fpds/tables.php?tabtype=t2&subtype=t &year=2008 (accessed April 6, 2014).

Orwell, G. (1984, orig. 1950). *Shooting an elephant and other essays.* San Diego: Harcourt Brace Jovanovich.

Osiel, M.J. (2001). *Mass atrocity, ordinary evil, and Hannah Arendt.* New Haven, CT: Yale University Press.

O'Toole, L.J., and Meier, K. (2004). "Parkinson's law and the new public management? Contracting determinants and service quality considerations in public education." *Public Administration Review,* 64: 342–353.

Parkin, D. (Ed.). (1985). *The anthropology of evil.* London: Blackwell.

Parkinson, J. (2006). *Deliberating in the real world: Problems of legitimacy in deliberative democracy.* New York: Oxford University Press.

Perlmutter, A. (1969). "The praetorian state and the praetorian army: Toward a taxonomy of civil-military relations in developing politics." *Comparative Politics*, 1: 382–404.

Perrett, R.W. (2002). "Evil and human nature." *Monist*, 85 (April): 304–319.

Perrow, C. (1999/1984). *Normal accidents: Living with high-risk technologies*. New York: Basic Books.

Perry, J. (2002). *Repairing communities through restorative justice*. Lanham, MD: American Correctional Association.

Peterson, L. (2003). Outsourcing government: Service contracting has risen dramatically in the last decade. Center for Public Integrity. Available at http://www.publicintegrity.org/2003/10/30/5634/outsourcing-government (accessed April 6, 2014).

Petrik, J. (2000). *Evil beyond belief*. Armonk, NY: M.E. Sharpe.

Pfiffner, J.P. (2009). *Torture as public policy*. Boulder, CO: Paradigm Press.

Physicians for Human Rights. (2008). *Broken laws, broken lives: Medical evidence of torture by U.S. personnel and its impact*. Cambridge, MA.

Piszkiewicz, D. (1995). *The Nazi rocketeers: Dreams of space and crimes of war*. Westport, CT: Praeger.

Polanyi, M. (1966). *The tacit dimension*. Garden City, NY: Doubleday Anchor.

Poole, R. (1991). *Morality and modernity*. London: Routledge, Chapman and Hall.

Power, S. (2002). *"A problem from hell": America and the age of genocide*. New York: Basic Books.

Prunier, G. (1995). *The Rwanda crisis: History of a genocide*. New York: Columbia University Press.

Rabinbach, A. (1990). *The human motor: Energy, fatigue and the origins of modernity*. New York: Basic Books.

Rapoport, A.C. (1960). "Praetorianism: Government with consensus." Ph.D. diss., University of California, Berkeley.

Reich, R. (2007). *Supercapitalism: The transformation of business, democracy, and everyday life*. New York: Knopf.

Reicher, S.D, Haslam, S.A., and Smith, J.R. (2012). "Working toward the experimenter: Reconceptualizing obedience with the Milgram paradigm as identification-based followership." *Perspectives on Psychological Science*, 7: 315–324.

Rejali, D. (2007). *Torture and democracy*. Princeton, NJ: Princeton University Press.

Return to Flight Task Group. (2005). *Final report*. Washington, DC: NASA.

Rhem, K.T. (2004). "Bush shows 'deep disgust' for apparent treatment of Iraqi prisoners." *American Forces Press Service*, April 30.

Rhodes, R. (2002). *Masters of death: The SS Einsatzgruppen and the invention of the Holocaust*. New York: Alfred A. Knopf.

Ricks, T.E. (2006). *Fiasco: The American military adventure in Iraq*. New York: Penguin.

Ricoeur, P. (1995). "Intellectual Autobiography." In Lewis Edwin-Hahn (Ed.), *The Philosophy of Paul Ricoeur, The Philosophy of Living Philosophers*, vol. XXII. Chicago: Open Court.

Robertson, G., and Roth, K. (2006). *Crimes against humanity: The struggle for global justice*. London: Penguin Books.

Rogers, W.P. (1986). *Presidential commission on the space shuttle Challenger accident: Report*. Washington, DC: U.S. Government Printing Office.

Romzek, B.S., and Dubnick, M.J. (1987). "Accountability in the public sector: Lessons from the Challenger tragedy." *Public Administration Review*, 47: 227–238.

Rorty, A. (2001). *The many faces of evil.* New York: Routledge.

Rosenbaum, E. (1997). Personal telephone conversation with author. August 4.

Rosenberg, S. (Ed.). (2007). *Deliberation, participation and democracy: Can the people govern?* London: Palgrave Macmillan.

Rosenbloom, D.H., and Piotrowski, S.J. (2005). "Outsourcing the Constitution and administrative law norms." *American Review of Public Administration,* 35: 103–121.

Rosholt, R.L. (1966). *An administrative history of NASA, 1958–1963.* Washington, DC: Scientific and Technical Information Division, National Aeronautics and Space Administration.

Ross, D. (1979). "The development of the social sciences." In A. Oleson and J. Voss (Eds.), *The organization of knowledge in modern America* (107–138). Baltimore, MD: Johns Hopkins University Press.

———. (1991). *The origins of American social science.* New York: Cambridge University Press.

Rothman, D.J. (1971). *The discovery of the asylum: Social order and disorder in the new republic.* Boston: Little, Brown.

Rubenstein, R.L. (1975). *The cunning of history.* New York: Harper and Row.

———. (1983). *The age of triage: Fear and hope in an overcrowded world.* Boston: Beacon Press.

Rummel, R.J. (1994). *Death by government.* New Brunswick, NJ: Transaction.

Russell, J.B. (1988). *The prince of darkness: Radical evil and the power of good in history.* Ithaca, NY: Cornell University Press.

Russell, N., and Gregory, R.J. (2011). "Spinning an organizational 'web of obligation'? Moral choice in Stanley Milgram's 'obedience' experiments." *American Review of Public Administration,* 41: 495–518.

Sandel, M. (2012). *What money can't buy: The moral limits of markets.* New York: Macmillan.

Sands, P. (2008). *Torture team: Rumsfeld's memo and the betrayal of American values.* New York: Palgrave Macmillan.

Sanford, J.A. (1981). *Evil: The shadow side of reality.* New York: Crossroad.

Sartre, J-P. (1948). "Les mains sales (Dirty hands)." In *No exit and three other plays.* New York: Vintage Books.

Sassen, S. (1998). *Globalization and its discontents.* New York: Free Press.

Saul, J.R. (1992). *Voltaire's bastards: The dictatorship of reason in the West.* New York: Random House.

Schlosser, E. (1994). "Reefer madness." *Atlantic Monthly,* 274: 45–59.

———. (1998). "The prison-industrial complex." *Atlantic Monthly,* 282: 51–77.

Schon, D.C. (1993). "Generative metaphor: A perspective on problem-setting in social policy." In A. Ortony (Ed.), *Metaphor and thought* (137–163). Cambridge, England: Cambridge University Press.

———. (1983). *The reflective practitioner: How professionals think in action.* New York: Basic Books.

Schooner, S.L. (2005). "Contractor atrocities at Abu Ghraib: Compromised accountability in a streamlined, outsourced government." *Stanford Law and Policy Review,* 2: 45–67.

Schrift, A.D. (Ed.). (2005). *Modernity and the problem of evil.* Bloomington: Indiana University Press.

Schwann, G. (1998). "The 'healing' value of truth-telling: Chances and social conditions in a secularized world." *Social Research,* 65 (4), 725–741.

Schwartz, H.S. (1990). *Narcissistic process and corporate decay.* New York: New York University Press.

Sereny, G. (1995). *Albert Speer: His battle with truth.* New York: Alfred A. Knopf.

Shapiro, E.R., and Carr, A.W. (1991). *Lost in familiar places: Creating new connections between the individual and society.* New Haven, CT: Yale University Press.

Shelden, R.G., and Brown, W.B. (2000). "The crime control industry and the management of the surplus population." *Critical Criminology,* 9 (1/2): 41–62.

Shirey, O.C. (1946). *The story of the 442nd combat team.* Washington, DC: Infantry Journal.

Shklar, J.N. (1984). *Ordinary vices.* Cambridge, MA: Harvard University Press.

Simon, H.A. (1976). *Administrative behavior.* New York: Free Press.

Singer, P.W. (2003). *Corporate warriors: The rise of the privatized military industry.* Ithaca, NY: Cornell University Press.

Small, A. (1916). "Fifty years of sociology." *American Journal of Sociology,* 21: 724–731.

Smith, P. (1990). *Killing the spirit: Higher education in America.* New York: Viking.

———. (1995). *Democracy on trial: The Japanese American evacuation and relocation in World War II.* New York: Simon and Schuster.

Smith, R.W. (1989). *The space telescope.* New York: Cambridge University Press.

Sofsky, W. (1997). *The order of terror: The concentration camp.* Princeton, NJ: Princeton University Press.

Speer, A. (1970). *Inside the Third Reich.* London: Weidenfeld and Nicholson.

Spicer, E.H. (1969). *Impounded people: Japanese Americans in the relocation centers.* Tucson: University of Arizona Press.

Stannard, D.E. (1992). *American Holocaust: The conquest of the new world.* New York: Oxford University Press.

Staub, E. (1992). *The roots of evil: The origins of genocide and other group violence.* New York: Cambridge University Press.

Steiner, H. (2002). "Calibrating evil." *Monist,* 85 (April): 183–194.

Stiglitz, J.E. (2010). *Free fall: America, free markets, and the sinking of the world economy.* New York: Norton.

Stivers, R. (1982). *Evil in modern myth and ritual.* Athens: University of Georgia Press.

Stone, D.A. (1988). *Policy paradox and political reason.* New York: HarperCollins.

Stover, E., and Weinstein, H. (2004). *My neighbor, my enemy: Justice and community in the aftermath of mass atrocity.* Cambridge: Cambridge University Press.

Strang, H., and Braithwaite, J. (Eds.). (2001). *Restorative justice and civil society.* Cambridge: Cambridge University Press.

Strasser, S. (Ed.). (2004). *The Abu Ghraib investigations.* New York: Public Affairs.

Stuhlinger, E.F., and Ordway, F.I. (1994). *Wernher von Braun: Crusader for space.* Malabar, FL: Krieger.

Stuhlinger, E., Ordway, F.I., McCall, J., and Bucker, G. (Eds.). (1963). *Astronautical engineering and science from Peenemünde to planetary space.* New York: McGraw-Hill.

Sullivan, D., and Tifft, L. (2006). *Handbook of restorative justice.* London: Routledge.

Sutherland, S.L. (1995). "The problem of dirty hands in politics: Peace in the vegetable trade." *Canadian Journal of Political Science,* 28: 479–498.

Suzuki, L. (1979). *Ministry in the assembly and relocation centers of World War II.* Berkeley: Yardbird Press.

Tateishi, J. (1984). *And justice for all: An oral history of the Japanese American detention camps.* New York: Random House.

Terry, L.D., and Stivers, C. (2002). "Democratic governance in the aftermath of September 11, 2001." *Public Administration Review,* 62 (September special issue): 16–17.

Thompson, G. (2008). "Fewer people entering the U.S. illegally, report says." *New York Times,* October 2. Available at www.nytimes.com/2008/10/03/us/03immig.html.

Trento, J.J. (1987). *Prescription for disaster: From the glory of the Apollo to the betrayal of the shuttle.* New York: Crown.

Turner, B.S. (Ed.). (1990). *Theories of modernity and postmodernity.* London: Sage.

Turse, N. (2012). *Kill anything that moves: The real American war in Vietnam.* New York: Henry Holt.

Twitchell, J.B. (1985). *Dreadful pleasures.* New York: Oxford University Press.

U.S. Department of War. (1943). *Japanese evacuation from the west coast, 1942 (General John DeWitt's final report).* Washington, DC: War Department.

U.S. House of Representatives. Select Committee (Tolan) Investigating National Defense Migration. (1942). *Preliminary report and recommendations on problem of evacuation of citizens and aliens from military areas.* 77th Congress, 2d session. Washington, DC: U.S. House of Representatives.

Van der Wal, Z., de Graaaf, G., and Lasthuizen, K. (2008). "What's valued most? Similarities and differences between the organizational values of the public and private sectors." *Public Administration,* 86: 465–482.

Van Pelt, R. (1994). "A site in search of a mission." In Y. Gutman and M. Berenbaum (Eds.), *Anatomy of the Auschwitz death camp* (93–156). Bloomington and Indianapolis: University of Indiana Press.

Vanderburg, W.H. (1985). *The growth of minds and cultures: A unified theory of the structure of human experience.* Toronto: University of Toronto Press.

———. (2000). *The labyrinth of technology.* Toronto: University of Toronto Press.

———. (2005). *Living in the labyrinth of technology.* Toronto: University of Toronto Press.

Vardi, Y., and Weitz, E. (2004). *Misbehavior in organizations: Theory, research and management.* Mahwah, NJ: Lawrence Erlbaum.

Vaughan, D. (1996). *The Challenger launch decision: Risky technology, culture, and deviance at NASA.* Chicago: University of Chicago Press.

Ventriss, C. (1993). "The 'publicness' of administrative ethics." In Terry L. Cooper (Ed.), *Handbook of administrative ethics.* New York: Marcel Dekker.

Vickers, G. (1995, orig. 1965). *The art of judgment.* Thousand Oaks, CA: Sage.

Volkan, V. (1988). *The need to have enemies and allies.* Northvale, NJ: Jason Aronson.

———. (1997). *Blood lines: From ethnic pride to ethnic terrorism.* Boulder, CO: Westview Press.

von Braun, W. (1963). "Management of the space program at a field center." In *Conference on space-age planning* (239–250). Washington, DC: National Aeronautics and Space Administration.

Waldo, D. (1948). *The administrative state.* New York: Ronald Press.

Wallach, M.A., Kogan, N., and Bem, D.J. (1962). "Group influences on individual risk taking." *Journal of Abnormal and Social Psychology,* 65: 75–86.

Warrick, J. (2008). "CIA tactics endorsed in secret memos: Waterboarding got White House nod." *Washington Post,* October 15: A01.

Weber, M. (1905, repr. 1958). *The Protestant ethic and the spirit of capitalism.* New York: Scribners.

Wegener, P.P. (1996). *The Peenemünde wind tunnels: A memoir.* New Haven, CT: Yale University Press.

Westermann, E.B. (2010). *Hitler's police battalions: Enforcing racial war in the east.* Lawrence: University Press of Kansas.

White House. (2004). Remarks by President Bush, April 30.

White, J. (2005). "Documents tell of brutal improvisation by GIs." *Washington Post,* Wednesday, August 3: A01.

Whitehead, A.N., and Russell, B. (1910). *Principia mathematica.* Oxford: Oxford University Press.

Wiebe, R.H. (1967). *The search for order, 1877–1920.* New York: Hill and Wang.

Wiesenthal, S. (1998). *The sunflower: On the possibilities and limits of forgiveness.* New York: Schocken Books.

Wijze, S. (2002). "Defining evil: Insights from the problem of dirty hands." *Monist,* 85 (April): 210–239.

Wilson, W. (1887). "The study of administration." *Political Science Quarterly,* 2: 197–222.

Wittgenstein, L. (1922). *Tractatus logico-philosphicus.* New York: Harcourt Brace and World.

Wyman, D.S. (1984). *The abandonment of the Jews: America and the Holocaust, 1941–1945.* New York: Pantheon Books.

Yahil, L. (1990). *The Holocaust: The fate of European Jewry, 1932–1945.* New York: Oxford University Press.

Yankelovich, D. (1991). *Coming to public judgment: making democracy work in a complex world.* Syracuse, NY: Syracuse University Press.

———. (1999). *The magic of dialogue: Transforming conflict into cooperation.* New York: Simon and Schuster.

Yanow, D. (1995). *How does a policy mean?* Washington, DC: Georgetown University Press.

Zimbardo, P. (2007). *The Lucifer effect: Understanding how good people turn evil.* New York: Random House.

Zycinski, J.M. (2000). "God, freedom and evil: Perspectives from religion and science." *Zygon,* 35 (September): 653–664.

# Index

# About the Authors

**Guy B. Adams** is professor emeritus of public affairs in the Harry S Truman School of Public Affairs at the University of Missouri. He is co-editor in chief of the *American Review of Public Administration*. His research interests are in the areas of public administration history and theory, public service ethics, and organization studies. He has over sixty scholarly publications, including books, book chapters, and articles in the top national and international public administration journals. He earned his doctorate in public administration in 1977 from the George Washington University in Washington, D.C.

**Danny L. Balfour** is professor of public administration in the School of Public, Nonprofit and Health Administration at Grand Valley State University in Grand Rapids, Michigan. He was the founding managing editor of the *Journal of Public Affairs Education* and serves on the editorial boards of several public affairs journals. His research and teaching interests are in the areas of public management, public service ethics, and the Holocaust. He has more than fifty scholarly publications, including book chapters and articles in the top national and international public administration journals. He earned his Ph.D. in public administration from the Florida State University in 1990.